**The Law of Accumulation
and Breakdown of the
Capitalist System**

The Law of Accumulation and Breakdown of the Capitalist System
Being also a Theory of Crises

HENRYK GROSSMANN

Translated and abridged by Jairus Banaji
Foreword and Introduction by Tony Kennedy

PLUTO PRESS

This edition first published in English in 1992 by
Pluto Press, 345 Archway Road, London N6 5AA

First published in German in 1929 as
*Das Akkumulations – Zusammenbruchsgesetz des
kapitalistischen Systems (Zugleich eine Krisentheorie),*
by C L Hirschfeld, Leipzig; reprinted 1970 by Verlag Neue
Kritik, Frankfurt am Main.

Translation and selection copyright © 1979 Jairus Banaji
Foreword and Introduction copyright © 1992 Tony Kennedy
This edition copyright © Pluto Press 1992

British Library Cataloguing in Publication Data
Grossmann, Henryk
    The law of accumulation and breakdown of the capitalist
    system.
    1. Marxism
    I. Title
    335.4

    ISBN 0–7453–0458–3 (hb)
    ISBN 0–7453–0459–1 (pb)

Library of Congress Cataloging-in-Publication Data
Grossmann, Henryk, 1881–1950.
    [Akkumulations – und Zusammenbruchsgesetz das kapitalistischen
    Systems. English]
        The law of accumulation and breakdown of the capitalist system :
    being also a theory of crises / Henryk Grossmann; translated and
    abridged by Jairus Banaji ; foreword and introduction by Tony
    Kennedy.
            p.   cm.
        Translation of: Das Akkumulations – Zusammenbruchsgesetz des
    kapitalistischen Systems (Zugleich eine Krisentheorie)–CIP t.p.
    verso.
        Includes bibliographical references and index.
        ISBN 0–7453–0458–3 (hb)
        ISBN 0–7453–0459–1 (pb)
        1. Capitalism. 2. Capital. 3. Saving and investment.
    4. Business cycles. 5. Marxian economics. I. Banaji, Jairus,
    1947– . II. Title.
    HB501.G713   1992
    330.12'2–dc20   91–26181
                                                                  CIP

Typeset in 10 on 12pt Times by Stanford DTP Services, Milton Keynes
Printed in Great Britain by Billing and Sons, Worcester

Contents

For Rana Sen (1952–1985)

Foreword

TONY KENNEDY

Henryk Grossmann's *The Law of Accumulation and Breakdown of the Capitalist System* was first published in 1929 in Leipzig.[1] Both date and place are highly significant. This study of capitalist collapse was published on the eve of the Wall Street crash that preceded the great world depression of the 1930s, the most profound and wide-reaching crisis in the history of capitalism. It was also published in Germany, the country at the epicentre of the crisis of Europe and the wider international balance of power, a crisis only resolved through a descent into fascism and war and intercontinental barbarism on a scale unprecedented in human history.

It was an inauspicious moment for the publication of a major contribution to Marxist theory. The international working-class upsurge that followed the end of the First World War and had received a powerful impetus from the Russian Revolution had everywhere been contained by the mid-1920s. The Stalinist degeneration of the Soviet Union and the official communist movement internationally removed the initiative from the left and put it on the defensive against the rising forces of reaction. In this climate of defeat and demoralisation, Grossmann's work was destined at first to receive a universally hostile response, and then to be ignored for decades.

Grossmann was already close to 50 when his major work was published. He was born in 1881 in Cracow, in what was then Austrian Galicia, into a Jewish mine-owning family. He studied at Vienna, under both the conservative economist Bohm-Bawerk and the Marxist historian Carl Grunberg. After the collapse of the Austro-Hungarian empire in 1918 he became a professional economist under the newly constituted Polish state. He had moved towards socialism during the First World War and, sympathetic to the Russian Revolution, he afterwards became a member of the Polish Communist Party. In 1922 he was appointed professor of economics at Warsaw university, where he remained until harassment from the reactionary Pilsudski regime forced him to emigrate in 1925.

In 1926 Grossmann was invited by his former teacher Grunberg to join the newly established Marxist Institute for Social Research at Frankfurt. The lectures he gave at Frankfurt over the next three years formed the basis of his 1929 book. Respected for his formidable erudition, Grossmann was appointed professor in Frankfurt in 1930. In these years, Grossmann is described as being 'the embodiment of a Central European academic: proper, meticulous and gentlemanly'.[2] Always more of an academic than a political activist, it seems that Grossmann never joined the Communist Party in Germany, though he remained a loyal defender of the Soviet Union.

In the 1930s and 1940s Grossmann found himself increasingly marginalised. He became embroiled in disputes with his colleagues in the Frankfurt school as they either took up revisionist economic theories or moved away from the critique of political economy towards studies of psychology and aesthetics. As they became increasingly hostile towards Stalinism, he became more isolated in his support for the Soviet Union. The biggest problem however was the impact of the triumph of Hitler on the Frankfurt school. Forced to flee to Paris in 1933, Grossmann moved again to London in 1935 and then to the USA in 1937, when the remnants of the Frankfurt school took refuge in New York. With his family in Europe and at odds with his former colleagues, Grossmann lived 'a lonely and isolated existence'.[3] He suffered a stroke and continuing ill-health before his return to East Germany at the end of the war. In 1949 he was offered a professorial post in Leipzig, but died the following year, at the age of 69.

Grossmann's personal tragedy was symbolic of the fate of a generation of Marxists in the inter-war period. His work on breakdown was repudiated by the social democrat Braunthal, by the Stalinist Varga and by the left communist Pannekoek with more or less equal vehemence and with strikingly similar misinterpretations of his central arguments. One of the few people who recognised the value of Grossmann's work was the left communist Paul Mattick, who continued to uphold the Marxist theory of breakdown up to his death in 1981.

Born in Germany in 1904, Mattick was trained as a tool and die maker and became active in revolutionary socialist politics in Berlin and Cologne after the First World War. In 1926 he emigrated to the USA where he became an influential Marxist propagandist over the next half century. As an exponent of a libertarian approach that owed more to Rosa Luxemburg and the Dutch left communists than to Lenin and the Bolsheviks, Mattick was unsympathetic to Grossman's political allegiance to the Soviet Union. Yet in 1933 he defended the adoption of Grossmann's breakdown theory by his small group, as he put it, 'without, in general, sufficiently knowing or even wanting to take account of Grossmann's political interpretation' of his own theory.[4] Whatever his reservations about Grossmann's politics, Mattick endorsed his theory and he forcefully repudiated the criticism that came from all sides that it advanced a mechanical and fatalistic conception of breakdown.

Mattick's writings, notably his *Marx and Keynes*, first published in 1969, helped to make Marx's theory of breakdown, and Grossmann's elaboration of it, available in English to a new generation of Marxists.[5] With the re-emergence of world recession in the 1970s, this tradition contributed to a revival of Marxist crisis theory and a new interest in Grossmann. Just as the financial crash of 1929 led to the depression of the 1930s, the international stock exchange crash of October 1987 was a harbinger of the global recessionary trends gathering momentum in the early 1990s. The persistent stagnation and decay of global capitalism provides a powerful vindication of Marx's critique of capitalist society. Grossmann's unsurpassed elaboration of this critique offers a rigorous scientific basis from which to interpret contemporary trends.

For Grossmann, writing in the 1920s, re-presenting Marx's theory of capitalist breakdown was no mere academic exercise. Nor was he concerned simply with describing tendencies towards periodic economic crises, of a more or less restricted character, nor even with trends towards more systematic and global recessions. He aimed to show that the essence of Marx's analysis of capitalist society was the identification of the inexorable tendency towards breakdown as the fundamental characteristic of the social system as a whole:

> The question I shall examine is whether fully developed capitalism, regarded as an exclusively prevalent and universally widespread system relying only on its own resources, contains the capacity to develop the process of reproduction indefinitely and on a continually expanding basis, or whether this process of expansion runs into limits of one sort or another which it cannot overcome.[6]

Grossmann's book provided an impressive theoretical demonstration of the latter position, through his presentation of the tendencies towards capitalist collapse; the events of the 1930s and 1940s provided an even more powerful confirmation of these tendencies in practice. Capitalism survived, but only after two decades of worldwide turmoil and devastation.

Capitalism revived and continued to expand in the post-war era but only at the cost of reproducing tendencies towards stagnation and decay at a global level. While capitalism boomed in the USA, Western Europe and

Japan, backwardness and poverty remained endemic throughout the third world. Even when a few third world economies underwent rapid expansion and industrialisation in the 1960s and 1970s, the impoverishment of whole areas of Latin America, Africa and Asia intensified. The return of financial instability and economic recession, to plague not merely the backward capitalist world, but the system as a whole in the 1970s and 1980s, confirmed that the tendency towards breakdown – and the recurrent crises that are both an expression of this tendency and a means of forestalling it – are the constant features of modern capitalist society. It is these real developments in world capitalism today that give Marx's revolutionary critique, and Grossmann's unsurpassed elaboration of it, such exceptional pertinence.

The abridged translation presented here was one result of the growing interest in the Marxist critique of political economy in the 1970s. There was a particular concern among Marxists in Britain both to develop Marxist crisis theory in relation to contemporary economic and political events and to make Grossmann's major work accessible to an English-speaking readership for the first time. Jairus Banaji produced this translation in 1979 for the Platform Tendency – a group of former Trotskyists then based in Bombay, Bangalore and Delhi, who argued that a renovation of Marxist theory was *essential* to any renewal of the socialist movement and that this process of renovation would have to start with a critical re-examination of what was most valuable or most fundamental in that theoretical tradition. The general perspectives and intense theoretical life of the Platform group was the context in which a study of Grossmann seemed obligatory, like the parallel discussions of the work of Rubin and Rosdolsky which was or would soon become available in English then.

Where possible English editions are cited in references, and corrections to some minor mathematical errors have been made in the tables.

Acknowledgements are due to Mike Freeman, John Gibson, Phil Murphy and Katia Mecklenberger.

Tony Kennedy
London, January 1992

Notes

1. Henryk Grossmann, *Das Akkumulations – Zusammenbruchsgesetz des kapitalistischen Systems (Zugleich eine Krisentheorie),* Leipzig: C L Hirschfeld, 1929, reprinted Frankfurt Am Main: Verlag Neue Kritik, 1970.
2. Martin Jay, *The Dialectical Imagination: A History of the Frankfurt School and the Institute for Social Research 1923–50,* London: Heinemann, 1973, p. 17.

3. Jay, *The Dialectical Imagination*, p. 151.
4. Paul Mattick, quoted in Russell Jacoby, 'The Politics of the Crisis Theory: Towards the Critique of Automatic Marxism II', *Telos*, 23, 1975, p. 29.
5. Mattick, *Marx and Keynes*, London: Merlin, 1971. Mattick and Grossmann's influence can be seen in: David Yaffe, 'The Marxian Theory of Crisis, Capital and the State', *Economy and Society*, 1973, 2, pp. 186–232, 'Class Struggle and the Rate of Profit', *New Left Review*, 80, July/August, 1973 and 'Inflation, the Crisis and the Post-war Boom' (with Paul Bullock), *Revolutionary Communist*, 3/4, November 1975; Tony Allen et al., 'The Recession, the Capitalist Offensive and the Working Class', *Revolutionary Communist Papers*, 3, July 1978 and 'The World in Recession', *Revolutionary Communist Papers*, 7, July 1981.
6. Grossmann, *Law of Accumulation*, p. 31.

Henryk Grossmann and the Theory of Capitalist Collapse

TONY KENNEDY

The survival of capitalism over the past century is widely held to be the most damning refutation of Marxism. The popular view is that Marx's prediction that the capitalist system was destined to collapse under the weight of its internal contradictions has been falsified by events. What better vindication could there be for the existing order, and what better repudiation of its critics? Indeed, in recent years many authoritative commentators have argued that, not only has capitalism survived since Marx's death, but that today it is stronger than ever before. They point to 40 years of unprecedented prosperity and stability in the West; to the dramatic expansion of 'newly industrialising countries', particularly in Asia and Latin America; and they celebrate the ascendancy of market forces over the stagnant Stalinist economies of the Soviet Union and Eastern Europe. The apparent success of capitalism has given a new confidence to right-wing critics of Marxism. In his 1986 book, *The Capitalist Revolution: Fifty Propositions about Prosperity, Equality and Liberty*, Boston economics professor Peter L Berger dismisses what he takes to be the central theses of Marxism:

> The list of ... falsified Marxist propositions is long and embarrassing – to mention but a few of the most important ones, the deepening 'immiseration' of the working class and the consequent ever-sharper polarisation of society, the inability of 'bourgeois' democracy to cope with modern class conflicts and the consequent ascendency of dictatorial regimes in the heartlands of capitalism, or the progressive exclusion of the working class from the culture of the capitalist classes.[1]

By the close of the 1980s the scale of the capitalist triumph appeared to be so great that even former Marxists were inclined to agree with critics like Peter Berger that Marx had got it all wrong. Prominent New Left historian Gareth Stedman Jones conceded despondently that 'Marx was far more successful in evoking the power of capitalism than in demonstrating in any conclusive fashion why it had to come to an end.'[2] The influential 'regulation school' Marxist Michel Aglietta emphasised the regenerative capacities of the capitalist system, arguing that 'it is possible to speak of an organic crisis of capitalism without implying its inevitable disappearance'.[3] The 'analytic' Marxist John Roemer summed up the prevailing consensus that 'the key economic models and theories that Marxism champions, such as the labour theory of value and the falling rate of profit, are simply wrong'.[4]

Yet developments in the capitalist world in the 1980s and 1990s have undermined the complacency of the right and suggested that the left's abandonment of Marx might be premature. The world capitalist recession has turned into a slump and confounded all the confident promises of an early return to stable and sustained growth. Meanwhile the transition from Stalinism to capitalism in the Soviet Union, Eastern Europe and China is proving to be highly volatile, with unpredictable consequences for the stability of the world capitalist order. A growing awareness that developments in the former Eastern bloc raise the likelihood of major tensions and realignments in the post-war international balance of power has done much to mute the celebrations over the collapse of Stalinism. Despite Berger's bold title, 'prosperity, equality and liberty' are still denied to millions, not only in the third world, but among the growing numbers of unemployed and homeless in the heartlands of his much vaunted 'capitalist revolution'. Indeed, while Marx's theory of immiseration meets with derision in some quarters, the fact remains that the numbers facing starvation and disease on a world scale today exceed the entire global population in Marx's time.

Yet despite the widespread recognition that capitalism faces serious problems, most radical critics of the system regard Marx's critique as obsolete and as of little use in interpreting contemporary patterns of development. In fact, the last few years have seen many erstwhile critics of capitalism naively swallow the right's line on rejuvenated capitalism and abandon opposition altogether. Marx's own prognosis for the capitalist system was proclaimed in categorical terms in a famous passage in the chapter 'The historical tendency of capital accumulation' at the close of the first volume of *Capital*:

Along with the constantly diminishing number of the magnates of capital, who usurp and monopolise all advantages of this process of transformation, grows the mass of misery, oppression, slavery, degradation, exploitation; but with this too grows the revolt of the working class, a class always increasing in numbers, and disciplined, united, organised by the very mechanism of the process of capitalist production itself. The monopoly of capital becomes a fetter upon the mode of production, which has sprung up and flourished along with, and under it. Centralisation of the means of production and socialisation of labour at last reach a point where they become incompatible with their capitalist integument. This integument is burst asunder. The knell of private property sounds. The expropriators are expropriated.[5]

Today's commentators on Marx reject his theory of capitalist collapse. They insist that his analysis bears little correspondence to the reality of capitalist production. In their repudiation of Marx's theory by reference to contemporary economic trends modern commentators follow a similar approach to that taken by a number of influential Marxists in the two decades after Marx's death. In a series of articles first published in the late 1880s, Eduard Bernstein, a leading theoretician of German social democracy, sought to repudiate Marx's theory by reference to the current stabilisation of the capitalist system:

Signs of an economic worldwide crash of unheard-of violence have not been established, nor can one describe the improvement of trade in the intervals between the crises as particularly short-lived. Much more does a ... question arise ... (1) whether the enormous extension of the world market, in conjunction with the extraordinary shortening of the time necessary for the transmission of news and for the transport of trade, has so increased the possibilities for adjustment of disturbances; and (2) whether the enormously increased wealth of the European states, in conjunction with the elasticity of the modern credit system and the rise of industrial cartels, has so limited the reacting force of local or individual disturbances that, at least for some time, general commercial crises similar to the earlier ones are to be regarded as improbable.[6]

Bernstein concluded that the socialist movement could no longer base its activity on the anticipation of capitalist collapse and intensifying class conflict. Instead it should seek to achieve gradual improvements within the existing order through collaborating with other classes and through parliamentary reforms. The bulk of the socialist movement rejected Bernstein's reformist perspectives. However, the leading theoreticians of the left, notably Karl Kautsky, were unable to advance a coherent defence of Marx's theory of breakdown. Indeed Kautsky went so far as to dismiss the whole issue, arguing that 'a special theory of breakdown was never proposed by Marx or Engels'.[7]

Bernstein's 'revision' of Marxism provided the theoretical foundations for reformism and set the terms for the debate about crisis theory and political strategy that continues to this day. Henryk Grossmann's *The Law of Accumulation and Breakdown of the Capitalist System* was a decisive intervention in what he described as the 'fierce controversies' raging around the status of the theory of breakdown in Marx's system that continued from the turn of the century into the 1920s. Grossmann emphasised the point that, though Bernstein's opponents rejected his reformist perspectives, they were unable to challenge the logic of his position:

> Bernstein was perfectly right in saying, against social democracy's views about the end of capitalism; 'If the triumph of socialism were truly an immanent economic necessity, then it would have to be grounded in a proof of the inevitable breakdown of the present order of society'.[8]

Grossmann contended that the socialist movement's commitment to the overthrow of capitalism required a theoretical proof of the system's tendency towards collapse. He insisted that if, by contrast, capitalism showed a consistent ability to develop the productive powers of society, and improve the conditions of the working class, then there was no material justification for socialism. Grossmann argued that in the long-running Bernstein–Kautsky debate 'there was no real dispute about the theory of economic breakdown of capitalism.'[9] In fact apart from a laudable, but ultimately ill-conceived, attempt by Rosa Luxemburg – the leading theoretician of the left – to provide an explanation of capitalist breakdown, Grossmann observed that the 'debate itself revolved around less important issues.' The result was 'an absolute chaos of conflicting views' on Marx's critique, 'quite irrespective of whether the individuals concerned are bourgeois writers or belong to the radical or moderate wing of the workers' movement'.[10]

Grossmann believed that the absence of any serious assessment of the theory of breakdown reflected a broader lack of interest in the structure and content of Marx's critique. At the same time he stressed that this had important political consequences inside the socialist movement. Thus by the late 1920s Kautsky could conclude that the First World War and the economic chaos and revolutionary upheaval that followed, far from indicating the capitalist system's tendency towards breakdown, confirmed that 'its capacity to adjust to new conditions was much stronger than its vulnerability'. Two years before the worldwide collapse of the financial system in 1929 Kautsky insisted that capitalism 'stands today, from a purely economic point of view, stronger than ever'.[11]

In introducing Grossmann's work we begin with his challenge to the superficial approach of contemporary theorists to Marx's theory and their general neglect of the method underlying Marx's *Capital*; the same deficiencies continue to dominate commentaries on Marxism today. We can then proceed to outline the place of the law of the tendency of the rate of profit to fall in his theory of breakdown and the importance of various counteracting tendencies in modifying the expression of this law in reality. Finally, we discuss the role of the class struggle in the breakdown of capitalism before finally reviewing the views of some contemporary Marxist scholars on the prospects of modern capitalism.

Marx's method

Grossmann maintained that the content and significance of the theory of breakdown could only be clarified through a 'reconstruction or definition of its place in the system as a whole'.[12] By this he meant that the key to the analysis lay in the totality of Marx's presentation founded on the law of value as the basic law of capitalist production:

> Under capitalism the entire mechanism of the productive process is ruled by the law of value, and just as its dynamic and tendencies are only comprehensible in terms of this law, its final end, the breakdown, is likewise only explicable in terms of it.[13]

Grossmann's emphasis on the importance of Marx's analysis of the inner laws governing capitalist production arose from his belief that both followers and opponents of Marxism had lost sight of the historically constructed character of capitalist production and the specific character of the social laws by which the system is governed. He insisted that the disputes surrounding the interpretation of Marx's work were largely rooted in the almost universal failure to appreciate the importance of its structure as the theoretical reflection of the internal dynamics of capitalist production. The source of many controversies, according to Grossmann, was a 'general tendency to cling to the results' of Marx's theory and an ignorance of 'the method underlying *Capital*'.[14]

Marx's method involved a presentation of the structure of capitalist society in terms of a theoretical movement from its simplest, and most fundamental, social relations towards progressively more complex and developed relations. To reveal the basic relations of capitalist society Marx used a method of abstraction which began by leaving aside the more complex and developed features of reality. Through a succession of stages Marx introduced these more complex relations so that the theoretical representation of capitalist production becomes a progressively fuller depiction of the system's developmental tendencies. Marx's method was thus to ascend from a simple, abstract presentation of capitalist production towards a successively fuller, concrete presentation. Grossmann characterised the movement as a process in which 'the investigation as a whole draws nearer to the complicated appearances of the concrete world'.[15]

The significance of Marx's theory lay in its totality. Marx's method of presentation, his practice of isolating specific social relations and analysing their characteristic movement, was not meant to suggest that capitalist reality itself was simply an aggregate of essentially compartmentalised phenomena whose interactions were arbitrary. His aim was to provide a comprehensive theoretical reproduction of the social laws governing the system. Hence every stage of Marx's analysis, and every formulation, has a provisional character in relation to capitalist reality. Marx's formulations cannot, therefore, be applied directly to any particular set of economic circumstances – not least because Marx's method itself assumes that the laws of capitalist production operate in a dynamic way, continually generating new trends and patterns of development. The utility of Marx's approach lies in a method that stresses the need to grasp the specific social character of the capitalist mode of production. Any discussion of prevailing patterns of capitalist development must appreciate the abstract nature of Marx's presentation. The problem of comprehending new developments involves establishing a series of mediating links which reveal their origins in the inner movement of capitalist production rather than trying to fit reality into the analysis presented in *Capital*.

Grossmann's awareness of these methodological principles formed the basis of his challenge to the opponents of the theory of breakdown. His main objection was that the failure to comprehend the method underlying Marx's work meant that the critics of breakdown at that time based their assessments of his theory on whether or not it directly corresponded to the prevailing economic circumstances. Grossmann argued that this approach involved two fundamental errors.

First it meant introducing into Marxist analysis the uncritical attitude of bourgeois economics towards the surface appearances of capitalist society.

Both Bernstein and his opponents regarded new developments within the system as self-evident facts requiring little further investigation. This led to a second mistake, that of searching Marx's work for formulations which seemed to correspond to the latest patterns of economic development. Instead of approaching new theoretical problems from a critical angle with the aim of developing an interpretation founded on the dynamic and contradictory movement of capitalist production, the new generation of Marxists tended to extract themes from Marx's analysis that seemed to provide a useful model for characterising the latest economic developments. This selective approach also encouraged a tendency to dispense with aspects of the analysis which seemed to be in conflict with immediate circumstances.

Grossmann pointed out that the desire to find some facet of Marx's theory which seemed to correspond to the most recent trends revealed little about the trends themselves. The main result was to generate doubts about the credibility of Marxism as a mode of analysis. Grossmann argued that this selective approach to Marx's theory, the tendency to divorce a given thesis 'from the path that led to its formulation', was ill-founded.[16] It meant converting abstract formulations, which had a provisional explanatory role in a broader theoretical system, into comprehensive portrayals of capitalist reality. For Grossmann this was bound to create the impression that Marx needed revising because an isolated thesis would always prove inadequate for comprehending the complex and changing patterns of capitalist development. The procedure necessarily led to the production of inflexible models of capitalist development. Nothing could be easier than to refute a formulation that was only meant to figure as a provisional conclusion within a broader theoretical system. The inflexible character of such models therefore tended to encourage yet further revisions of the theory. As Grossmann observed, this approach reinforced the view that Marxism had little definite content and that it had become little more than 'a matter of interpretation'.[17]

The logical form which Marx used in *Capital* – the dialectical method of presentation – was designed to lay bare the inner nature of capitalist production. Marx aimed to depict in theoretical form the development of a social system which is simultaneously a process of producing the material needs of society and a process for ensuring the profitable expansion of private capital. He maintained that there was a real, living contradiction in this twofold character of capitalist production. Capitalism cannot fulfil both the social and the private objectives of production in a stable and harmonious way. The criterion of profitability tends to create barriers to fulfilling social need and the consequent clash between the needs of society and the constraints on capitalist production threatens its very survival.

The dialectical method forms the foundation of Marx's theory of a system characterised by a fundamental conflict between the interests of private capital and those of society as a whole. A revised Marxism which ignores the methodological basis of the theory necessarily loses sight of this contradiction. Grossmann criticised the neglect of Marx's method because this meant separating the examination of economic developments from Marx's conception of the contradictory nature of capitalist production. The inevitable outcome was a version of Marxism which could not sustain a coherent anti-capitalist outlook.

The theory of breakdown

Grossmann observed that Marxists had often criticised Marx because he 'nowhere ever produced a comprehensive description of his theory of crisis'. But, Grossmann continued, 'this objection rests on a crude misunderstanding: the object of Marx's analysis is not crisis, but the capitalist process of reproduction in its totality'.[18] The theory of breakdown was, for Grossmann, something more than the conception of capitalist crisis. In fact he indicated that the idea of economic crisis found a parallel formulation in bourgeois economics (business cycle theory) whereas the theory of breakdown definitely did not. The theory of breakdown, as formulated by Grossmann, is a theory of the limitations of capitalism as a mode of production capable of ensuring social progress. At its heart lies Marx's analysis of the contradictory nature of capitalist production.

Marx's *Capital* opens with a presentation of the contradiction of capitalist production in its simplest form – the commodity. A product of human labour takes the form of a commodity not because it fulfils some human need, but because it is sold on the market. As a commodity the product therefore possesses a twofold character: it is both useful (a use value) and exchangeable (a value). The distinction within the commodity between its material, bodily, form and its socially-constructed existence as a product for exchange is the most elementary form of the contradiction of capitalist production.

Marx examines the simple exchange between two commodities to show how the contradiction develops. The commodity, in being exchanged for another of equivalent value, expresses its value in the material form of another commodity. The social aspect of the commodity is therefore expressed in the use value form of another commodity. Thus the use value/value relation internal to the commodity form develops, in the act of exchange, into a contradictory relation between two commodities. At this level of simple exchange the significance of the contradiction is not apparent. After all, the question of which of the two commodities is expressing its value in the useful form of the other is accidental: either can change places without affecting the character of the relationship.

Marx moves on to consider the situation in which one commodity (the money commodity) comes to function as the bodily expression of the value not of one other but of all commodities. Here the contradiction between value and use value acquires a clearer expression. The money form tends to become attached to one or two commodities (gold or silver) which are universally accepted as the material representatives of value. In effect, the contradiction between use value and value assumes a fixed form in the exchange of commodity for money. However, the contradiction between the technical and social aspects of capitalist production is still not fully apparent and appears to have a purely formal character.

At this early stage of his presentation Marx points out that the very separation of the economic process into two phases – production and exchange – creates 'the possibility and no more than the possibility' of crises, since there can be no guarantee that production will be followed by sale. At the same time he warns that 'the conversion of this mere possibility into a reality is the result of a long series of relations, that, from our present standpoint of simple circulation, have as yet no existence'.[19] To discover this series of relations we have to investigate the contradiction further.

The formal possibility of crisis begins to emerge as a reality when the production of value begins to take precedence over the production of use value. This is the result of the further extension of commodity exchange, involving the transformation of human labour power itself into a commodity. This apparently formal process involves a profound social and historical change through which producers are converted into a class of propertyless wage labourers, while ownership of the means of production becomes the preserve of a non-producing capitalist class. As the capital–wage labour relation becomes dominant in society, the motive of production changes. The objective is now the reproduction of this social relation on an expanded scale through the appropriation of surplus value from the wage labouring class. The creation of value and surplus value, rather than the production of use values, now becomes the system's defining motive. From this moment the contradiction between the narrow motive of capital accumulation and the broader material interests of society emerges as a living contradiction.

In his exploration of the way the production process is subordinated to the interests of capital, Marx introduces a number of new categories. Thus the concept of *constant capital*, that portion of capital invested in means of production, reveals the fact that under the rule of capitalist social relations, the productive forces of society are employed for the purpose of enriching capital rather than society. In a similar way, the concept of *variable capital*, the portion of total capital spent on living labour power, reveals how human labour is organised for capital rather in the interests of workers. Conservative, as well as radical, critics have dismissed such concepts as ingenious creations of Marx's mind. For Marx however, the subordination of society's productive powers to the interests of capital is a real feature of capitalist production. Theory is obliged to grasp this peculiar aspect of capitalist social reality.

In his presentation of the theory of breakdown Grossmann continually emphasises the importance of Marx's focus on the twofold nature of capitalist production. He points out that the ability of the individual labourer to set in motion a greater mass of means of production is the fundamental indicator of progress because it reflects the possibility of producing more in a given expenditure of labour time:

> Ever since the beginnings of history it has always been the capacity of the individual worker with his labour power L to set in motion a greater mass of means of production M that has signalled technological and economic progress.[20]

The rationale for society devoting more and more of its labour time to the production of means of production is that it enables more than proportional increases in the generation of consumable wealth. For example, if under a given set of conditions 10 cars could be produced in 10 working days of 8 hours it would be in the interest of society to devote 5 working days to producing a better machine if this allowed the production of more than 10 cars during the other 5 days. The tendency to devote more of society's labour time to the production of means of production is confirmed by the growing mechanisation of the process of producing means of production.

The expansion of the means of production relative to living labour is a self-evident feature of economic progress. It is also evident that capitalism develops society's impetus to extend its productive powers more rigorously than all previous modes of social organisation. In doing so, however, capitalism endows the productive powers of society with a specific social character: 'The elements of production M and L figure not only in their natural form, but at the same time as values c [constant capital] and v [variable capital]'.[21] Grossmann went on to argue that 'Marx emphasises ... not the changes in the technical composition of capital (M:L) but changes in the organic composition of capital ($c{:}v$).' This is because 'the valorisation process, and not the technical process of production, is the characteristic driving force of capitalism'.[22]

Grossmann pointed out that organic composition of capital 'is a value composition determined by the technical composition and reflecting its changes'.[23] For him the problem was to identify the specific capitalist form of the general tendency towards the development of society's productive forces, the drive to increase the mass of means of production set in motion by each labourer. In other words, how is the tendency for M to increase relative to L reflected in the social relationship $c{:}v$? For Grossmann it was evident that under capitalism the general tendency to economise on living labour by using more means of production must lead to a tendency towards a rising organic composition of capital, or an increase in the ratio of constant to variable capital.

Grossmann noted a widespread lack of interest among commentators on Marx with his discussion, in *Capital Volume Three*, of the rising organic composition of capital. He regarded it as symbolic of a general failure to appreciate Marx's emphasis on the twofold social character of capitalist production. For Grossmann the rising organic composition of capital was crucial to Marx's whole presentation of the laws of capitalist development. In technical terms living labour and means of production may be regarded as mere factors of the production process; their material functions within production are obviously distinct but such technical differences are of no particular scientific interest. But this is far from the case when we consider the matter from the point of view of capitalist production and the distinct social functions which constant and variable capital perform for the capitalist production process.

The employment of labour power – purchased out of the variable component of capital – is the source of the surplus value required to sustain the process of capital accumulation. Yet the variable portion tends to decline in relation to constant capital, and therefore total capital. This means that as capital accumulation proceeds there is a tendency for the mass of surplus value to increase at a slower rate than the total capital required to generate that surplus value.

The employment of better production methods in the production of goods consumed by the working class does have an indirect effect on increasing the mass of surplus value. Higher productivity cheapens the value of such goods and thereby reduces the cost of acquiring labour power for the capitalist class. More of the product of a given working day can therefore be appropriated as unpaid surplus value. Yet the working day is finite. Such increases in the rate of surplus value extracted from each worker cannot equal the rate of increase in the constant capital employed by each worker.

The tendency for the mass of surplus value to increase at a slower rate than the total capital employed is expressed in the *tendency of the rate of profit to fall*. The rate of profit is the total mass of surplus value, or profit, as a portion of the total capital employed. According to Marx: 'The progressive tendency of the general rate of profit to fall is … *an expression peculiar to the capitalist mode of production*, of the progressive development of the social productivity of labour'.[24] For Marx the tendency of the rate of profit to fall is the form in which the general development of human productive powers appears when organised under the sway of capitalist social relations. Grossmann viewed Marx's discussion, in *Capital Volume Three*, of the tendency of the rate of profit to fall as the proof that Marx's critique is a theory of the breakdown of the capitalist system. The central theme of Grossmann's presentation of the theory of breakdown is that barriers to the generation of wealth emerge out of the capital accumulation process itself.

Capital accumulation generates enormous increases in the production of social wealth. Indeed it appears to capitalist entrepreneurs and their economic commentators that capital accumulation and increasing wealth are by nature the same process. But in reality capitalism provides merely a glimpse of society's productive potential. The development of society's productive mechanism comes into conflict with the specific aim of capitalist production – the production of surplus value for the purpose of further capital accumulation. In the course of accumulation a growing scarcity of profits emerges in relation to the size of the capital seeking a profit.

This produces a paradoxical 'overproduction'. Overproduction does not take place with respect to any measure of social need; indeed the overproduction of capital is always accompanied by generalised want. Capital is overproduced in the sense that the available surplus value is insufficient to reproduce the entire capital on a profitable basis. In such a situation productive resources are allowed to lie idle and further expansion is delayed until the conditions of profitability improve. According to Grossmann the very existence of overproduced, idle capital in a situation where wants go unsatisfied confirms the validity of the theory of breakdown. It shows that the systematic development of society's productive powers is, indeed, a profound threat to capitalism. Grossmann emphasised that economic crises both expressed the tendency towards breakdown and acted to offset it: 'crises are simply a healing process of the system, a form in which equilibrium, that is, valorisation, is again re-established, even if forcibly and with huge losses. From the standpoint of capital every crisis is a "crisis of purification" ... [a] form in which the breakdown tendency is temporarily interrupted and restrained from realising itself completely'.[25]

No other aspect of Marx's theory has provoked more confusion and hostility than his elaboration of the law of the tendency of the rate of profit to fall. This is not surprising since, as Marx states, beneath the

> horror of the falling rate of profit is the feeling that capitalist production meets in the development of the productive forces a barrier which has nothing to do with the production of wealth as such; and this peculiar barrier testifies to the limitations and the merely historical, transitory character of the capitalist mode of production.[26]

However, exponents of Marxism too have renounced the thesis, declaring that no capitalist would rationally invest if it led to a fall in the rate of profit. But the rational calculation of the individual capitalist does not enter into the question of the tendency of the rate of profit to fall. Marx's analysis is concerned with the dynamics of the system as a whole. The tendency of the rate of profit to fall indicates that the very conditions for the continuation of capital accumulation, the generation of an increasing mass of surplus, also throws up obstacles to the preservation of the accumulation process. The tendency of the rate of profit to fall shows that production for profit is an inadequate basis for the consistent development of society's material conditions of life.

Much of the confusion around the tendency of the rate of profit to fall stems from a misunderstanding of the structure of Marx's work. Grossmann argued that the falling rate of profit is a tendency that arises out of the capital accumulation process conceived in its pure operation. In other words it illustrates the tendency towards the breakdown of the capitalist system presented theoretically in terms of its pure operation. Grossmann stressed that an 'abstract, deductively elaborated theory never coincides with actual appearances' and that the further analysis must examine 'how far the tendency of the pure law is modified in its realisation'. Indeed the question that concerned Grossmann was not so much whether or not the capitalist system exhibited a tendency to breakdown but 'why has capitalism not already broken down?'.[27] We will return to this issue in the discussion on the countertendencies to capitalist collapse.

The reproduction schemes

The debate around the reproduction schemes in *Capital Volume Two* is a classic illustration of the danger of extracting a formulation from the body of Marx's work and trying to use it directly as some sort of model of economic realities. In *Capital Volume One*, Marx presents an analysis of the process of capitalist production, touching on questions of exchange only to highlight the outward forms taken by the relations of production. In *Capital Volume Two* he focuses on the circulation process, analyses its specific characteristics and assesses the extent to which propositions in *Volume One* have to be modified.

The purpose of the reproduction schemes, which appear in *Volume Two*, is to emphasise that although capitalist production is above all concerned with the production and expansion of value, the reproduction of this process necessitates the production of particular use values in determinate proportions. There are two main aspects to the schemes. First Marx assumes that the process of social reproduction in value terms, whether in a simple form or an expanded form, proceeds in harmony. The purpose of this assumption is to isolate the impact of value reproduction on the use value side of production. Second, Marx presents the use value aspect of reproduction in terms of two broad social categories – the production of means of production and the production of means of consumption. The total production process is depicted as an interaction between two departments of production, *department I* producing means of production and *department II* producing means of consumption.

The basic error of commentators on the reproduction schemes from Bernstein to the present is to take them as a faithful description of the actual process of capitalist reproduction. They interpret a highly abstract conceptual device as a model that is directly applicable to the real world. The result is that they use Marx's provisional and artificial assumption of a stable process of social reproduction as a proof that capital accumulation really does proceed harmoniously.

The assumption of the possibility of a harmonious reproduction process was common to leading authorities within the European Marxist movement such as Rudolf Hilferding and Otto Bauer in the early decades of the twentieth century. Even Rosa Luxemburg, who firmly rejected any notion of stable capitalist development, shared the harmonist interpretation of the schemes. She argued that Marx, when constructing the schemes, had forgotten one crucial factor – the problem of realising surplus value. She insisted that the schemes were faulty because, in considering only the relations between capitalists and workers, the issue of realisation was irresolvable. Workers obviously could not constitute a market for the surplus product since it had been appropriated from them without payment. Nor could capitalists constitute a market for one another's surplus product. The implication, she insisted, was that surplus value could only be realised outside the capitalist system, in markets provided by 'non-capitalist' regions of the world. Luxemburg's view was that the scheme for extended reproduction was therefore unable to explain 'the actual and historical process of accumulation'.[28] In her view, 'it falls down so soon as we consider the realisation of surplus value'.[29]

That the reproduction schemes do not resolve the problem of realisation or explain the real process of accumulation is undeniable. The problem however lies not in the reproduction schemes but in Luxemburg's critique. As we have seen, the schemes are an examination of the circulation process in its pure form, holding consideration of the interaction of production and circulation until *Capital Volume Three*. Why Marx should have discussed the contradiction between the production and realisation processes of capital in the context of an examination of the circulation alone is a mystery to which Luxemburg never gave an answer. In fact, by using Marx's discussion of the problem of realisation contained in *Capital Volume Three* to dismiss the reproduction schemes, Luxemburg merely followed her harmonist opponents in imagining that Marx's schemes attempt to portray the capitalist production process in its totality.

The outcome was not merely confusion about the schemes and Marx's method. Luxemburg also converted Marx's analysis of the inner contradictions of capitalist production into one of an external contradiction between two separate processes – capitalist production and non-capitalist realisation. While Grossmann acknowledged Luxemburg's subjective commitment to the theory of breakdown, he considered that her attempt to establish a rigorous materialist basis for this position had failed:

> Her deduction of the necessary downfall of capitalism is not rooted in the immanent laws of the accumulation process, but in the transcendental fact of an absence of non-capitalist markets. Luxemburg shifts the crucial problem of capitalism from the sphere of production to that of circulation.[30]

The Austrian Marxist Otto Bauer set about defending Marx's reproduction schemes from Luxemburg's attack. Taking account of Luxemburg's technical criticisms of Marx's schemes he produced the most elaborate harmonist reproduction scheme. Grossmann argued that Bauer's scheme matched 'all the formal requirements that one could impose on a schematic model of this sort'.[31] Bauer concluded that a harmonious process of accumulation was possible. To explain the occurrence of crises, he resorted to the idea of potential imbalances or disproportions between the rate of accumulation and the growth of the wage labour force. Grossmann upbraided Bauer for his 'underlying lack of methodological clarity':

He confuses the purely fictitious trajectory of accumulation represented by the scheme with the actual trajectory of accumulation ... His mistake lies in his supposing that the scheme is somehow an illustration of the actual processes in capitalism and in forgetting the simplifications that go together with it.[32]

Despite Grossmann's insistence that the schemes cannot be used to depict the actual development tendencies of capitalism, Paul Mattick – who otherwise regarded Grossmann's work as a major contribution to the defence of the theory of breakdown – argued that he made an 'unnecessary concession' to the view that the reproduction schemes could 'demonstrate the possibility of frictionless exchange between the departments of production'.[33] In seeking to demonstrate the possibility of equilibrium Bauer had followed the operation of his scheme for only four years. Grossmann continued the calculations over a period of 35 years. Without changing any of the specifications outlined by Bauer, Grossmann showed that the scheme, far from proving the possibility of harmonious expansion, eventually broke down.

It is important to clarify that Grossmann's demonstration of the impossibility of equilibrium is *not* an arithmetical proof of the tendency towards capitalist breakdown. To claim this would be to make the same methodological mistake as Bauer and others in drawing conclusions about reality directly from the abstract reproduction schemes. Grossmann's treatment of Bauer simply proves the impossibility of equilibrium even in his abstract model, with all its simplifying assumptions. Given the prevailing confusions about Marx's method it is not surprising that many readers of Grossmann interpreted his academic exercise of arithmetically disproving Bauer's already methodologically flawed analysis as a proof of the theory of breakdown. This perhaps explains Mattick's impatience with Grossmann's indulgence in the exercise.

Counteracting tendencies

Grossmann repeatedly emphasised that Marx's theory of breakdown does not 'directly correspond with the appearances of bourgeois society in its day to day life'.[34] He observed, in presenting the theory of breakdown, that 'many real factors pertaining to the world of appearances are consciously excluded from the analysis.'[35] While this method allowed Marx 'to determine the direction in which the accumulation of capital works' it nevertheless meant that 'the results of this analysis have only a provisional character.'[36] The objective of representing the workings of the capitalist system in a comprehensive form therefore requires that the analysis be pursued further.

Marx moved further in this direction in *Capital Volume Three*, subtitled 'capitalist production as a whole'. As Grossmann observed, this meant that in addition to discussing the tendency of the rate of profit to fall it was also necessary to consider 'several countertendencies that hinder the complete working out of the breakdown'.[37] Grossmann's work is divided equally between a discussion of the fundamental tendency to breakdown and an elaboration of various countertendencies. The formal division in the mode of presentation, however, is not meant to suggest that the two conflicting movements relate to one another in an external and arbitrary fashion. The countertendencies are generated in the course of the accumulation process itself. Grossmann discusses a series of countertendencies in terms of two broad categories; those which are internal to the mechanism of capital accumulation and those which arise through the world market and the global extension of capitalist social relations. The implications of Marx's method emerge most forcefully in Grossmann's analysis of the world market, a subject that has caused confusion among Marxists since the turn of the century.

Grossmann pointed out that, in the course of his analysis of capitalist production, Marx abstracted from the issue of foreign trade. He goes on to note that subsequent commentators regarded this as a major omission that implied that Marx had 'built his system on the unproven and improbable assumption that there are no non-capitalist countries'. Grossmann insisted that this objection arose out of an ignorance of Marx's method:

> The grotesque character of the entire exposition is quite obvious. It is the product of a whole generation of theoreticians who go straight for results without any philosophical background, without bothering to ask by what methodological means were those results established and what significance do they contain within the total structure of the system.[38]

Marx did not forget the question of the world market; he consciously left the issue aside because it is irrelevant to the task of conceptualising the fundamental contradictions of capitalist production. However he fully recognised the importance of the world market as an integral feature of capitalist development:

> Capitalist production rests on the *value* or the transformation of the labour embodied in the product into social labour. But this is only

[possible] on the basis of foreign trade and of the world market. This is at once the pre-condition and the result of capitalist production.[39]

As we have seen, under capitalism the products of labour share a common social character as values despite their different useful properties. The world market is contained in the very concept of value because it is the fullest development of this social form of the product. The conversion of the product of the whole world of producers into commodities for exchange is the highest expression of the social character of value production. Furthermore, the fundamental objective of capitalist production – the continual expansion of capital through the appropriation of the social product as surplus value – gives an impetus to the extension of commodity relations on a global scale. There is in effect an inherent universalising tendency within capitalist production.

Nevertheless, in terms of the structure of Marx's analysis of capitalist society, a detailed investigation of the world market must *follow* the exploration of the inner nature of capitalist production. This is because the global extension of exchange relations, though posed abstractly in the concept of value, is concretely realised in the form of counteracting tendencies to capitalist breakdown. It is not the inner nature of the value form itself that provides the practical impetus to the formation of the world market and the globalisation of capitalist production relations. It is the concrete development of that form, in the tendency of the rate of profit to fall and capitalist breakdown, that prompts the extension of capitalist social relations.

Grossmann's discussion of the globalisation of capitalist production in terms of counteracting the tendency to breakdown yielded useful insights into the dynamics of modern imperialism. He noted that there was 'a big difference between the capital exports of today's monopoly capitalism and those of early capitalism', that unlike the modern era the export 'of capital was not "typical" of the capitalism of that epoch, it was a transient, periodic phenomenon'.[40] By contrast, in contemporary conditions the overproduction of capital had ceased to be a 'merely passing phenomenon', and had started 'to dominate the whole of economic life'.[41] He concluded: 'Under these circumstances the overabundance of capital can be surmounted only through capital exports. These have therefore become a typical and indispensable move in all the advanced capitalist countries.'[42]

Grossmann provided a theory of imperialism organically linked to Marx's theory of the fundamental tendencies of capitalist production. While recognising the dynamic character of new patterns of capitalist development, he showed that these could be explained in terms of the underlying social laws governing capitalist production that were presented in Marx's *Capital*. Grossmann's demonstration of the capacity of Marx's theory to take account of new developments in capitalist society was one of his most important contributions. By showing how new trends modified the tendency to breakdown he demonstrated the open-ended and dynamic character of Marxist theory. He confirmed the vitality of Marxist theory by showing how it could grasp changing patterns of development on the basis of its understanding of the totality of capitalist social relations.

Breakdown and class struggle

Grossmann's presentation of the theory of breakdown provided the basis for restoring the connection between the critique of political economy and the theory of revolution that was at the heart of Marx's work. For Grossmann class struggle was the 'subjective bearer of change' within the objective conditions provided by the emergence, stagnation and breakdown of the capitalist system. Marx had a twofold interest in the class struggle. He was concerned with studying the class struggle as an expression of the existing conflict in society. But, more importantly, he was concerned with informing the active participation of the working class in the historical process. Marx's theory of class struggle was not merely a description of the existing state of society, but that 'part of his historical theory which endows it with concrete and profound meaning'.[43] In a society in a constant state of transition, the working class was the dynamic force for progress.

Grossmann emphasised that in discussing the trends towards breakdown it was not a question of the effect of economic factors on class relations, but of the totality of capitalist relations of production:

> In the materialist conception of history the social process as a whole is determined by the economic process. It is not the consciousness of mankind that produces social revolutions, but the contradictions of material life, the collisions between the productive forces of society and its social relations.[44]

For Grossmann the historical limit of capitalist society lay in proletarian revolution; the tendency towards breakdown, while an objective tendency of the system, is fully realised only in the overthrow of capitalism. It is thus impossible to abstract the class struggle (politics) from the tendency towards breakdown (economics). Just as capital itself is both the driving force and the limitation of capitalist development, so proletarian revolution offers the potential to unleash the productive potential of society from the constraints imposed by capitalist social relations.

In a letter to Mattick in 1931 Grossmann clarified his position against those who alleged that his book contained a theory of the 'automatic breakdown' of capitalism independent of the intervention of class struggle:

> It should be evident that the notion that capitalism must 'by itself' or 'automatically' collapse is alien to me ... But I did wish to show that the class struggle alone is *not* sufficient ... As a *dialectical* Marxist, I know that both sides of the process, objective and subjective elements, mutually influence each other. In the class struggle both these factors blend. One cannot 'wait' until *first* the 'objective' conditions are met, and only *then* let the 'subjective' elements go to work. That would be an insufficient and mechanical interpretation which is alien to me ... My breakdown theory does not intend to exclude the active intervention, but rather hopes to show when and under what conditions such an objective revolutionary situation can and will arise.[45]

Grossmann's dialectical approach thus enabled him to advance a coherent revolutionary perspective on the transformation of capitalist society. He transcended the mechanical and fatalist perspective on capitalist breakdown offered by Luxemburg in the earlier debate. He reminded those who would underestimate the role of the subjective factor that 'obviously, as Lenin remarks, "there are no absolutely hopeless situations"'.[46] In the final analysis, capitalism will not collapse by itself, and if it is not overthrown, there is always the possibility it will continue.

Marxism today

The method of producing theories by generalising from the most striking features of the contemporary capitalist economy has produced a spiralling instability among radical critics of the capitalist order over the 60 years since Grossmann's work was published. The career of the British economist John Strachey well exemplifies the results of this approach in the three decades after 1929. In response to the world slump of the 1930s, Strachey argued that the collapse of capitalism was imminent and took up a political position close to the official communist movement. Once the post-war boom was underway, Strachey argued that the capitalist system had overcome its problems and could continue indefinitely. He ended his political career on the right wing of the British Labour Party.[47]

In the 1950s and 1960s the continuation of the post-war expansion in the advanced capitalist world encouraged theories such as 'state monopoly capitalism' and the 'permanent arms economy' which interpreted this phase of relative stability as a new epoch of capitalist development. A focus on technical factors, such as the growth of state intervention, the spread of multinational corporations and the arms race, rather than on questions of production and class conflict, was characteristic of these theories. Meanwhile the continuing backwardness of the third world led to theories of 'underdevelopment' and 'unequal exchange' which anticipated that continuing prosperity in the North would coexist with continuing impoverishment in the South.[48]

The re-emergence of recessionary trends in the advanced capitalist countries in the 1970s, at the same time as a number of formerly backward countries underwent a process of rapid industrialisation and development, threw radical theory into disarray. The result was further variations of versions of Marxism that had already been revised so far as to become scarcely recognisable. The fragmentation of radical economic theory was apparent in the increasingly rapid turnover of theories such as 'Fordism', 'peripheral Fordism', 'post-Fordism', 'the new international division of labour' and so on. Each only claimed to offer a partial explanation of global trends and consistently emphasised technical factors – changes in the labour process, the globalisation of production, the impact of high-tech communications systems on the financial markets – rather than offering any wider social analysis.[49]

The more radical economists fixed on superficial aspects of society the more quickly their theories were repudiated. Rather than reconsider their own method, they moved away from an untrustworthy empirical reality towards pure theory. Desperate to escape the dead-end that all various revisions of Marxism had reached and despairing of the possibility of producing a coherent and unified theory of complex economic trends, they sought to reorient the intellectual project. The objective of comprehending capitalist society was replaced by an obsession for testing propositions in isolation from any social considerations.

The new wave of academic Marxists set about applying the rules of formal logic to Marx's theory and they were soon able to declare central tenets of Marx's theory disproven. In fact, it was fairly easy to dismiss Marx by using a system of logic which started from the presumption of an essential harmony in the relations among varied phenomena: their conclusions were already assured by the simple act of starting out with the method of formal logic. Exponents of this approach merely pronounced as conclusions what was already given in their methodological assumptions. The outcome of this speculative exercise was to replace Marx's emphasis on the contradictory, socially-constructed, character of capitalist production relations with an idealist conception of capitalism as a process of formal interaction among technically defined factors of production.

The desire to abandon the realm of capitalist social relations and embrace the academic form exemplifies the latest school of 'analytic Marxists'. The analytical school has systematised the introduction of all the fundamentals of bourgeois economics into a Marxist framework. Whereas earlier schools rejected Marx's theory of breakdown, they retained some notion of crisis, even if this was relegated to the sphere of circulation. By contrast the analytic Marxists explicitly reject the notion that capitalism is a contradictory system. They celebrate the role of pure theory and, in doing so, presume that capitalism is a harmonious economic system. Their project is to assimilate into Marxism elements of all the fragmented theories that are currently popular among the liberal intelligentsia.

According to John Roemer, Marxism must embrace 'general equilibrium theory, game theory and the arsenal of modelling techniques developed by neoclassical economics'. He goes on to state: 'The revised Marxism I present is shaped by the insights that the tools of contemporary economics – that is, neoclassical economics – can bear.'[50] Elsewhere Roemer provides a flavour of how this new brand of Marxism differs from other schools of thought: 'what distinguishes Marxism ... from these other approaches, is not easy to define.'[51] John Elster, another leading exponent of the analytical approach, laments: 'Although I remember being upset by Paul Samuelson's statement on the centenary of the publication of *Capital I* that Marx was basically "a minor post-Ricardian", I now largely subscribe to that view, if taken exclusively as an evaluation of the economic theories found in *Capital II* and *III*.' For Elster, Marx's 'most important achievement was the analysis of the capitalist factory and the capitalist entrepreneur'.[52] On the other hand, the 'quasi-deductive procedure used in ... the opening chapters of *Capital I* ... is barely intelligible'.[53] In other words, according to Elster, Marx's insights amount to a few descriptive passages; the rest is dead wood.

In his critique of bourgeois economics, Marx wrote that 'the last form is the *academic form*.' He characterised this as systematising a tendency in the bourgeois outlook to deny 'actual contradictions in the life of society'.[54] For adherents of the academic form, economic contradictions and social conflict were of no interest; their preoccupation was with learned discourse and formal rigour. Marx ridiculed the scientific pretensions of the academics, arguing that they merely replaced the polemical style of earlier apologists for capitalism with a spurious erudition. He noted that the academic form included what it took to be 'the "best" from all sources ... peacefully gathered together in a miscellany' with little discrimination between insights and confusions.[55] The result, as he observed, was that real insights simply floated 'as oddities in its mediocre pap'. In the academic form even 'the genuine thought of a Smith or a Ricardo, and others – not just their vulgar elements – is made to appear insipid.'[56] Little could Marx have anticipated that the academic form would be embraced by those calling themselves Marxists. The analytic Marxists have even succeeded in making Marx's theory of exploitation appear insipid.

In adopting the idealist method of bourgeois apologists for capitalism, the analytical Marxists in the 1990s imagine that the scientific status of a theory depends on its internal logical coherence. Whether or not it reflects the actual course of social development becomes irrelevant. Nevertheless, the academic form of radical economic theory differs in one crucial respect from bourgeois economic theory. Bourgeois economists do not have to account for the theoretical deficiencies of their approach. In periods of economic crisis the capitalist class does not admit the faulty character of its ideology. Indeed, it declares the correctness of its ideas more forcefully, blames rival social interests for economic ills and prepares to fight to defend its system. By contrast, theories that are critical of capitalism, no matter how tame, cannot rely on the patronage of ruling interests. Capitalism has not created an alternative social constituency whose material interests are reflected in a theory which sets out to re-work the idealised conception of the capitalist system held by capitalists. Marxism is obliged to seek its confirmation in material reality and found itself on social forces which have an active interest in challenging the rule of capital. A Marxism which celebrates the realm of pure speculation is simply waiting to be discredited by developments in social reality and ridiculed by its bourgeois opponents. Indeed the striking feature of analytic Marxism is that it has a narrower basis than any of its predecessors and thus its appeal is likely to be even more transient. Analytical Marxism symbolises little more than the shift of an increasingly isolated radical intelligentsia towards an accommodation with a pro-capitalist world view.

The irony of today's radical academic critics of Marx is that their criticisms have much in common with those of generations of right-wing critics of Marx. Conservative commentators have long attempted to discredit Marxism by questioning the scientific status of the method informing his work. Such a criticism of Marx was made in 1896 by the Austrian economist Eugen von Bohm-Bawerk, in one of the first and most famous conservative critiques of *Capital*. Bohm-Bawerk claimed that Marx founded his theory 'on no firmer ground than the formal dialectic'.[57] Reality, he insisted, was 'turned and twisted' to make it conform to the dialectic. Grossmann cites a contemporary right-wing commentator who, though impressed by the 'grand style' of Marx's theory of crisis, argued that it 'flowed from his application of the "dialectical method"' rather than a concrete investigation of capitalism.[58] In similar terms the leading pre-war American economist Joseph Schumpeter claimed that Marx's views on crisis could not 'be made to follow logically from his "laws" of the capitalist process'.[59]

Right-wing commentators contend that there is a dualism in Marx's theory. On the one hand, Marx claims to investigate a concrete social phenomenon – capitalist production. On the other hand, he employs a philosophical method to order the concepts used to depict the system. In their view Marx's theory is not a study of the real character of capitalist production, but an exercise in dialectical reasoning. They go on to argue that concepts such as value, surplus value, constant and variable capital have nothing to do with grasping reality; they were invented by Marx to make his peculiar brand of speculative thinking hang together. The dualist interpretation of Marx, in effect, argues that contradictions do not exist within capitalism. Rather there is a contradiction between the nature of capitalist production and Marx's abstract, dialectical mode of presenting economic reality. Today's academic Marxists in their rejection of Marx's conceptual framework share this view that Marx merely indulged in an illogical mode of reasoning.

Such an assessment of his work was, in fact, already familiar to Marx. In the 1873 'afterword' to the second German edition of *Capital Volume One*, he discussed the apparent conflict between the 'severely realistic' character of the material analysed and the abstract form in which it is presented.[60] Marx defended his method by pointing out that capitalist production itself is a contradictory social process. He insisted that the descriptive and formal methods of bourgeois economics were really the highest form of idealism since they failed to grasp the contradictory nature of capitalist production. The dialectical method, he claimed, was undeniably abstract in form. But its content was the conception of capitalist production in its concrete existence as an economic order fraught with contradictions.

Marx recognised that his method of presentation 'may appear as if we had before us a mere a priori construction' in the sense that the entire argument in *Capital* seems to be determined by an arbitrary choice of method.[61] Yet in contrast to today's revisionists with their unsustained assertions in favour of the formal logical approach, this is not the case.

Marx's method of presentation is not his starting point but the result of his enquiries into capitalist production. In his investigations into capitalist production he first sought to 'appropriate the material in detail, to analyse its different forms of development, to trace out their inner connection'.[62] Only then did he seek to present the 'actual movement' in theoretical form. Marx adopted the dialectical method because it was the only means adequate to depict the fundamental conclusion of his enquiries – that capitalism is an internally contradictory mode of production.

Grossmann's work is a challenge to the schematic approach to theoretical investigation that has dominated the Marxist movement for most of the twentieth century. He shows that the quest for definitive conclusions in the investigation of capitalist social reality is antithetical to Marxism. Capitalism, as a system in which the basic social contradictions are both generated and contained in new and complex economic forms, embodies an inherent dynamic for change. The theoretical reflection of capitalist social reality must be able to comprehend the fundamental nature of these social contradictions and recognise their evolving character. Only a theory founded on a method that embraces the social contradictions of the capitalist order can hope to explain the source of contemporary economic problems. In doing so it can give direction to the quest to resolve those contradictions in the interests of society. Grossmann's great service was to have shown that Marx's method is the essential foundation of a revolutionary critique of capitalist society.

Notes

1. Peter Berger, *The Capitalist Revolution: Fifty Propositions about Prosperity, Equality and Liberty*, Aldershot: Wildwood House, 1986, p. 5.
2. Gareth Stedman Jones, 'editorial', *Marxism Today*, February 1990.
3. Michel Aglietta, *A Theory of Capitalist Regulation – the US Experience*, trans. David Fernbach, London: Verso, 1987, p. 163.
4. John Roemer, *Free to Lose: An Introduction to Marxist Economic Philosophy*, London: Radius, 1988, p. 2.
5. Karl Marx, *Capital, a Critical Analysis of Capitalist Production*, vol. 1, London: Lawrence and Wishart, 1954, trans. Samuel Moore and Edward Aveling, p. 715.
6. Eduard Bernstein, *Evolutionary Socialism*, New York: Schocken, 1961, pp. 79-80.
7. Grossmann, *Law of Accumulation*, p. 40.
8. Grossmann, *Law of Accumulation*, p. 39.
9. Grossmann, *Law of Accumulation*, p. 41.
10. Grossmann, *Law of Accumulation*, p. 41.

11.   Karl Kautsky, *Materialistische Geschichtsaufassung*, Berlin, 1927, p. 559.
12.   Grossmann, *Law of Accumulation*, p. 29.
13.   Grossmann, *Law of Accumulation*, p. 38.
14.   Grossmann, *Law of Accumulation*, p. 29.
15.   Grossmann, *Law of Accumulation*, p. 30.
16.   Grossmann, *Law of Accumulation*, p. 29.
17.   Grossmann, *Law of Accumulation*, p. 29.
18.   Grossmann, *Law of Accumulation*, p. 83.
19.   Marx, *Capital*, vol. 1, 1954, p. 115.
20.   Grossmann, *Law of Accumulation*, p. 31.
21.   Grossmann, *Law of Accumulation*, p. 32.
22.   Grossmann, *Law of Accumulation*, p. 79–80.
23.   Grossmann, *Law of Accumulation*, p. 80.
24.   Marx, *Capital, a Critique of Political Economy*, vol. 3, London: Lawrence and Wishart, 1959, p. 213 (emphasis in the original).
25.   Grossmann, *Law of Accumulation*, p. 84.
26.   Marx, *Capital*, vol. 3, 1959, p. 242.
27.   Grossmann, *Law of Accumulation*, p. 131.
28.   Rosa Luxemburg, *Accumulation of Capital*, London: Monthly Review Press, 1968, p. 348.
29.   Rosa Luxemburg, *Accumulation of Capital*, p. 354.
30.   Grossmann, *Law of Accumulation*, p. 42.
31.   Grossmann, *Law of Accumulation*, p. 67.
32.   Grossmann, *Law of Accumulation*, p. 69.
33.   Paul Mattick, *Economic Crisis and Crisis Theory*, London: Merlin, 1981, p. 109.
34.   Grossmann, *Law of Accumulation*, p. 130.
35.   Grossmann, *Law of Accumulation*, p. 130.
36.   Grossmann, *Law of Accumulation*, p. 130.
37.   Grossmann, *Law of Accumulation*, p. 134.
38.   Grossmann, *Law of Accumulation*, p. 165.
39.   Marx, *Theories of Surplus Value*, Part III, London: Lawrence and Wishart, 1972, p. 253.
40.   Grossmann, *Law of Accumulation*, p. 194.
41.   Grossmann, *Law of Accumulation*, p. 194.
42.   Grossmann, *Law of Accumulation*, p. 194.
43.   Grossmann, 'The Evolutionist Revolt Against Classical Economics', *The Journal of Political Economy*, vol. 51, nos. 5 and 6, p. 522.
44.   Grossmann, *Law of Accumulation*, p. 52.
45.   Quoted in R. Jacoby, 'The Politics of the Crisis Theory: Towards the Critique of Automatic Marxism II', *Telos*, 23 1975, p. 37.
46.   Grossmann, *Law of Accumulation*, p. 95.
47.   Compare John Strachey, *The Coming Struggle for Power*, London: Gollancz, 1932, and *Contemporary Capitalism*, London: Gollancz, 1956.

48. See Andre Gunder Frank, *Latin America – Underdevelopment or Revolution*, New York: Monthly Review Press, 1970 and Arghiri Emmanuel, *Unequal Exchange: A Study of the Imperialism of Trade*, New York, 1972.

49. See Alain Lipietz, *The Enchanted World – Inflation, Credit and the World Crisis*, trans. Ian Patterson, London: Verso, 1983, *Mirages and Miracles – the Crisis of Global Fordism*, trans. David Macey, London: Verso, 1987, and Michel Aglietta, *A Theory of Capitalist Regulation – the US Experience*, trans. David Fernbach, London: Verso, 1987, for examples of the theories of Fordism and post-Fordism.

50. John Roemer, *Free to Lose*, p. vii.

51. John Roemer, *Value, Exploitation and Class*, London: Harmood, 1986, p. 5.

52. John Elster, *Making Sense of Marx*, London: Cambridge University Press, 1985, pp. 513–14.

53. John Elster, *Making Sense of Marx*, p. 37.

54. Marx, *Theories of Surplus Value*, part II, p. 502.

55. Marx, *Theories of Surplus Value*, part II, p. 502.

56. Marx, *Theories of Surplus Value*, part II, p. 502.

57. Eugen von Bohm-Bawerk, *Karl Marx and the Close of his System*, Philadelphia: Orion, 1984, p. 101.

58. Grossmann, *Law of Accumulation*, p. 88.

59. Joseph Schumpeter, *Capitalism, Socialism and Democracy*, London: Unwin, 1987, p. 39.

60. Marx, *Capital*, vol. 1, pp. 27–8.

61. Marx, *Capital*, vol. 1, p. 28.

62. Marx, *Capital*, vol. 1, p. 28.

Introduction

HENRYK GROSSMANN

The present book forms part of a larger work to appear soon on the tendencies of development of capitalism in the theory of Marx. The origins of this work lie in lectures prepared in the course of 1926–7 at the *Institut fur Sozialforschung* for the University of Frankfurt.

The results of my research are twofold: (1) for the first time ever the method underlying *Capital* has been subjected to a reconstruction and (2) on this basis important areas of Karl Marx's system of theory have been presented from a fundamentally new perspective. One of the new findings is the theory of breakdown which is expounded below and which forms the cornerstone of the economic system of Marx. For decades this theory was at the centre of fierce controversies of theory. Yet in all that time no one ever attempted a reconstruction or definition of its place in the system as a whole.

It would be a useless task to increase the dogmas surrounding Marxism with a new interpretation and simply reinforce the view that Marxism has become purely a matter of interpretation. My view is that the unsatisfactory state of the literature on Marx is ultimately rooted in the fact – which will appear strange to some – that until today no one has proposed any ideas at all, let alone any clear ideas, about Marx's method of investigation. There has been a general tendency to cling to the results of the theory: these have been the focal point of interest, on the part of both critics as well as defenders. In all this the method has been totally ignored. The basic principle of any scientific investigation – that however fascinating a conclusion might appear, it is worthless divorced from an appreciation of the way in which it was established – was forgotten. A conclusion can after all only become a matter of conflicting interpretation when it is completely divorced from the path that led to its formulation.

A proper exposition of Marx's method of investigation will have to be left to my major work. The short methodological remarks that follow appear to me to be indispensable only insofar as they bear on the understanding of the arguments of this book.

29

The real world of concrete, empirically given appearances is that which is to be investigated. But in itself this is much too complicated to be known directly. We gain an approach to it only by stages. To this end we make various simplifying assumptions that enable us to gain an understanding of the inner structure of the object under investigation. This is the first stage of cognition in Marx's method of approximation to reality. It is the particular methodological principle that finds its specific reflection in Marx's reproduction schemes, which form the starting-point of his entire analysis, and which already underlie the arguments of *Capital Volume One*. Among the numerous assumptions connected with the reproduction schemes are the following: that the capitalist mode of production exists in an isolated state (foreign trade is ignored); that society consists of capitalists and workers alone (abstract from all so-called 'third persons' in the course of our analysis); that commodities exchange at value; that credit is ignored; that the value of money is assumed constant, and so on and so forth.

It is clear that thanks to these fictitious assumptions, we achieve a certain distance from empirical reality, even while the latter remains the target of our explanations. It follows that conclusions established on such a structure of assumptions can have a purely provisional character and therefore that the initial stage of the cognitive process must be followed by a second, concluding stage. Any set of simplifying assumptions will go together with a subsequent process of correction that takes account of the elements of actual reality that were disregarded initially. In this way, stage by stage, the investigation as a whole draws nearer to the complicated appearances of the concrete world and becomes consistent with it.

Yet an almost incredible thing happened – people saw that Marx works with simplifying assumptions but they failed to notice the purely provisional nature of the initial stages and ignored the fact that in the methodological construction of the system each of the several fictitious, simplifying assumptions is subsequently modified. Provisional conclusions were taken for final results. Otherwise it is quite impossible to understand how E Lederer could criticise Marx's method the way he does. He argues that simplification is part of any theory but he himself would not wish to go as far in this direction as Marx because 'excessive simplification only creates problems in the way of our understanding. If, like Marx we suppose the whole economic universe to be composed only of workers and capitalists, then the sphere of production becomes too simple' (1925, p. 368).

This pure misunderstanding of Marx's method explains why F Sternberg reproaches Marx for 'having analysed capitalism under the quite unrealistic assumption that there is no non-capitalist sector. Such an analysis works with assumptions that have not been demonstrated' (1926, p. 301). K Muhs goes so far as to say that 'Marx obviously indulged in massive orgies of abstraction' and introduced 'impossible because irrational assumptions that were bound to defeat any analysis of the historic process' (1927, p. 10).

Anyone who has grasped the essence of Marx's method will immediately be struck by the totally superficial character of these criticisms, and a critique of them would be quite superfluous. It is also not difficult to see why in the existing debates on Marx's theory the greatest confusion could and was bound to arise. Marx's method of approximation to reality is defined by two stages, sometimes even three. Entire phenomena and problems are tackled at least twice, initially under a set of simplifying assumptions, and later in their final form. As long as this remains an obscure mystery, we shall repeatedly run up against contradictions between the individual parts of the theory. To take one example, this is the source of the famous 'contradiction' discovered by Bohm-Bawerk between *Capital Volumes One and Three*.

The problem analysed in this book was tackled by Marx in three stages. Initially he examines the contradictions that define the process of reproduction in its normal trajectory, or he examines simple reproduction. At a second stage of his analysis, he focuses on the impact of the accumulation of capital with its resulting tendency towards breakdown. Finally, in the third stage Marx investigates the factors that modify this tendency.

The question I shall examine is whether fully developed capitalism, regarded as an exclusively prevalent and universally widespread economic system relying only on its own resources, contains the capacity to develop the process of reproduction indefinitely and on a continually expanding basis, or whether this process of expansion runs into limits of one sort or another which it cannot overcome. In examining this problem the moments specific to the capitalist mode of production have to be drawn in. Ever since the beginnings of human history it has always been the capacity of the individual worker with his labour power L to set into motion a greater mass of the means of production M that has indicated technological and economic progress. Technological advance and the development of mankind's productivity are directly expressed in the growth of M relative to L. Like every other form of economy, socialism too will be characterised by technological advance in its immediately natural form $M:L$.

The specific nature of capitalist commodity production shows itself in the fact that it is not simply a labour process in which products are created by the elements of production M and L. Rather the capitalistic form of commodity production is constructed dualistically – it is simultaneously a labour process for the creation of products and a valorisation process. The elements of production M and L figure not only in their natural form, but at the same time as values c and v respectively. They are used for the production of a sum of values w, and indeed only on condition that over and above the used up value magnitudes c and v there is a surplus s (that is, $s = w - c + v$). The capitalist expansion of production, or accumulation of capital, is defined by the fact that the expansion of M relative to L occurs on the basis of the law of value; it takes the specific form of a constantly expanding capital c relative to the sum of wages v, such that both components of capital are necessarily valorised. It follows that the reproduction process can only be continued and expanded further if the advanced, constantly growing capital $c + v$ can secure a profit, s (surplus value). The problem can then be defined as follows – is a process of this sort possible in the long run?

The following study is divided into three chapters. The first chapter surveys the existing literature on Marx's theory of breakdown and describes the views of more recent Marxists about the end of capitalism. The second chapter is an attempted reconstruction of the Marxian theory of accumulation and breakdown (this being the basic element of the theory of crisis) in its pure form, unaffected by the operation of 'countertendencies'. The concluding chapter attempts to grasp these counteracting tendencies which modify the law of breakdown in its pure form. By this means it seeks to establish a certain basic consistency between the actual reality of capitalism and the law in its pure operation.

Here it is not a matter of describing in detail the actual processes that go on in the environment of capitalism. On principle I shall abstain from presenting the extensive and rather exhausting factual material. The work is intended to bear a theoretical character, not a descriptive one. To the extent that factual material is presented, the aim is to illustrate the various theoretical propositions and deductions. I have only tried to show how the empirically ascertainable tendencies of the world economy which are regarded as defining characteristics of the latest stage of capitalism (monopolistic organisations, export of capital, the struggle to divide up the sources of raw materials, etc) are only secondary surface appearances that stem from the essence of capital accumulation as their primary basis. Through this inner connection it is possible to use a single principle, the Marxian law of value, to explain clearly all the appearances of capitalism without recourse to any special *ad hoc* theories, and to throw light on its latest stage – imperialism. I do not need to labour the point that this is the only form in which the tremendous consistency of Marx's economic system can be clearly drawn out.

Because I deliberately confine myself to describing only the economic presuppositions of the breakdown of capitalism in this study, let me dispel any suspicion of 'pure economism' from the start. It is unnecessary to waste paper over the connection between economics and politics; that there is a connection is obvious. However, while Marxists have written extensively on the political revolution, they have neglected to deal theoretically with the economic aspect of the question and have failed to appreciate the true content of Marx's theory of breakdown. My sole concern here is to fill in this gap in the Marxist tradition.

1 The Downfall of Capitalism in the Existing Literature

The point at issue

Already prior to Marx certain representatives of political economy had a clear presentiment of the historically ephemeral character of the bourgeois mode of production. Jean C L Simonde de Sismondi was the first to uphold it against David Ricardo. He argued that in the course of time every mode of production becomes 'intolerable' and 'the social order, continually threatened, can only be maintained by force' (cited Grossmann, 1924, pp. 63–4). However, in terms of capitalism, this conclusion was based not on an economic analysis of its mode of production but purely on historical analogies. Therefore Marx was right to say that:

> at the bottom of his [Sismondi's] argument is indeed the inkling that *new* forms of the appropriation of wealth must correspond to productive forces and the material and social conditions for the production of wealth which have developed within capitalist society; that the bourgeois forms are only transitory and contradictory forms. (1972, p. 56)

A quarter of a century after Sismondi, Richard Jones developed the same insights when he described capitalism 'as a transitional phase in the development of social production' (cited Marx, 1972, p. 428). But like Sismondi, Jones gained his insight into the historically transitory character of capitalism through a mainly historical-comparative analysis of successive forms of economy.

The development of the productive power of social labour is the driving force of historical evolution. When the earliest modes of production proved unable to develop the productive forces of society any further, they were bound to disintegrate:

Hence the necessity for the separation, for the rupture, for the antithesis of labour and property (by which property in the conditions of production is to be understood). The most extreme form of this rupture, and the one in which the productive forces of social labour are also most powerfully developed, is capital. (Marx, 1972, p. 423)

Elsewhere Marx writes:

It is one of the civilising aspects of capital that it enforces this surplus-labour in a manner and under conditions which are more advantageous to the development of the productive forces, social relations and the creation of the elements for a new and higher form than under the preceding forms of slavery, serfdom, etc. (1959, p. 819)

At a certain point in its historical development capitalism fails to encourage the expansion of the productive forces any further. From this point on the downfall of capitalism becomes economically inevitable. To provide an exact description of this process and to grasp its causes through a scientific analysis of capitalism was the real task Marx posed for himself in *Capital*. His scientific advance over Sismondi and Jones consisted precisely in this. But how did Marx carry through this analysis? He says, at a certain stage:

The monopoly of capital becomes a fetter upon the mode of production which has flourished alongside with and under it. Centralisation of the means of production and the socialisation of labour at last reach a point where they become incompatible with their capitalist integument. This integument is burst asunder. The knell of capitalist private property sounds. (1954, p. 715)

Marx refers to an antagonism between the productive forces and their capitalist shell. What is this, however? There is nothing more erroneous than the prevalent identification of the development of productive forces with the growth of c in relation to v. This simply confuses the capitalist shell in which human productivity obtains a form of appearance with the essence of that productivity itself. The development of productivity has in itself nothing to do with the capitalist valorisation process which, as a process of formation of values, has its roots in *abstract human labour*. The antagonism that Marx refers to is between the forces of production in their material shape as elements of the labour process – as means of production and labour power – and these same forces in their specifically capitalist shell, in the shape they assume as values c and v in the valorisation–process. In *Capital Volume Three* Marx attacks:

> the confusion and identification of the process of social production with the simple labour-process ... To the extent that the labour-process is simply a process between man and nature, its simple elements remain common to all social forms of development. But each specific historical form of this process further develops its material foundations and its social forms. Whenever a certain stage of its maturity has been reached, the specific historical form is discarded and gives way to a higher one ... A conflict then ensues between the material development of production and its social form. (1959, pp. 883–4)

The form of the productive forces peculiar to capitalism, their capitalist shell ($c{:}v$) becomes a fetter on the form they share in common with all modes of production ($M{:}L$). The solution of this problem forms the specific task of this book.

It is quite characteristic of the intellectual crisis, even decay, of contemporary bourgeois economics that it denies that there is any such problem as accumulation. The apologetic optimism of bourgeois economics has simply extinguished all interest in a deeper understanding and analysis of today's mechanism of production. Economists like J B Clark (1907) and Alfred Marshall (1890) imagine that the psychological and individual motivations driving capitalists to 'save' account for the entire problem of the accumulation of capital. They do not bother to ask if there are objective conditions that determine the scope, the tempo and finally the maximal limits of the accumulation of capital. If accumulation is purely a function of the subjective propensities of individuals and the number of these individuals grows constantly, how do we explain the fact that the tempo of accumulation shows periodically alternating phases of acceleration and slow down? How do we account for the fact that the tempo of accumulation in the advanced capitalist countries is often slower than that in the less developed, although the number of those individuals is obviously greater in the former?

Elsewhere Marshall tries to explain things with the banal observation that the extent of the demand for capital depends on the level of the rate of interest. But Marshall breaks off his analysis where the real problems begin. Prior to the First World War the USA was massively in debt to Europe despite high domestic interest rates. On the other hand, in 1927 the

USA exported capital sums totalling 14.5 billion dollars, and this export of capital showed no signs of abating, although the rate of interest at home had already fallen to 3.5 per cent. This also contradicts the analogous view of G Cassel that the 'low rate of interest that prevails during a depression obviously acts as a powerful stimulus to the expanded production of fixed capital' (1923, p. 570).

Why, despite the low rate of interest in the USA, did the expansion of production come to a halt in that country, or why was capital exported and not invested at home? If one answers that higher rates of interest prevailed abroad, the problem is only displaced. For why did the rate of interest fall in the USA? Because of an 'oversupply' of capital there? Then under what conditions does such an oversupply of capital arise?

This brings us back to the problem that is completely ignored in contemporary economics. In this respect Marx was closer to classical economy in the way he posed the problem. But whereas classical economy presumed the possibilities of an unlimited accumulation of capital, Marx predicted insuperable limits to the development of capitalism and its inevitable economic downfall.

How did Marx conduct this proof? This brings us to the well-known debate regarding the form in which Marx grounded the 'necessity of socialism'. K Diehl tells us that 'Marx's theory of value never formed the fundamental basis of his socialistic principles' (1898, p. 42). According to him, Marx's socialism is grounded not in the Marxist law of value, but in his materialist conception of history. As proof of the argument that the labour theory of value contains little that is specifically socialist, Diehl cites the case of Ricardo who likewise saw in labour the most suitable measure of value. For Diehl the moral postulate of a just distribution of income forms the only possible link between socialism and the law of value. However, as there is no such postulate in Marx, Diehl rejects the idea that Marx himself draws any such connection.

This widespread conception is totally false. Under capitalism the entire mechanism of the productive process is ruled by the law of value, and just as its dynamic and tendencies are only comprehensible in terms of this law its final end, the breakdown, is likewise only explicable in terms of it. In fact Marx provided such an explanation.

The idea that capitalism 'creates its own negation with the inexorability of a natural process' was already enunciated in *Capital Volume One* in the section on the historical tendency of capitalist accumulation (1954, pp. 713–15). But Marx did not explicitly state how this negating tendency asserts itself, how it must lead to breakdown of capitalism or through what immediate causes the system meets its economic downfall. If we then turn to the corresponding chapter of *Capital Volume Three* dealing with the 'law of the tendency of the rate of profit to fall', we are immediately disappointed (1959, pp. 207–26). The very causes that affect the process of accumulation also produce the fall in the rate of profit. But is this fall a symptom of the breakdown tendency? How does this tendency work itself out? Methodologically speaking, this is where Marx should have demonstrated the breakdown tendency. Indeed Marx does ask, 'Now what must be the form of this double-edged law of a decrease in the *rate* of profit and a simultaneous increase in the absolute *mass* of profit arising from the same causes?'. We feel now the decisive answer will come. But it does not.

Already in 1872 a Petersburg reviewer of *Capital Volume One* wrote: 'The scientific value of such an inquiry lies in the disclosing of the special laws that regulate the origin, existence, development and death of a given social organism and its replacement by another, higher one' (Marx, 1954, p. 28). Citing these words with the comment that they provide 'a striking description' of his own method, Marx says about the dialectical method that:

> it includes in its comprehension and affirmative recognition of the existing state of things, at the same time also, the recognition of the negation of that state, of its inevitable breaking up; because it regards every historically developed social form as being in fluid movement, and therefore takes into account its transient nature not less than its momentary existence. (p. 29)

In this sense Eduard Bernstein was perfectly right in saying, against social democracy's views about the end of capitalism: 'If the triumph of socialism were truly an immanent economic necessity, then it would have to be grounded in a proof of the inevitable economic breakdown of the present order of society' (Vorwarts, 26 March 1899). However Bernstein himself believed that such a proof was impossible and that socialism could not therefore be deduced from any economic compulsions. In Marx's theory of the 'negation of the negation' Bernstein could see only the 'pitfalls of the dialectical method of Hegel', a product 'of one of the residues of Hegel's dialectic of contradictions', a 'schema of development constructed on Hegelian lines' (Bernstein, 1899, p. 22). The theory of breakdown was, according to him, a 'purely speculative anticipation' of a process that had barely sprouted. This critique was based exclusively on the empirical fact that the material position of certain strata of the working class had improved. For Bernstein this was proof that 'the actual development had proceeded in a quite different direction' to that predicted by Marx. As if Marx had ever denied the possibility of such improvements in the position of the working class at specific stages of capitalist development.

How did Karl Kautsky answer Bernstein's critique? If Kautsky had tried to show that relative wages may fall even while real wages (measured in product terms) rise, and that even in this favourable situation the social misery and dependence on capital of the working class increase, he would have contributed to deepening Marx's theory. But Kautsky simply rejected the theory of breakdown, arguing that 'a special theory of breakdown was never proposed by Marx or by Engels' (1899, p. 42). Kautsky rejected the notion that the Marxist theory of breakdown establishes a tendency for the position of the working class under capitalism ultimately to deteriorate, in the strong sense of an absolute worsening of its situation, an absolute growth of its economic misery.

In fact Kautsky proposed the very opposite idea. According to him Marx and Engels were distinguished from the other currents of socialism by the circumstance that apart from the tendencies that depress the proletariat, they also foresaw, unlike other socialists, positive tendencies that elevate its position. They foresaw 'not simply an increase in its misery ... but also an increase in its training and organisation, its maturity and power' (p. 46). 'The notion that the proletariat increases in maturity and power is not only an essential part of Marx's theory of the breakdown of capitalism, it is its defining part' (p. 45). Thus Kautsky quietly ignored Bernstein's argument that for the triumph of socialism to be an immanent economic necessity it would have to be traced to underlying economic causes.

Yet the same Kautsky, who in dealing with Marx's theory one-sidely accentuated the tendencies that elevate the working class, would observe some years later that from a certain stage on these positive tendencies come to a standstill, that a retrograde movement gains the upper hand: 'The factors that led to an increase in real wages in the last few decades have already been wiped out' (1908, p. 54). Kautsky analyses these various factors. He shows that the trade unions have been continuously pushed back on the defensive while the capitalists, united in various associations, have enormously expanded in strength:

> All of which means that the period of rising real wages for one stratum of the working class after another has come to an end, and many sections will even face a period of wage cuts. This holds true not only for periods of temporary depression, but even for periods of prosperity. (p. 549)

A year later (1909) Kautsky noted that:

> It is remarkable that already in the last few years of prosperity, when industry worked continuously and there was a constant complaint of labour-shortage, workers proved unable to increase their real wages, and that they even fell. For various strata of the German working class this has been proved in unofficial studies. In America there is an official acknowledgement of this fact for the entire working class. (1909, p. 87)

Kautsky sees the facts, but his description does not go beyond this purely empirical level. Having rejected Marx's theory of breakdown, he finds it impossible to account for them in terms of Marxist theory. What deeper causes govern the movements of wages and what their fundamental tendency is he does not explain. Thus in the famous 'debate on revisionism' there was no real dispute about the theory of the economic breakdown of capitalism because both Kautsky and Bernstein abandoned Marx's theory of breakdown; the debate itself revolved around less important issues that were partly terminological.

This remarkable result of the Bernstein–Kautsky debate was not the only consequence of the fateful omissions in the exposition of *Capital Volume Three*. Right down to today there rules an absolute chaos of conflicting views, quite irrespective of whether the individuals concerned are bourgeois writers or belong to the radical or moderate wing of the workers' movement. Both the 'revisionist' professor M Tugan-Baranovsky and the 'Marxist' Rudolf Hilferding rejected the idea of a breakdown of capitalism – of absolute, unsurpassable limits to the accumulation of capital – replacing it with the theory of a possible unlimited development of capitalism. It was a great historical contribution of Rosa Luxemburg that she, in a conscious opposition to the distortions of these 'neo-harmonists' adhered to the basic lesson of *Capital* and sought to reinforce it with the proof that the continued development of capitalism encounters absolute economic limits.

Frankly Luxemburg's effort failed. According to her exposition, capitalism simply cannot exist without non-capitalist markets. If this line of reasoning were true, the breakdown tendency would have been a constant symptom of capitalism from its very inception, and it would be impossible to explain either periodic crises or the characteristic features of the latest stage of capitalism called 'imperialism'. Yet Luxemburg herself had the feeling that the breakdown tendency and imperialism only appear at an advanced stage of accumulation and find their sole basis in this stage. 'There is no doubt that the explanation for the economic roots of imperialism must be deduced from the laws of capital accumulation' (Luxemburg, 1972, p. 61).

However Luxemburg herself provided no such deduction and even made no attempt in this direction. Her own deduction of the necessary downfall of capitalism is not rooted in the immanent laws of the accumulation process, but in the transcendental fact of an absence of non-capitalist markets. Luxemburg shifts the crucial problem of capitalism from the sphere of production to that of circulation. Hence the form in which she conducts her proof of the absolute economic limits to capitalism comes close to the idea that the end of capitalism is a distant prospect because the capitalisation of the non-capitalist countries is the task of centuries. Moreover the collapse of the capitalist system is conceived in a mechanical fashion. Once capital rules the entire globe, the impossibility of capitalism will become evident. The result is to anticipate in theory a situation in which capitalism will be automatically destroyed, although we know that there are no absolutely hopeless situations. Luxemburg thus renders the theory of breakdown vulnerable to the charge of a quietist fatalism in which there is no room for the class struggle.

No other attempts were ever made to examine the problem of the 'catastrophe' of capitalism, as the neo-harmonists deliberately called it. Some examples will show the fantastic confusion that prevails today on this decisively important aspect of Marx's theory.

The conception of breakdown in the existing literature

First I shall deal with VG Simkhovitch, professor at the University of Columbia, New York, then with the German professors Werner Sombart and A Spiethoff and finally with the Frenchman Georges Sorel. Then I shall deal with the socialists H Cunow, A Braunthal, G Charasoff, Boudin, M Tugan-Baranovsky, Otto Bauer and Rudolf Hilferding.

Simkhovitch rightly disputes the view of Anton Menger that Marx's socialism is rooted in the moral interpretation of the theory of value. According to him this would simply wipe out the distinction between the early utopian socialism and modern scientific socialism (Simkhovitch, 1913, p. 2). Like Diehl, Simkhovitch argues that the Marxist notion of breakdown is anchored not in the theory of value but in a historically constructed proof. The decisive element is the materialist conception of history expounded in the *Communist Manifesto* which, Simkhovitch argues, 'contains no reference at all to any theory of value' (p. 4). Thus while Bernstein saw in the Marxist theory of breakdown a schema of development constructed on Hegelian lines, derived in a purely speculative manner from Hegel's dialectic, Simkhovitch sees in it a reflection and generalisation of actual circumstances and tendencies that prevailed empirically at the time of the writing of the *Manifesto*. Marx's theory of immiseration was, accordingly, drawn from historical experience.

In *Capital*, according to Simkhovitch, 'Marx remained in his theory a typical free trader of the classical variety' (p. 69). Only this position could allow Marx to establish his theories of immiseration and breakdown. Of course, Marx lived to see the introduction of the ten-hour day and factory legislation. 'But it was too late; Marx's theory had acquired a finished shape and formulation. As a theory it was profound, but it bore no relation whatever to the social changes going on before his very eyes' (p. 70). From the wage fund theory Marx accepted the assumption that the working class could never improve its situation. To support this view he used Andrew Ure's theory of the impact of machinery on labour (p. 70). 'Marx constructed his theory of wages and population around these facts. This data tended to suggest that in industrial society technological improvements led to a surplus population, immiseration of the unemployed and low wages' (p. 71). Through the setting free of workers such improvements would lead to the formation of a reserve army which would in turn keep wages low. Hence Marx, according to Simkhovitch, 'precluded the possibility of any wage increases that might threaten the continuous expansion of capital' (p. 73). According to Marx, says Simkhovitch, 'the progress of accumulation sets free an ever greater mass of workers, the result is an increasing pauperisation of the working class' (p. 76).

After this description of Marx's theory, its critique becomes all too easy. Simkhovitch claims to test the theory in the light of data on wages. He concludes that the 'experience of all the industrial countries without exception shows a continuous and unprecedented improvement in the position of the working classes' (p. 93). With this reference to empirical facts Simkhovitch imagines he has disposed of the whole of Marx's system, 'because its cornerstone is the theory of immiseration' (p. 82).

Simkhovitch does not notice that he has confused two things which have nothing to do with one another and which, in Marx, stand quite independent of one another. The empirical fact of the displacement of workers through machinery has nothing to do with the Marxist theory of immiseration or with the process by which workers are 'set free' due to the general law of capitalist accumulation and its historical tendency. The setting free of workers through machinery which Marx describes in the descriptive portion of his book is an empirical fact. The theory of immiseration and breakdown as expounded in the chapter on accumulation is a theory derived in a deductive manner, on the foundation of the law of value, from the fact of capitalist accumulation. It is a theory that makes no sense apart from the law of value.

The setting free of workers through the introduction of better machinery is a result of the technological relation $M:L$. It is an expression of technological advance, and as such something characteristic of any mode of production, including the planned economy of socialism. The Marxist theory of immiseration and breakdown, on the other hand, flows from the fact that in the capitalist accumulation process means of production and labour-power are applied in their value forms c and v. These value forms are the primordial source of the absolute necessity for valorisation, with all its consequences: imperfect valorisation, the reserve army, etc:

> The fact that the means of production, and the productiveness of labour, increase more rapidly than the productive population, expresses itself ... capitalistically in the inverse form that the labouring population always increases more rapidly than the conditions under which capital can employ this increase for its own self-expansion. (Marx, 1954, p. 604)

Sombart's treatment of the theory of breakdown is characterised by superficiality and an almost incredible ignorance of the facts. According to him, Marx founds the necessity for the proletarian revolution on his theory of crises and his theory of immiseration. He claims that the theory of crises was proposed initially in the *Manifesto* and not developed by Marx or Engels or by anyone after that. The same is supposed to hold true of the theory of immiseration. It is a striking sign of Sombart's theoretical illiteracy that in a work of two volumes running into a thousand pages and devoted to the theme of 'Marxism', the Marxist theory of accumulation is not mentioned once with the problem of the downfall of capitalism. Sombart's hopeless empiricism is obvious in the way he tries to finish off Marx's theory. The two theories in question are described as an expression of the 'situation' or the 'mood' generated by the 'circumstances of that time'. This epoch has been relegated to the past, however, and recourse to experience is enough to establish the weakness and untenability of those theories.

Sombart's claim that after its formulation in ˈ ̣e *Manifesto*, the theory of crises was never developed any further by Marx, can be shown to be baseless by a mere glance at the dozens of important passages in *Capital Volumes Two and Three* and the pages of the relevant section of *Theories of Surplus Value* (Part 2, Chapter 17) . Later we shall see that the Marxian theory of immiseration was not a formulation based on the 'circumstances of the time' but a deduction drawn logically from the Marxian theory of value and accumulation.

A Spiethoff's great 'discovery' in the field of crisis theory is his attempt to explain crises in terms of the overproduction of means of production relative to means of consumption. Spiethoff tries to present Marx's own theory as an underconsumptionist one; the final breakdown of capitalism is supposed to follow as a consequence of the insufficient consumption of the masses (1919, p. 439). Where Spiethoff finds such a formulation in Marx he does not say. But it enables him to prove Marx's theory false by recourse to facts. 'The actual course of development was quite different to the one Marx supposed' (p. 440). Capitalism does not suffer from restricted consumption, according to him. The sharpest market fluctuations are found in the spheres of industry that produce means of production, not in those that produce the means of consumption.

Elsewhere Spiethoff adds some further elements to his description of Marx's theory of crises; 'Marx's starting point is the falling tendency of the rate of profit' (1925, p. 65). Whether and what sort of connection there is between this tendency of the rate of profit and crises – the question which is so fundamental to any understanding of the Marxian theory of crises – is quietly ignored. He simply produces a few quotations from *Capital* and then explains that Marx confused general tendencies pertaining to the final collapse of capitalism with short-term fluctuations. But because Spiethoff himself cannot grasp the logical relationship between these two elements he passes over the real kernel of Marx's theory of crises and breakdown without the least understanding and interprets the theory as one of disproportionality and underconsumption at the same time.

Whatever Sorel has to say about the theory of breakdown only proves that for him the economic side of Marx's system remains a closed book. He tries to justify his own lack of comprehension by raising it to the status of a general principle. In other words, one does not really need to understand the Marxian theory of breakdown, for the 'final catastrophe' is simply a 'social myth' designed to rally the proletarian masses for class struggle. The basis of this entire conception is the view that 'men of action would lose all sense of initiative if they reasoned things out with the rigour of a critical historian' (Sorel, 1907, p. 59).

To take yet another version of bourgeois criticism, Thomas G Masaryk (1899) argues that Marx and Engels expected the collapse of bourgeois society in their own lifetime. He ascribes to Marx the argument that the ever-growing concentration of capital would lead to a breakdown. In fact, Masaryk's view is gratuitous and false. Marx argued only that due to the process of concentration, competitive capitalism is transformed into a monopoly capitalism. The breakdown was derived by him from completely different causes. To refute Marx, Masaryk appeals to the fact that the middle classes have not in fact disappeared and that even the position of the working class has improved. In his conception Marx supposedly derived the necessity of a breakdown from the proletarianisation of the middle classes. There could not be an easier refutation of Marx's system. But as for theoretical arguments against the theory of accumulation and breakdown Masaryk can think of none. Joseph A Schumpeter repeats the same banal dogmas against Marx. For him Marx was an underconsumptionist – he derived crises from the 'discrepancy between society's capacity to produce and its capacity to consume' (1914, p. 97).

Among Marx's critics Robert Michels takes special place as he has devoted a whole book (1928) to the question of immiseration and breakdown. In this book Michels proposes to clarify the issues involved once and for all and to show that Marxism has been 'scientifically overvalued', a fact which is only explicable, according to him, due to the 'crass ignorance' that prevails about Marx's predecessors and contemporaries. A comparison between Marx and writers of the seventeenth and eighteenth centuries would prove that Marx was hardly original. Most of Marx is to be found not only among the socialists, but even among contemporary liberals and clericalists. Indeed, as early as 1691, John Locke had a certain presentiment of the existence of a reserve army and its tendency to become pauperised (p. 55).

Yet in direct contradiction to the view that Marx simply plagiarised the early theory of pauperisation from writers of the past, Michels expounds the opposite view that Marx's theory was simply a reflection of the specific relations in which the young industrial countries of Europe found themselves on the outbreak of the February revolution in Paris, 1848 (p. 195). Still, Marx had a lot to recommend him over countless numbers of his predecessors. What the latter often stated only in the form of isolated observations, empirical accidents and even episodes, appeared in Marx in the form of 'the causal connections and overall plasticity of a system' (p. 196).

About what sort of 'causal connections' or what 'system', you find in Michels not even a dying word, as he is thoroughly incapable of any theoretical analysis. Michels obviously believes that independent ideas are quite unnecessary for a writer and are infinitely replaceable by 'erudition'. He can think only politically and historically. To him knowledge contains no room for theory. Can we wonder that with such an attitude Michels is quite incapable of grasping the simplest elements of theory and fills hundreds of pages in his book, in one massive confusion, with things that have absolutely nothing to do either with Marx or with the Marxist 'theory of immiseration'? Anyone at all who has ever written about poverty becomes immediately transformed into a 'predecessor' of Marx.

Because Michels ignores the specific nature of Marx's theory of immiseration (its derivation from the specific moments of the capitalist process of reproduction), and because his study concentrates on an amorphous 'poverty' (the opposition of rich and poor), he can trace the 'predecessors of Marx' back into the seventeenth century and even further back, into antiquity and the bishops of the ancient church. Finally because Michels has no notion of the theory that was worked out by Marx, nowhere mentions the actual moments that lead to a disruption of the capitalist mechanism in the course of accumulation, he sees 'poverty' as the sole source of the revolutionary hopes of Marxist socialism. But he knows that Marx himself supported trade union struggles as a means of improving the position of the class and is therefore forced to conclude that 'there is an indisputable contradiction here' (p. 127).

Even more strange than the interpretation of the theory of breakdown by the bourgeois economists was its description in the writings of Marxists and socialists.

The oldest representative of the theory that traces the breakdown of capitalism to a lack of non-capitalist market outlets is H Cunow. Marx's diagnosis of the tendencies of development of capitalism was basically correct Cunow argues, but he misjudged their tempo because he regarded the market outlets of that time as given. Capital's ability to win new spheres for investment and trade in the final decades of the century had a mitigating impact on the breakdown tendency. The expansion of foreign markets 'not only created an outlet that could absorb the constantly recurring superabundance of commodities' but could also, through this mechanism, 'diminish the tendency towards the outbreak of crises' (Cunow, 1898, p. 426). Without the conquest of new markets in the 1870s and 1880s, English capitalism would long ago have faced a contradiction between the absorptive capacities of her existing markets and the gigantic growth of her capitalist accumulation.

Cunow criticises Bernstein for mistakenly generalising from a specific stage of development and projecting its special tendencies across all stages without asking whether the conditions would always exist for an extension of the world market to keep pace with the expansion of production (p. 424). Cunow himself ruled this out. Up to the 1870s England enjoyed a monopoly on the world market, after which Germany and the United States emerged as industrial competitors. This in turn was followed by the industrialisation of India, Japan, Australia and Russia, and would soon be followed by that of China (p. 427). To Cunow the breakdown of capitalism was only a matter of time (p. 427). Fifteen years later Luxemburg took over this theory word for word and tried to deepen it theoretically.

The theory of breakdown developed by Cunow and later defended by Luxemburg and her followers, such as F Sternberg, is the only one dealt with by A Braunthal. He knows of no other theory of breakdown, and he regards the very conception as fundamentally incompatible with Marx's system. He accentuates the tendencies towards the concentration and centralisation of capital and the polarisation between the classes, and rejects a theory of breakdown because it is incompatible with Marx's theory of class struggle.

> For any work in the present a theory of breakdown clearly leads to pure passivity ... If one took the theory to its logical conclusion, the proletariat's present task would consist only of organisational and educational preparation for the revolution. Any activity immediately directed to the present, any class struggle for the present goals would be basically useless. For in that case all objective development leads to a pauperisation of the proletariat, and it makes no sense to put oneself into opposition to such development. (Braunthal, 1927, p. 43)

Nikolai Bukharin likewise fails to provide a serious account of the theory of breakdown and simply ends up with nebulous phrasemongering about 'contradictions'. Bukharin tears all the threads that tie the breakdown of capitalism to actual tendencies of economic development. His theory of breakdown is the following:

> Capitalist society is a 'unity of contradictions'. The process of movement of capitalist society is a process of the continual reproduction of the capitalist contradictions. The process of *expanded reproduction* is a process of the *expanded reproduction* of these *contradictions*. If this is so, it is clear that these contradictions will blow up the entire capitalist system as a whole. (1972, p. 264)

Satisfied with the results of his analysis, Bukharin then proclaims, 'We have reached the *limit* of capitalism' (p. 264). 'Even this general ... explanation of the collapse of capitalism postulates a limit which is in a certain sense objective. This limit is given to *a certain degree by the tension of capitalist contradictions*' (pp. 264–5). He decrees: 'It is a fact that imperialism means catastrophe, that we have entered into the period of the collapse of capitalism, no less' (p. 260).

The exactness of Bukharin's analysis is amazing. He obviously believes that pure assertions will do by way of proof. Bukharin calls his 'contradiction' phraseology dialectical. The lack of any concrete proof-procedure, the complete inability to conduct a theoretical analysis, is covered up with the term dialectical and this is the 'solution' of the problem. Bukharin's statement that it is a fact that we have entered a period of the breakdown of capitalism may very well be true, but it is precisely a question of explaining this fact causally, of establishing by way of theory, the necessity for a tendency to break down under capitalism. As for what kind of sharpening of 'contradictions' we might expect, Bukharin naturally refers us to his book *Economics of the Transformation Period*, where his hopes about the breakdown of capitalism are shifted on to a 'second round' of imperialist wars and the gigantic destruction of productive forces caused by war. Bukharin's theory of breakdown turns out to be nothing but a reformulation of Russia's own experiences during the War:

> Today we are able to watch the process of capitalist collapse not merely on the basis of abstract constructions and theoretical perspectives. The collapse of capitalism has started. The October Revolution is the most convincing and living expression of that. (1971, p. 266)

As for the causes of this collapse in Russia:

> The revolutionisation of the proletariat was doubtless connected to the economic decline, this to the war, the war to the struggle for markets, raw materials and spheres of investment, in short with imperialist politics in general. (p. 267)

So according to Bukharin, the collapse of capitalism flows from the destruction of the economic base. But this latter is not grounded in economic forces, in inexorable economic laws of the capitalist mechanism itself, but in war, in a force that exists outside the economy and which exerts a disintegrating influence on the apparatus of production from the outside. It would be useless to search Bukharin for any other cause of the breakdown of capitalism than the ravages created by war. The breakdown flows from transcendental causes whereas, for Marx, it is an immanent consequence of the very laws that regulate capitalism.

If, like Bukharin, we expect the breakdown of capitalism to flow from a second round of imperialist wars, then it is necessary to point out that wars are not peculiar to the imperialist stage of capitalism. They stem from the very essence of capitalism as such, during all its stages, and have been a constant symptom of capital from its historical inception. Later I shall show that far from being a threat to capitalism, wars are a means of prolonging the existence of the capitalist system as a whole. The facts show precisely that after every war capitalism has entered on a period of new upsurge.

In a more profound study than anything offered by Bukharin, G Charasoff correctly underlines the strict connection between Marx's theory of breakdown at the end of *Capital Volume One* and the theory of the falling rate of profit: 'All the propositions of the theory of breakdown are basically intended to be only different expressions of a single fundamental fact – the fall in the rate of profit' (Charasoff, 1910, p. 3). The fall in the rate of profit is according to Marx only an expression of the fact that with the advance of technology an ever smaller mass of living labour is required to set capital, or dead labour, into motion. With the incessant development of social productivity, the rate of profit must fall and capitalism becomes intrinsically unstable. There is an intensified competition and concentration of capitals, 'overproduction becomes inevitable, the reserve army forms with the force of a natural law and the final catastrophe supervenes' (p. 4).

However Charasoff himself disputes the correctness of this idea, on two grounds. First he disputes the fact of the falling rate of profit (pp. 294–7). This law in his opinion is obviously wrong. Secondly he doubts whether the breakdown as such can be deduced from the tendential fall in the rate of profit (p. 299). Charasoff feels that in Marx the breakdown is connected to the falling rate of profit, but what this connection is he himself cannot show. In this sense he fails to demonstrate the economic necessity of the breakdown from the laws pertaining to the system itself. Therefore he ends up saying that 'the fall (in the rate of profit) has to be consciously produced' (p. 316). This alone will enable Marxism to overcome its 'fatalistic character' according to which socialism is a product 'mainly of the external collapse of capitalism and not of the conscious assaults' of the masses (p. 318). By struggling on its wage demands, the working class consciously reduces the rate of profit and prepares the ground for the generalised crisis.

Boudin likewise accepts the idea that the downfall of capitalism is inevitable. He correctly says that this can only be understood and explained with the help of Marx's theory of value. 'According to the theory of Marx', he writes, 'the purely economic-mechanical breakdown of capitalism is a result of the inner contradictions of the law of value' (1909, p. 173). But Boudin offers no proof of this. He simply offers a description of the concentration and centralisation of capital that flows from competition in which the bigger capitalists beat the small, and concludes that if the laws of capital were to operate unhindered, no capitalists would be left to form any sort of social class (p. 172). Boudin does not get past generalities of this kind. It is not surprising, therefore, that he finally falls back on Cunow's theory of the necessity for non-capitalist markets as a condition of existence of capitalism. The industrialisation of non-capitalist countries is 'the beginning of the end of capitalism' (p. 264). Capitalism's inability to find outlets for its surplus product is the basic cause of periodic disturbances 'and will finally lead to its breakdown' (p. 255).

It should be obvious that not only Tugan-Baranovsky but also the socialist neo-harmonists Rudolf Hilferding and Otto Bauer are completely hostile to the idea that capitalism contains unsurpassable economic limits. Tugan-Baranovsky says that:

> the absolute limit to any further expansion of production is given in the quantum of productive forces at the disposal of society; capitalism is defined by an incessant but futile striving to reach these limits. Capital can never actually reach them. (Tugan-Baranovsky, 1901, p. 31)

Therefore 'capitalism can never collapse from purely economic causes, whereas it is doomed for moral reasons' (Tugan-Baranovsky, 1904, p. 304). Elsewhere he says that there 'are no grounds for supposing that capitalism will ever meet with a natural death; it has to be destroyed through conscious, human will, destroyed by the class exploited by capital, by the proletariat' (Tugan-Baranovsky, 1908, p. 90).

Tugan-Baranovsky upholds this idea because he opposes the materialist conception of history and grounds socialism moralistically in the conscious will of the proletariat as something divorced from the objective course of economic development. Yet the same idea is taken over by Bauer, Hilferding and Kautsky, who stand on the terrain of historical materialism. According to Bauer, objective limits are indeed imposed on accumulation by the size of a given population. Within these demographic limits unfettered accumulation occurs. Of course in reality accumulation is accompanied by violent crises, but only because accumulation surpasses the given demographic limits; in relation to the population at the disposal of capital there is either an overaccumulation or an underaccumulation of capital. Yet these periodic crises are only momentary disruptions of the equilibrium of capitalist accumulation.

> The periodic occurrence of phases of prosperity, crisis and depression is only the empirical expression of the fact that the mechanism of the capitalist mode of production automatically eliminates over- or underaccumulation, and always adjusts the accumulation of capital to the growth of population. (Bauer, 1913, p. 871)

Thus for Bauer crises are passing phenomena that are automatically overcome by the mechanism of capitalist production. The schematic equilibrium of the reproductive process is also Hilferding's peculiar obsession; crises are a reality only because production is not regulated. With a proportional distribution of capital in the individual branches of industry, there would never be overproduction. In a case like that capitalism could expand without limits; 'production can be expanded indefinitely without leading to the overproduction of commodities' (Hilferding, 1981, p. 241). On the few occasions that Hilferding refers to breakdown, he hastens to add that it will be 'political and social, not economic; for the idea of a purely economic collapse makes no sense' (p. 366). When the bourgeois economist Ludwig von Mises argues that the modern organisation of exchange and credit are a threat to the continued existence of capitalism, that 'the development of the means of circulation must necessarily produce crises under capitalism' (Mises, 1912, p. 472), Hilferding can only deride this 'latest representative of the breakdown theory' (Hilferding, 1912 p. 1027). Far from leading to the breakdown of capitalism, the credit system is to him a means of transferring the entire productive mechanism from the hands of the capitalists into those of the working class:

> The socialising function of finance capital facilitates enormously the task of overcoming capitalism. Once finance capital has brought the most important branches of production under its control, it is enough for society, through its conscious executive organ – the state conquered by the working class – to seize finance capital in order to gain immediate control of these branches of production ... Even today, taking possession of six large Berlin banks would mean taking possession of the most important spheres of large-scale industry. (Hilferding, 1981, pp. 367–8)

This entire conception corresponds to the dream of a banker aspiring for power over industry through credit. It is the putschism of Auguste Blanqui translated into economics.[1]

The breakdown of capitalism was either rejected completely, or grounded in a political voluntarism. No economic proof of the necessary breakdown of capitalism was ever attempted. And yet, as Bernstein realised in 1899, the question is one that is decisive to our whole understanding of Marxism. In the materialist conception of history the social process as a whole is determined by the economic process. It is not the consciousness of mankind that produces social revolutions, but the contradictions of material life, the collisions between the productive forces of society and its social relations:

If one wants to prove that capitalism cannot continue for ever, one has to prove the necessary breakdown of capitalist economy and its inevitable transformation into socialist economy. Once this is established, one has proved the necessary transformation of capitalism into its opposite and one has then brought socialism out of the realm of utopia into that of science. (Tugan-Baranovsky, 1905, p. 209)

I shall show later that Marx provides all the elements necessary for this proof.

How Kautsky finally abandoned Marx's theory of accumulation and of breakdown

In his latest book (1927) Kautsky abandons his earlier method of distorting Marx under the guise of defending him, in order openly to oppose the basic ideas of *Capital*. In the chapter called 'the downfall of capitalism', he asks, 'will capitalism end the same way that feudalism did before it?' That it will is a pure assumption, according to Kautsky, and one which 'Marx and Engels never completely rid themselves of' (p. 539). Here we have a good example of Kautsky's method of distortion. He tries to create the impression that at one time Marx and Engels supported the idea of the economically necessary downfall of capitalism, but tried to rid themselves of it without ever fully succeeding. In fact the idea of the necessary downfall of capitalism is absolutely basic to Marx's theory of accumulation and crises in both *Capital Volumes One* and *Three*.

According to Kautsky, the notion of breakdown contradicts the facts. Like the bourgeois critics of Marx he argues that the Marxian theory of immiseration is an empirical deduction from the conditions prevailing in the 1840s. It was valid in the terms of the frightful ravages caused by capitalism in the working classes of the early nineteenth century. But after 1847, Kautsky continues, England saw the repeal of grain tariffs, the institution of a ten-hour working day and the beginnings of a new epoch of expanding industry and unionism: 'In industries covered by the Factory Acts the condition of the working class improved significantly' (p. 541). Political methods likewise contributed to improving the economic position of the workers:

As democracy expanded the proletariat of the large towns increasingly gained control of their administration and, even in the midst of bourgeois society, gained the capacity to improve their conditions of

welfare and life to such a degree that their general conditions of health
improved perceptibly. (p. 542)

Kautsky concludes that 'it is no longer possible to maintain that the capitalist mode of production prepares its own downfall through the very laws
of its own development' (p. 541). Kautsky's argument is based entirely on
the fact that the position of the working class improved after the conditions described in the *Communist Manifesto*. From this fact he draws the
conclusion that Marx's theory of the development of the productive forces
under capitalism is untenable, especially the idea, basic to Marx, that from
a certain stage onwards capitalism is a fetter on the productive forces. To
this Marxist theory Kautsky counterposes the directly opposite conception: 'If earlier modes of exploitation ultimately led to a destruction of the
productive forces, despite short spasms of expansion, industrial capital is
defined by its tendency to augment them' (p. 539).

A few pages later Kautsky says that in '*Capital Volume One*, 1867,
Marx spoke an entirely different language' (p. 541) to that of two decades
earlier. In *Capital* Marx is supposed to have abandoned the theory of pauperisation. Yet the essential aspects of Marx's theory of immiseration and
breakdown were first presented only in *Capital*. This was possible, despite
his acknowledgement that the position of the working class had improved,
because he did not derive the inevitable pauperisation of the working class
under capitalism from the empirical conditions of England in the 1840s,
but by way of a deduction from the very nature of capital or the law of
accumulation peculiar to capitalism.

The worsening position of the working class and the growth of the
reserve army are certainly not the primary facts from which the breakdown is deduced; rather they are the necessary consequences of the accumulation of capital at a specific stage of capitalism. It is the accumulation
of capital that forms the primary cause that leads ultimately to the economic failure of capitalism due to an imperfect valorisation of the accumulated capital. Characteristically Kautsky completely ignores the theory
of accumulation and breakdown formulated in the chapter on the general
law of capitalist accumulation. This is especially obvious in the way he
refutes Luxemburg's view as:

Yet another hypothesis that attempts to deduce the ineluctable necessity for a final economic breakdown of capitalism from the conditions
of its process of circulation – despite, or rather precisely because of its
expansion of the productive forces – in direct opposition to Marx who
proved the exact opposite in *Capital Volume Two*. (p. 546)

So in *Volume Two* Marx is supposed to have proved the possibility of an unfettered development of the productive forces under capitalism. Kautsky finally has to appeal to Bauer's reproduction scheme, describing it as 'the most important critique' (p. 547) of Luxemburg's theory. Bauer likewise defends the thesis of a possible unlimited accumulation (Bauer, 1913, p. 838).

Tugan-Baranovsky was the first to suppose that Marx's reproduction schemes at the end of *Capital Volume Two* are proof that Marx himself was convinced of the possibility of a crisis-free, unlimited development of the productive forces of capitalism. Tugan-Baranovsky admits that Marx never explicitly formulated the thesis of equilibrium that allegedly underlies the reproduction schemes and that these schemes were never developed logically by Marx: 'The logical deductions that flow from them, which Marx himself totally neglected, are a blatant contradiction with the ideas he professed before constructing the schemes' (1913, p. 203). Naturally Tugan-Baranovsky has to clarify this astonishing contradiction, and he tries to do this by seeing the system prior to the construction of the schemes as an older, outdated draft of Marx's theory. Because Marx never reworked this earlier portion his earlier 'analysis remained incomplete' (p. 203).

In accepting Bauer's theory Kautsky rejects the notion of a final limit to capitalist accumulation, and stands on the same ground as Tugan-Baranovsky 25 years earlier.[2] But if Tugan-Baranovsky was at least aware of the contradiction contained in an harmonist interpretation of the reproduction schemes, it is characteristic of Kautsky, Bauer and Hilferding that they are not in the least bothered by it. When the contradiction is apparent they abandon Marx's theory and stick to their own harmonist interpretations. To Kautsky crises are only temporary disruptions caused by the lack of proportionality between individual branches. But 'the correct proportionality is always re-established' (1927, p. 548).

Kautsky is not content simply with abandoning Marx's theory of the final economic end of capitalism. He becomes an unconditional admirer of capitalism. During the great catastrophe of the War:

> capitalism did not collapse. It showed us that its elasticity, its capacity to adjust to new conditions, was much stronger than its vulnerability. It stood the test of war and stands today, from a purely economic point of view, stronger than ever. (p. 559)

Kautsky's faith in the economic future of capitalism, his optimistic enthusiasm for it, are carried so far that like Bernstein he concludes that capitalism is always capable of surmounting all obstacles; that not only has no one ever produced a theoretical proof of its economically necessary down-fall, but that such a proof is impossible. The practical experiences of capi-talism 'more than testify to its capacity to survive and to adjust to the most manifold and even desperate situations' (p. 559). 'Three decades ago', Kautsky says:

> I dealt with the problem of crises. Since then capitalism has survived so many crises, has shown its capacity to adapt to so many new, often quite astonishing and extraordinary demands that today it seems to me, from a purely economic point of view, far more capable of survival than it did some decades back. (p. 623)

It is quite sad to watch a thinker of such exceptional merit, towards the closing stages of his active life, rejecting his entire life's work at a single stroke. The conclusions Kautsky draws constitute an abandonment of sci-entific socialism. If there is no economic reason why capitalism must nec-essarily fail, then socialism can replace capitalism on purely extra-economic – political or psychological or moral – grounds. But in that case we abandon the materialist basis of a scientific argument for the necessity of socialism, the deduction of this necessity from the economic movement. Kautsky himself senses this:

> The prospects for socialism depend not on the possibility or necessity of a coming collapse or decline of capitalism but on the hopes we must have that the proletariat attains sufficient strength, that the productive forces grow sufficiently to provide abundant means for the welfare of the masses ... finally, that the necessary economic knowledge and con-sciousness develop in the working class to ensure a fruitful application of these productive forces by the class – these are the preconditions of socialist production. (p. 562)

Kautsky displaces the question from economics to politics, from the sphere of economic laws to the sphere of justice. Once problems of distri-bution become decisive, socialism retrogresses three-quarters of a century to its historical starting-points, to Pierre Joseph Proudhon and his demand for just distribution. To abandon materialism as our basis is to abandon socialism in favour of reformism.

Once the economic basis for the destruction of capitalism is given up, where is the certainty that the proletariat, having become the decisive class, will define its goal as the destruction of capitalism? Will it not perhaps prefer to reconcile itself with the existing order of society? Why should the working class come out against capitalism when it is not only capable of an unfettered development of the forces of production, but secures for it a constant improvement in its conditions of life and ever increasing protection through social reforms?

Capitalism is doing all that, Kautsky assures us, and yet the working class will realise socialism. According to Kautsky – despite all the developments of the productive forces, despite all the improvements in the position of the working class, despite all advances in social legislation – class antagonisms become progressively sharper, not milder, under capitalism so that the conscious intervention of the proletariat is something inevitable. Kautsky enumerates a series of subsidiary moments that will lead to a sharpening of class antagonisms: 'Here, and not in the accumulation of capital or the growth of crises, will the fate of socialism be decided' (p. 563). Kautsky fails to realise that he is simply moving in circles. If the causes of sharper class struggle are economically conditioned, then his own standpoint proves the necessary collapse of capitalism, with only this difference; that the causes given by Marx (growing accumulation and its consequences in insufficent valorisation and crises) are replaced by other causes. Or – and this is the second alternative – these causes are not economically conditioned, in which case the growth of class oppositions are traced to the consciousness of the working class as something pure, something cut loose from the economic movement. In truth this is the ultimate basis on which Kautsky's socialism is grounded – the realisation of socialism purely voluntaristically, through the conscious will of the workers, without any economic failure of capitalism and despite improvements in the conditions of life of the proletariat.

Notes

1. At the Kiel convention of the Social Democratic Party (May 1927) Hilferding explained in his report:

   I have always rejected any theory of economic breakdown. In my opinion Marx himself proved the falsehood of all such theories. After the War a theory of this sort was represented mainly by the Bolsheviks who thought we were on the verge of the collapse of the capitalist system. No such collapse followed. There is no reason to regret that. I have always been of the opinion that the downfall of the capitalist system is not something one waits for fatalistically, not something that will flow from the inner laws of this system, but that it must be the conscious act of the will of the working class. Marxism has never been a fatalism but, on the contrary, the most intense activism.

   With the same logic Hilferding might have argued that the conscious will of
   workers who force wages up through strike action proves that there are no
   economic laws governing the movement of wages.

2. At that time Kautsky had attacked Tugan-Baranovsky, from an underconsumptionist standpoint, in his articles on theories of crisis.

2   The Law of Capitalist Breakdown

Is there a theory of breakdown in Marx?

Even if Marx did not actually leave us a concise description of the law of breakdown in any specific passage he did specify all the elements required for such a description. It is possible to develop the law as a natural consequence of the capitalist accumulation process on the basis of the law of value, so much so that its lucidity will dispose of the need for any further proofs.

Is it correct that the term 'theory of breakdown' stems from Bernstein, not Marx? Is it true that Marx nowhere ever spoke of a crisis that would sound the deathknell of capitalism, that 'Marx uttered not a single word that might be interpreted in this sense', that this 'stupid idea' was smuggled into Marx by the revisionists? (Kautsky, 1908, p. 608) To be sure, Marx himself referred only to the breakdown and not to the theory of breakdown, just as he did not write about a theory of value or a theory of wages, but only developed the laws of value and of wages. So if we are entitled to speak of a Marxist theory of value or theory of wages, we have as much right to speak of Marx's theory of breakdown.

In the section on the law of the tendency of the rate of profit to fall in the course of accumulation where Marx shows how the accumulation of capital proceeds not in relation to the level of the rate of profit, but in relation to its mass, he says, 'This process would soon bring about the collapse of capitalist production if it were not for counteracting tendencies that have a continuous decentralising effect alongside the centripetal one' (1959, p. 246). So Marx observes that the centripetal forces of accumulation would bring about the breakdown of capitalist production, were it not for the simultaneous operation of counteracting tendencies. However, the operation of these counteracting tendencies does not do away with the action of the original tendency towards breakdown: the latter does not cease to exist. So Marx's statement is only intended to explain why this tendency towards breakdown does not enforce itself 'soon'. To deny this is to distort the clear sense of Marx's words.

However it is scarcely a matter of words which 'might be interpreted in this sense', and so on. Where the mere interpretation of words leads to is quite obvious from the directions in which Kautsky drags Marx's theory. For us the question is: suppose initially we abstract from the counteracting tendencies that Marx speaks of, how and in what way can accumulation bring about the breakdown of capitalist production? This is the problem we have to solve.

Preliminary methodological remarks

We have to show how, as a result of causes which stem from the economic process itself, the capitalist process of reproduction necessarily takes the form of cyclical and therefore periodically recurring movements of expansion and decline and how finally it leads to the breakdown of the capitalist system. However if the investigation is to be fruitful and to lead to exact results, we shall have to choose a method that can ensure this exactness.

What should we regard as the characteristic, determining condition of the reproductive cycle? Lederer identifies this as the price movements in the course of the business cycle: in periods of expansion commodity prices, including the price of labour power, rise; in periods of crisis and depression they fall. Therefore his way of posing the question is the following: how is a general increase of prices possible in periods of expansion? Expansions in the volume of production such as characterise periods of boom are, according to Lederer, only possible due to price increases. Therefore price increases are what he has to explain first. Lederer sees the creation of additional credit as the sole impulse behind price increases. Consequently he attributes to this factor the major role in determining the shape of the business cycle.

Spiethoff's explanation is quite different: 'An increase in capital investments forms the true hallmark and causal factor of every boom' (1925, p. 13). Here not one word is said about price increases and we could just as well choose a whole series of other forces as our basic indicators without moving one step further in explaining the problem. For the question is not one of which appearances are characteristic or typical of the business cycle, but which are necessary to it in the sense that they condition it. That price increases generally occur during an upswing does not mean that they are necessarily connected with it. If like Lederer, we were to assume that upswings presuppose rising prices we would be totally stumped by the American booms which were sometimes characterised by falling prices. That a wrong starting-point has been chosen is obvious. Both rising prices and expanded outlays on production are in themselves matters of indifference to the capitalist entrepreneur.

The capitalist process of production has a dual character. It is a labour process for the production of commodities, or products, and it is at the same time a valorisation process for obtaining surplus value or profits. Only the latter process forms the essential driving force of capitalist production, whereas the production of use values is for the entrepreneur only a means to an end, a necessary evil. The entrepreneur will only continue production and extend it further if it enables him to enlarge his profits. Expanded outlays on production, or accumulation, are only a function of valorisation, of the magnitude of profits. If profits are expanding production will be expanded, if valorisation fails production will be cut. Furthermore, both situations are compatible with constant, falling or rising prices.

Of these three possible price situations the assumption of constant prices is the one most appropriate to theory, in the sense that it is the simplest case and a starting point from which the other two more complicated cases can be examined later. The assumption of constant prices thus forms a methodologically valid theoretical fiction with a purely provisional character; it is, so to speak, a coordinate system within economics, a stable reference point that makes possible exact measurement of quantitative variations in profitability in the course of production and accumulation.

The basic question we have to clarify is how are profits affected by the accumulation of capital and vice versa. Do profits remain constant in the course of accumulation, do they grow or do they decline? The problem boils down to an exact determination of variations in surplus value in the course of accumulation. In answering this question we also clarify the cyclical movements or conjunctural oscillations that define the process of accumulation.

These considerations underlie Marx's analysis: 'Since the production of *exchange value* – the increase of exchange value – is the immediate aim of capitalist production, it is important to know how to measure it' (1972, p. 34). In order to establish whether an advanced capital value has grown during its circuit or by how much it has grown in the course of accumulation, we must compare the final magnitude with the initial magnitude. This comparison, which forms the basis of any rational capitalist calculation, is only possible because – in the form of costs of production and prices of the end product – value exists under capitalism as an objectively ascertainable independent magnitude. As something which is objectively ascertainable on the market, value constitutes both the basis of capitalist calculation and its form of appearance. Its explanation is thus the starting-point of any theoretical analysis.

From the very beginnings of free capitalism attempts were made to grasp the independent character of value – its aspect as an objective, external entity – in numerical terms. H Sieveking tells us that 'the rational approach to economics was enormously speeded up by the introduction of book-keeping' (1921, p. 96). The ability to calculate the yield on a sum of values originally invested is a vital condition for the existence of capital:

> as value in motion, whether in the sphere of production or in either phase of the sphere of circulation [money phase or commodity phase – TK] capital exists ideally only in the form of money of account, primarily in the mind of the producer of commodities, the capitalist producer of commodities. This movement is fixed and controlled by book-keeping, which includes the determination of prices, or the calculation of the prices of commodities. The movement of production, especially of the production of surplus value ... is thus symbolically reflected in imagination. (Marx, 1956, p. 136)

Through prices the fluctuations of a given capital value in the course of its circuit become expressed in money, which serves as measure of value required for accounting. And with respect to this measure of value Marx proceeds from the assumption, which is purely fictitious and which forms the basis of his analysis, that the value of money is constant. At first sight this appears to be all the more surprising in the sense that, in his polemic with Ricardo's 'invariable measure of value', Marx emphasised that gold can only serve as a measure of value because its own value is variable. In reality the values of all commodities, including gold, are variable. But science needs invariable measures: 'the interest in comparing the value of commodities in different historical periods is, indeed, not an *economic* interest as such, but an academic interest' (Marx, 1972, p. 133).

From historical surveys of the development of thermometry we know that a reliable measure of heat variations was established through the fundamental work of Amonton, with the discovery of two fundamental points (boiling-point and the absolute null point of water) for any liquid used as the measure of heat variations. This alone could establish the constant reference points with which it became possible to compare the variable states of heat (Mach, 1900, p. 8).

There are no such constant reference points for gold as the measure of value. So an exact measure of the value fluctuations of commodities would be impossible. On the one hand changes in the value of the money commodity may differ from the changes in the value of individual commodity types. In this case we have no exact measure to ascertain how far, say, the rising prices of a given commodity have been caused through changes in its own value and how far through changes in the value of the money commodity. In this case, suppose we were studying variations in the magnitude of surplus value; then, with a variable value of money, it would be difficult to tell whether a given increment in value (or price) was not something merely apparent and caused purely by changes in the value of money:

> In all these examples there would, however, have been no actual change in the magnitude of capital value, and only in the money expression of the same value and the same surplus value ... there is, therefore, but the appearance of a change in the magnitude of the employed capital. (Marx, 1959, pp. 139–40)

Alternatively the value of money varies in the same proportion as the values of other commodities, for instance due to general changes in productivity – a limiting case that is scarcely possible in reality. In that case there would have been enormous absolute changes in the real relations of production and wealth, but these actual changes would be invisible on the surface, because the relative proportions of individual commodity values would remain the same. The price index would not register the actual changes in productivity.

Thus it was entirely valid for Marx to substitute the 'power of abstraction' for the missing constant reference points, so falling into line with Galileo's principle: 'measure whatever is measurable, and make the non-measurable measurable'. For instance to ascertain the impact of changes in productivity on the formation of value and surplus value, Marx is forced to introduce the assumption that the value of money is constant. This assumption is therefore a methodological postulate that equips Marx with an exact measure for ascertaining variations in the value of industrial capital during its circuit. It is an assumption underlying all three volumes of *Capital*.

The variability of the measure of value, or of money, is only one of the causes of price changes. Such changes can just as well stem from causes that lie on the commodity side of the exchange relation. Here we should distinguish two cases. Either these variations of price are, from a social point of view, consequences of actual changes in value. (This is the case that preoccupies Marx initially, and it is these changes he wants to measure.) Or these variations of price represent deviations of prices from values, which do not in any case affect the total social mass of value because price increases in one sector of society correspond to price reductions in another.

The specific task that Marx set himself of measuring as exactly as possible increases in value over and above the initial magnitude of the advanced capital, forced him to exclude price changes of the latter sort. Price fluctuations that represent deviations from value are the result of changing configurations of supply and demand. Now if one proceeds from the assumption that supply and demand coincide then prices will coincide with values. Motivated by specific methodological considerations, Marx starts off his analysis with the assumption that supply and demand coincide. He assumes a state of equilibrium with respect to supply and demand, both on the commodity market and on the labour market, in order to be able to cover the more complicated cases later. Hence whenever production is expanded it is presupposed that this occurs proportionally in all the spheres so that the equilibrium is not destroyed. The reverse case, where production expands disproportionally, is taken up later.

Variations analysed at later stages are likewise exactly measurable only due to the simplifying assumptions that define this hypothesised state of equilibrium, which is not only directly reflected in the reproduction schemes but which forms the starting-point of the analysis as its coordinate system. Marx's *Capital* has a mathematical-quantitative character. Only these methodological devices allow an exact analysis of the accumulation process.[1]

Can accumulation proceed indefinitely without halts in the process of reproduction? To say 'yes' and to regard this as something self-evident without undertaking an actual analysis is to misunderstand the question completely. For instance professor Kroll argues that if commodities were exchanged at equilibrium prices, where supply equals demand, then there would be no conjunctural oscillations. He supposes that any decline in profitability is because wages are too high (Kroll, 1926, p. 214). But why were they not too high previously? What can 'too high' mean when we have no basis of comparison in the form of a 'normal case' such as represented by the reproduction scheme? If all the elements are variable, then the influence of any individual factor is impossible to assess. The causal relation that Kroll observes between the level of wages and falling profitability is not something we can presuppose; it has to be demonstrated. Therefore a scientific analysis is in principle bound to take as its starting point the case where wages are held constant in the course of accumulation, and it has to find out whether in such cases profits do not fall in the course of accumulation.

If they do, then it would be a logically exact proof that falling profitability, or crises, bear no causal connection with the level of wages but are a function of the accumulation of capital. The assumption of equilibrium, or of constant prices, is nothing but the method of variation applied to the problem of the business cycle in a form that excludes from the analysis all oscillations produced by changes in the volume of credit, prices, etc; it studies only the impact of the accumulation of capital, on quantitative changes in surplus value.

This is the assumption behind Marx's analysis of the crisis; 'The *general conditions* of crises, in so far as they are independent of *price fluctuations* ... must be explicable from the general conditions of capitalist production' (1969, p. 515). According to Marx crises can result from price fluctuations. But they were of no concern to him. Marx takes as the object of his analysis 'capital in general'; he is concerned only with those crises that stem from the nature of capital as such, from the essence of capitalist production. However this essence is only penetrable when we abstract from competition and thus confine ourselves to 'the examination of capital in general, in which prices of commodities are assumed to be *identical* with the *values* of the commodities' (p. 515). This identity of price and value is in turn only possible if the apparatus of production is assumed to be in a state of equilibrium. Marx makes an assumption of this sort. The same holds for credit. Credit crises are possible and do occur. But the question is, are crises necessarily connected with the movement of credit? Hence on methodological grounds we must first exclude credit and then see whether crises are possible. Marx says:

> In investigating why the general *possibility of crisis* turns into a *real* crisis, in investigating the *conditions* of crisis, it is therefore quite superfluous to concern oneself with the forms of crisis which arise out of money as *means of payment* [credit – HG]). This is precisely why economists like to suggest that this *obvious* form is the *cause* of crises. (pp. 514–5)

Once we have shown that even in a state of equilibrium, where prices and credit are ignored, crises are not only possible but inherent, then we have proved that there is no intrinsic connection between the movement of prices and credit on the one hand and crises on the other; 'that is to say, crises are possible without credit' (p. 514).

Bourgeois economists try to explain the movement of market prices by competition or the changing relations of supply and demand. But why does competition exist? This question they do not pose. Competition becomes some mysterious quality that one simply assumes or submits to without exploring its causes. 'Competition exists only in industry', Sternberg tells us, 'because the law of rising returns is fully valid for industry, or individual entrepreneurs struggle to control the market by cheapening their commodities' (Sternberg, 1926, p. 2). But why should they struggle to control the market, why should there not be outlets for the 'rising returns' of industry? This is not something logically necessary or obvious, and simply to assume it is to start off by presupposing what has to be proved. With this mystical force which has been left unexplained, he then tries to explain all other phenomena.

Marx was perfectly right in saying that 'competition has to shoulder the responsibility of explaining all the meaningless ideas of the economists, whereas it should be the economists who explain competition' (1959, p. 866). In fact:

> a scientific analysis of competition is not possible, before we have a conception of the inner nature of capital, just as the apparent motions of the heavenly bodies are not intelligible to any but him, who is acquainted with their real motions, motions which are not directly perceptible by the senses. (Marx, 1954, p. 300)

But how do we grasp the inner nature of capital? Marx's answer is, since individual capitalists 'confront one another only as commodity owners, and everyone seeks to sell his commodity as dearly as possible … the inner law enforces itself only through their competition, their mutual pressure upon each other, whereby the deviations are mutually cancelled' (1959, p. 880). So in reality the inner law of capitalism enforces itself through the mutual cancellation of deviations of supply and demand, which only means that it is through this process that the mechanism preserves its equilibrium.

The inner law only works itself out in reality through the constant deviation of prices from values. But in order to gain a theoretical perception of the law of value itself, we have to assume it as already realised, that is, we abstract from all deviations from the law. This does not mean that competition is discarded; rather it is conceived in its latent state, as a special case where its two opposing forces are in equilibrium. Only this 'normal case' draws out the various economic categories – value, wages, profit, ground-rent, interest – in their pure form, as independent categories. This is the starting point of Marx's analysis. He states:

> let us assume that the component value of the commodity product, which is formed in every sphere of production by the addition of a new

quantity of labour … always splits into constant proportions of wages, profit and rent, so that the wage actually paid always coincides with the value of labour-power, the profit actually realised with the portion of the total value that falls to the share of each independently functioning part of the total capital by virtue of the average rate of profit, and the actual rent is always limited by the bounds within which ground rent on this basis is normally confined. In a word, let us assume that the division of the socially produced values and the regulation of the prices of production take place on a capitalist basis, but with competition eliminated. (1959, pp. 869–70)

Starting from this methodological basis is it possible to ask – what is the impact of the accumulation of capital on the process of reproduction? Can the equilibrium which is presupposed be sustained in the long run or do new moments emerge in the course of accumulation which have a disruptive effect on it?

The equilibrium theory of the neo-harmonists

In approaching this problem I shall refrain from constructing any schemes of my own and demonstrate the real facts through Bauer's reproduction scheme (see Table 2.1). In Chapter 1 we saw the neo-harmonists Hilferding, Bauer and others join the company of Tugan-Baranovsky in reproducing a version of JB Say's old proportionality theory in order to prove that capitalism contains unlimited possibilities of development.

No doubt, as an answer to Luxemburg's theory, the reproduction scheme constructed by Bauer represents a distinct progress over all earlier attempts of this kind. Bauer succeeded in constructing a reproduction scheme which, apart from some mistakes, matches all the formal requirements that one could impose on a schematic model of this sort.[2]

Bauer's scheme shows none of the defects that Luxemburg ascribed to the reproduction scheme of Marx. First it takes account of incessant technological advances and incorporates this in the form of an ever-increasing organic composition of capital. Consequently what Luxemburg calls the 'cornerstone of Marxist theory' is preserved. Second, it avoids Luxemburg's criticism that 'there is no obvious rule in this accumulation or consumption', for Bauer's scheme does specify rules to which accumulation must correspond – constant capital grows twice as fast as variable capital – the former by ten per cent, the latter by five per cent per annum. Third, although capitalist consumption increases absolutely, increases in productivity and the mass of surplus value allow a progressively greater portion of the surplus value to be earmarked for the purposes of accumulation. Fourth, Bauer's scheme preserves the symmetry between *Departments I* and *II* required by Luxemburg. In Marx's scheme *Department I* always accumulates half its surplus value, whereas accumulation in *Department II* is anarchic and jerky. In Bauer's scheme both departments annually devote the same percentage of surplus value to accumulation. Finally the rate of profit behaves according to the Marxist law of its tendential fall. No wonder Luxemburg herself preferred the cautious warning:

> Naturally I shall not let myself be drawn into a discussion of Bauer's tabulated calculations. His position and his critique of my book depend mainly on the theory of population which he counterposes to my ideas as the basis of accumulation, and which in itself really has nothing to do with any mathematical models. (1972, p. 90)

Table 2.1: Bauer's reproduction scheme

Year	Dept.	c	v	k	a_c	a_v	AV	k/s	$a_s + a_v/s$
1.	One	120 000 +	50 000 +	37 500 +	10 000 +	2500 =	220 000		
	Two	80 000 +	50 000 +	37 500 +	10 000 +	2500 =	180 000		
		200 000 +	100 000 +	75 000 +	20 000 +	5000 =	400 000	75.00%	25.00%
2.	One	134 666 +	53 667 +	39 740 +	11 244 +	2683 =	242 000		
	Two	85 334 +	51 333 +	38 010 +	10 756 +	2567 =	188 000		
		220 000 +	105 000 +	77 750 +	22 000 +	5250 =	430 000	74.05%	25.95%
3.	One	151 048 +	57 567 +	42 070 +	12 638 +	2868 =	266 200		
	Two	90 952 +	52 674 +	38 469 +	11 562 +	2643 =	196 300		
		242 000 +	110 250 +	80 539 +	24 200 +	5511 =	462 500	73.04%	26.96%
4.	One	169 124 +	61 738 +	44 465 +	14 186 +	3087 =	292 600		
	Two	96 876 +	54 024 +	38 909 +	12 414 +	2701 =	204 924		
		266 000 +	115 762 +	83 374 +	26 600 +	5788 =	497 524	72.02%	27.98%

$$\frac{k + a_c + a_v}{c + v} \quad \text{(rate of profit)}$$

Year 1. 33.3%
2. 32.6%
3. 31.3%
4. 30.3%

Key:
c = constant capital
v = variable capital
k = capitalists' consumption (personal)
a_c = accumulated as constant capital
a_v = accumulated as variable capital
AV = value of annual product
s = surplus value ($= k + a_c + a_v$)

The critique that I shall make of Bauer's scheme starts from a quite different perspective from Luxemburg's (see Table 2.1). I shall show that Bauer's scheme reflects and can reflect only the value side of the reproduction process. In this sense it cannot describe the real process of accumulation in terms of value and use value. Secondly Bauer's mistake lies in his supposing that the scheme is somehow an illustration of the actual processes in capitalism, and in forgetting the simplifications that go together with it. But these shortcomings do not reduce the value of Bauer's scheme. As long as we examine the process of reproduction initially from the value side alone.

The conditions and tasks of schematic analysis

In the following sections I propose to accept Bauer's assumptions completely. But the problem is not simply to explain crises – the periodic expansions and contractions of the business cycle under capitalism – and their causes but also to find out what are the general tendencies of development of the accumulation of capital. Initially we make the favourable assumption that accumulation proceeds on the basis of dynamic equilibrium of the kind reflected in Bauer's scheme.

On this assumption Luxemburg's criticism that 'the question of markets does not even exist for Bauer' although periodic crises 'obviously stem from disproportions between production, that is the supply of commodities, and market, that is demand for commodities' (1972, p. 121) becomes meaningless and untenable. For Marx worked out the problem of accumulation and the whole analysis of *Capital Volume One* on the conscious assumption that commodities sell at value, which is only possible when supply and demand coincide. Marx studied the tendencies of accumulation in abstraction from all disturbances arising out of disproportions between supply and demand. Such disturbances are phenomena of competition that help us to explain deviations from the 'trend line' of capitalism, but not this trend line itself.

For Marx these phenomena are the 'illusory appearances of competition' and for that reason he abstracts from the movement of competition when investigating the general tendencies. Once these general tendencies have been established it is an easy task to explain the periodic deviations from the basic line of development, or the periodic crises. In this sense the Marxist theory of accumulation and breakdown is at the same time a theory of crises.

With Bauer we shall assume a productive mechanism in which constant capital amounts to 200 000 and variable capital to 100 000. The other assumptions are that: 120 000 of this constant capital is apportioned to *Department I* (means of production) and 80 000 to *Department II* (means of consumption); that the variable capital is equally divided between both spheres [50 000 each – TK]; that the constant capital expands by 10 per cent a year and the variable capital by 5 per cent; that the rate of surplus value is 100 per cent and that in any given year the rate of accumulation is equal in the two departments.

Proceeding from these assumptions, Bauer has constructed a reproduction scheme which in his view manifests perfect equilibrium year after year despite annual accumulation of capital and despite the fact that there are no non-capitalist markets in which the surplus value might be realised. With this scheme Bauer thinks he has established 'a perfect basis for tackling the problem raised by Luxemburg' (1913, p. 838). He rejects her theory of the crucial role of the non-capitalist countries in the realisation of surplus value; surplus value can be realised entirely within capitalism. As long as the expansion of capital is proportional to the growth of population – for the given levels of productivity – the capitalist mechanism creates its own market. As for the question whether the accumulation of capital encounters insuperable limits, Bauer's answer is no:

This condition of equilibrium between accumulation and the growth of population can only be maintained, however, if the rate of accumulation rises sufficiently fast to enable the variable capital to expand as rapidly as population despite the rising organic composition of capital. (p. 869)

But can the rate of accumulation proceed so fast? Bauer does not pose this decisive question even once. He simply took the basic point at issue as something self-evident, as if the speed with which the rate of accumulation rises depended solely on the will of the capitalists. From his position it followed that capitalism would be destroyed not through any objective limits on the growth of accumulation but by the political struggle of the working class. The masses would be drawn to socialism only through painstaking, day-to-day educational work. Socialism can only be the product of their conscious will.

Tugan-Baranovsky showed some time back that a conception of this sort means giving up the materialist conception of history. If capitalism really could develop the productive forces of society without hindrance, the discontent of the working class would lack any psychological basis. He pointed out that if we hope for the downfall of capitalism purely in terms of the political struggle of the masses trained in socialism, then 'the centre of gravity of the entire argument is shifted from economics to consciousness' (1904, p. 274). Rosa Luxemburg wrote in similar terms some twelve years later:

> If we assume, with the 'experts', the economic infinity of capitalist accumulation, then the vital foundation on which socialism rests will disappear. We then take refuge in the mist of pre-Marxist systems and schools which attempted to deduce socialism solely on the basis of the injustice and evils of today's world and the revolutionary determination of the working classes. (1972, p. 76)

Why was classical economy alarmed by the fall in the rate of profit despite an expanding mass of profit?

In Bauer's scheme the portion of surplus value reserved for the individual consumption of the capitalists (k) represents a continuously declining percentage of surplus value. But it grows absolutely despite increasing accumulation from year to year, thereby providing the motive that drives capitalists to expand production. We might imagine that Bauer's harmonist conclusions are confirmed by his table. The percentage fall in the rate of profit is of no concern because the absolute mass of profit can and does grow as long as the total capital expands more rapidly than the rate of profit falls. As Marx states:

> the same development of the social productiveness of labour expresses itself with the progress of capitalist production on the one hand in a tendency of the rate of profit to fall progressively and, on the other, in a progressive growth of the absolute mass of appropriated surplus value, or profit. (1959, p. 223)

And:

> The number of labourers employed by capital, hence the absolute mass of the labour set in motion by it, and therefore the absolute mass of surplus labour absorbed by it, the mass of the surplus value produced by it, and therefore the absolute mass of the profit produced by it, *can* consequently increase, and increase progressively, in spite of the progressive drop in the rate of profit. And this not only *can* be so. Aside from temporary fluctuations it *must* be so, on the basis of capitalist production. (1959, p. 218)

If this is so, however, the question arises – why should the capitalist be so worried if the rate of profit falls as long as the absolute mass of his profit grows? To ensure this growth all he needs to do is to accumulate industriously; accumulate at a rate that exceeds the fall in the rate of profit. Moreover why was classical economy dominated by a deep sense of disquiet, of real 'terror' before the falling rate of profit? Why is it a veritable 'day of judgement' for the bourgeoisie (Marx, 1969, p. 544), why were Ricardo's followers in 'dread of this pernicious tendency' (p. 541), why does Marx say that 'his law is of great importance to capitalist production' (1959, p. 213), why does he say that the law of the falling rate of profit 'hangs ominously over bourgeois production' (1969, p. 541) when, in contrast, vulgar economists 'pointed self-consolingly to the increasing mass of profit' (Marx 1959, p. 223)? The existing Marxist literature has no answer to any of these questions.

In other words is the falling rate of profit a real threat to capitalism? Bauer's scheme appears to show the opposite. By the end of year four both the fund for accumulation and the fund for capitalist consumption have grown absolutely. And yet, precisely with Bauer's scheme it will be shown that there are economic limits on accumulation, that Bauer's harmonist conclusions about the possibilities of unlimited development represent a banal delusion.

The views of classical economists on the future of capitalism (D Ricardo and J S Mill)

Marx's theory represented only the final stage of a fairly long development. It was directly linked to the theory of the classical economists and absorbed specific elements from the latter in a modified and deepened form. Ricardo had already reached the conclusion that due to the rising costs of basic means of subsistence the 'natural tendency of profits then is to fall' (1984, p. 71). Because profit is the motive behind capital the:

> motive for accumulation will diminish with every diminution of profit, and will cease altogether when their [the capitalists] profits are so low as not to afford them an adequate compensation for their trouble and the risk they must necessarily encounter in employing their capital productively. (p. 73)

Ricardo viewed the distant future of capitalism with a sense of apprehension, stating that 'if our progress should become more slow; if we should attain the stationary state, from which I trust we are yet far distant, then will the pernicious nature of these laws become more manifest and alarming' (p. 63).

The roots of Ricardo's theory of breakdown are discernible in the imperfect valorisation of capital that defines advanced stages of accumulation. The actual phenomenon, the tendency for the rate of profit to fall, was correctly perceived by Ricardo but he explained it in terms of a natural process rooted in the declining productivity of agriculture. Marx had only to replace this natural basis with a social one intrinsic to the specific nature of capitalism.

The theory of breakdown acquired a more developed form in the work of J S Mill despite the several distortions produced by his false theories of wages (the wage fund theory) and ground rent, his erroneous views on the relation of fixed capital to the level of the rate of profit, and by his general lack of clarity about the decisively important role of profit for the existence of capitalism. Mill viewed the 'stationary state' as the general direction of the advance of modern society but, unlike Ricardo, he contemplated the tendency with a sense of equanimity: 'I cannot regard the stationary state of capital and wealth with the unaffected aversion so generally manifested towards it by political economists of the old school' (Mill, 1970, p. 113). His standpoint was one of a petty-bourgeois reformism that sought to appease capital with the idea that a stationary state of capital would in no sense jeopardise the general progress of 'human improvements'. In his utopianism Mill seems to have forgotten that the accumulation of capital is an essential condition of capitalist production, that the capitalists have not the least interest in human improvements; they are interested only in the level of profitability. In this respect Ricardo and his school showed a more correct understanding of the vital conditions of capitalism than Mill himself.

However if we ignore these obviously essential points we have to concede that Mill showed a far clearer insight into the breakdown tendency and its causes, as well as into many of its counteracting moments. Mill's central argument is that if capital continued to accumulate at its existing rate and no circumstances intervened to raise its profits, only a short time would be needed for the latter to fall to the minimum. The expansion of capital would then soon reach its ultimate limit (pp. 94–7). A general overstocking of the market would occur. To Mill the basic difficulty was not the lack of markets but the lack of investing opportunities.

Counteracting circumstances can to some extent displace or postpone this ultimate limit. Among such circumstances Mill lists: 1) worsening conditions for workers, 2) devaluation or destruction of capital, 3) improvements in technology, 4) foreign trade that procures cheaper supplies of raw materials and means of subsistence, 5) export of capital to the colonies or to foreign countries. We shall go into these circumstances in more detail later.

A comparison between the sections in *Capital Volume Three* on the tendency of the rate of profit to fall and the theory of breakdown developed by Mill shows that Marx linked up his own theory to the one proposed by Mill. Even if Marx gave it a much deeper foundation and made it consistent with his law of value, Mill's seminal role is indisputable. In its external structure it shows the same logical construction one finds in Ricardo and in Marx. Marx also tackles the problem in two stages – first the tendency towards breakdown, then the counteracting tendencies – and refers to the fact that the process of capital accumulation 'would soon bring about the collapse of capitalist production if it were not for counteracting tendencies, which have a continuous decentralising effect alongside the centripetal one' (1959, p. 246). Marx mentions all the counteracting tendencies adduced by Mill, even if he adds some others and to some extent ascribes a different theoretical meaning to them.

The Marxist theory of accumulation and breakdown

If we are going to discuss the tendencies of development of a system, in this case – along with Bauer – the tendency of accumulation to adjust to the growth of population, then it is not enough simply to look at one or two years. We have to view the development of the system over a much longer span of time. Bauer did not do this. He restricted his calculations to just four cycles of production. This is the source of his mistakes.[3] The problem is precisely whether accumulation under the conditions postulated by Bauer is possible in the long run. If Bauer had followed through the development of his system over a sufficiently long time-span he would have found, soon enough, that his system necessarily breaks down.

If we follow Bauer's system into year 36, holding firm to all the conditions postulated by him, we see that the portion of surplus value reserved for capitalist consumption (k) which amounts to 86213 in the fifth year and grows over the following years, can only expand up to a definite highpoint. After this it must necessarily decline because it is swallowed up by the portion of surplus value required for capitalisation.

The failure of valorisation due to overaccumulation

Despite the fall in the rate of profit accumulation proceeds at an accelerated tempo because the scope of accumulation expands not in proportion to the level of profitability, but in proportion to the weight of the already accumulated capital: 'beyond certain limits a large capital with a small rate of profit accumulates faster than a small capital with a large rate of profit' (Marx, 1959, pp. 250–1).[4]

Table 2.2: Bauer's reproduction scheme continued

Year	c	v	k	a_c	a_v	AV	k/s	a/s
5	292 600 +	121 500 +	86 213 +	29 260 +	6077 =	535 700	70.9%	29.1%
6	321 860 +	127 627 +	89 060 +	32 186 +	6381 =	577 114	69.7%	30.3%
7	354 046 +	134 008 +	91 904 +	35 404 +	6700 =	622 062	68.6%	31.4%
8	389 450 +	140 708 +	94 728 +	38 945 +	7035 =	670 866	67.35%	32.7%
20	1 222 252 +	252 961 +	117 832 +	122 225 +	12 634 =	1 727 634	46.6%	53.4%
21	1 344 477 +	265 325 +	117 612 +	134 447 +	13 266 =	1 875 127	44.3%	55.7%
25	1 968 446 +	322 503 +	109 534 +	196 844 +	16 125 =	2 613 452	33.9%	66.1%
34	4 641 489 +	500 304 +	11 141 +	464 148 +	25 015 =	5 642 097	0.45%	99.55%
35	5 105 637 +	525 319 +	0 +	510 563 +	14 756*=	6 156 275	0	
36								

(1. capital available: 5 616 200, population available: 551 584; 2. capital in operation: 5 499 015, active population: 540 075; 3. surplus capital: 117 185, reserve army: 11 509)

5 499 015 + 540 319 + 0 + 540 075** + 0***

*   required: 26 265, deficit 11 509
**   deficit: 21 545
*** deficit: 27 003
       (total deficit for year 36, ** + ***, 48 548)

$$\frac{k + a_c + a_v}{c + v} \quad \text{(rate of profit)}$$

	%
year 5	29.3
6	28.4
7	27.4
8	26.5
34	9.7
35	9.3
36	8.7

We can see that after ten years [that is, by year eleven – TK] the original capital expands from a value of 300 000 to 681 243, or by 227 per cent, despite a continuous fall in the rate of profit. In the second decade the rate of expansion of capital amounts to 236 per cent, although the rate of profit falls even further from 24.7 per cent to 16.4 per cent. Finally in the third decade the accumulation of capital proceeds still faster, with a decennial increase of 243 per cent, when the rate of profit is even lower. So Bauer's scheme is a case of a declining rate of profit coupled with accelerated accumulation. The constant capital grows rapidly, it rises from 50 per cent of the total product in the first year to 82.9 per cent of the annual product by year 35. Capitalist consumption (k) reaches a peak in year 20 and from the following year on declines both relatively and absolutely. In year 34 it reaches its lowest level only to disappear completely in year 35.

It follows that the system must break down. The capitalist class has nothing left for its own personal consumption because [in order to sustain the assumptions of the scheme; constant capital rising by 10 per cent and variable capital by 5 per cent annually – TK] all existing means of subsistence have to be devoted to accumulation. In spite of this there is still a deficit of 11 509 on the accumulated variable capital (av) required to reproduce the system for a further year. In year 35 *Department Two* produces consumer goods to a total value of 540 075 [the 525 319 advanced as variable capital at the beginning of the year plus 14 756 accumulated variable capital – TK] whereas, on Bauer's assumption of a 5 per cent increase in population, 551 584 of variable capital is required.

Bauer's assumptions cannot be sustained any further; the system breaks down. From year 35 on any further accumulation of capital under the conditions postulated would be quite meaningless. The capitalist would be wasting effort over the management of a productive system whose fruits are entirely absorbed by the share of workers.

If this state persisted it would mean a destruction of the capitalist mechanism, its economic end. For the class of entrepreneurs, accumulation would not only be meaningless, it would be objectively impossible because the overaccumulated capital would lie idle, would not be able to function, would fail to yield any profits: 'there would be a steep and sudden fall in the general rate of profit' (Marx, 1959, p. 251).

This fall in the rate of profit at the stage of overaccumulation is different from the fall at early stages of the accumulation of capital. A falling rate of profit is a permanent symptom of the progress of accumulation through all its stages, but at the initial stages of accumulation it goes together with an expanding mass of profits and expanded capitalist consumption. Beyond certain limits however, the falling rate of profit is accompanied by a fall in the surplus value earmarked for capitalist consumption (in our scheme this appears in year 21) and soon afterwards of the portions of surplus value destined for accumulation. 'The fall in the rate of profit would then be accompanied by an absolute decrease in the mass of profit ... And the reduced mass of profit would have to be calculated on an increased total capital' (Marx, 1959, p. 252).

This Marxist theory of the economic cycle which sees the growing valorisation of social capital as the determining cause of accumulation – of the upswing – and its imperfect valorisation as the cause of the downturn into crisis has been fully confirmed by recent empirical studies. W C Mitchell (1927) has shown for the United States, J Lescure (1910) for France, and Stamp (1918) for Great Britain, that in periods of boom profits show an uninterrupted rise, whereas in periods of crisis the level of profitability declines. However, the agreement is at a purely factual level. Lescure supposes that reductions in profitability are due to shifts in commodity prices and prime costs. He overlooks the fact that profitability depends on the magnitude of capital, that is, on the relationship between the rate of increase of profits and that of capital. Overaccumulation is possible, and at a specific stage of accumulation inevitable, even for a given level of commodity prices and a given level of prime costs. Further expansion of production can become unprofitable even if the level of profits remains the same, indeed even if it rises. To understand these complicated relationships it is not enough simply to observe the movement of prices. A more sophisticated method is required, and here the assumption of constant prices for all elements of cost is crucial to the exactness of the investigation. Variations in costs (means of production, wages, interest) only encourage or constrain phases of boom or stagnation, they do not actually produce these phases themselves.

The formation of the reserve army of labour and of idle capital due to overaccumulation

Imperfect valorisation due to overaccumulation is, however, only one side of the accumulation process; we have to look at its second side. Imperfect valorisation due to overaccumulation means that capital grows faster than the surplus value extortable from the given population, or that the working population is too small in relation to the swollen capital. But soon overaccumulation leads to the opposite tendency.

Towards the closing stages of the business cycle the mass of profits (s), and therefore also its accumulated constant (a_c) and variable (a_v) portions, contract so sharply that the additional capital is no longer sufficient to keep accumulation going on the previous basis. It is therefore no longer sufficient to enable the process of accumulation to absorb the annual increase in population. Thus in year 35 the rate of accumulation requires a level of $510\ 563\ a_c + 26\ 265\ a_v = 536\ 828$. But the available mass of surplus value totals only 525 319. The rate of accumulation required to sustain the scheme is 104.6 per cent of the available surplus value; a logical contradiction and impossible in reality.

From this point onwards valorisation no longer suffices to enable accumulation to proceed in step with the growth of population. Accumulation has become too small, which means that a reserve army is inevitably formed and grows larger year by year. Given our analysis of the reproduction process in terms of a schematic model whose presupposition is dynamic equilibrium, there can, by definition, be no surplus population or reserve army of labour. The latter emerges only at an advanced stage of accumulation and as its product. The assumption which is made initially can no longer be sustained and is violated. The extension of Bauer's scheme shows that in year 35 there are 11 509 unemployed workers who form a reserve army.

In addition, because only a part of the working population now enters the process of production, only a part of the additional constant capital ($510\ 563\ a_c$) is required for buying means of production. The active population of 540 075 requires a total constant capital of 5 499 015; the result is that 117 185 represents a surplus capital with no investment possibilities.

The scheme is a lucid exposition of the condition Marx had in mind when he called the corresponding section of *Capital Volume Three* 'Excess Capital and Excess Population' (pp. 250–9). Overaccumulation, or imperfect valorisation, ensues because the population base is too small. And yet there is overpopulation, a reserve army. We cannot speak of a logical contradiction here. 'The so-called plethora of capital', Marx writes:

> always applies essentially to a plethora of capital for which the fall in the rate of profit is not compensated through the mass of profit ... This plethora of capital arises from the same causes as those which call forth relative overpopulation, and is, therefore, a phenomenon supplementing the latter, although they stand at opposite poles – unemployed capital at one pole, and a population of unemployed workers at the other. (1959, p. 251)

And a few pages later:

> It is no contradiction that this overproduction of capital is accompanied by more or less considerable relative overpopulation. The circumstances which increased the productiveness of labour, augmented the mass of produced commodities, expanded markets, accelerated accu-

mulation of capital both in terms of its mass and its value, and lowered the rate of profit – these same circumstances have also created, and continuously create, a relative overpopulation, an overpopulation of labourers not employed by the surplus capital owing to the low degree of exploitation at which alone they could be employed, or at least owing to the low rate of profit they would yield at the given degree of exploitation. (p. 256)[5]

A classic illustration is the United States today (March 1928) where, together with a superfluity of capital, shortage of investment opportunities and massive speculation in real estate and shares, there is a surplus working population of 4 million unemployed workers. This not because too much surplus value has been produced but because in relation to the accumulated mass of capital too little surplus value is available.

The fact that the means of production, and the productiveness of labour, increase more rapidly than the productive population, expresses itself, therefore, capitalistically in the inverse form that the labouring population always increases more rapidly than the conditions under which capital can employ this increase for its own self-expansion (Marx, 1954, p. 604).

We must be careful to distinguish the formation of the reserve army due to a crisis of valorisation from the 'setting free' of workers through machinery. The displacement of workers by machinery, which Marx describes in the empirical part of *Capital Volume One* (Chapter 15, 'Machinery and Modern Industry'), is a technical fact produced by the growth of M relative to L and as such is not a specifically capitalist phenomenon. All technological advance rests on the fact that labour becomes more productive, that it is economised – or set free – in relation to a given product. That machinery sets free labour is an incontrovertible fact that needs no proof; it belongs to the very concept of machinery as a labour saving means of production. This process of the setting free of workers will occur in any mode of production, including the planned economy of socialism.

From this it follows that Marx could not possibly have deduced the breakdown of capitalism from this technical fact. In Chapter 25 of *Capital Volume One,* where Marx derives the general law of capitalist accumulation, the setting free of the worker through the introduction of machinery is not mentioned. Here what Marx emphasises are not the changes in the technical composition of capital ($M:L$) but changes in the organic composition of capital ($c:v$): 'The most important factor in this inquiry is the composition of capital and the changes it undergoes in the course of the process of accumulation' (Marx, 1954, p. 574). Marx adds that: 'Wherever

I refer to the composition of capital, without further qualification, its organic composition is always understood' (p. 574).

The technical composition forms only one aspect of the organic composition; the latter is something more. It is the value composition of capital as it is determined by, and reflects, changes in the technical composition. Consequently Marx converts the technical side of the labour process, the relation $M:L$, into a value relation, $c:v$. Under capitalism, the means of production M and L figure as components of capital, as values, and they have to be valorised, that is, yield a profit.

The valorisation process, and not the technical process of production, is the characteristic driving force of capitalism. Wherever valorisation falters the production process is interrupted, even if from the standpoint of the satisfaction of needs production as a technical process may be desirable and necessary. The existing literature has totally ignored the fact that the process of setting free labour that Marx describes in the chapter on accumulation, and which is reflected in the formation of the reserve army, is not rooted in the technical fact of the introduction of machinery, but in the imperfect valorisation of capital specific to advanced stages of accumulation. It is a cause that flows strictly from the specifically capitalist form of production. Workers are made redundant not because they are displaced by machinery, but because, at a specific level of the accumulation of capital, profits become too small and consequently it does not pay to purchase new machinery and so on. Profits are insufficient to cover these purchases anyway.

The portion of surplus value destined for accumulation as additional constant capital (a_c) increases so rapidly that it devours a progressively larger share of surplus value. It devours the portion reserved for capitalist consumption (k), swallows up a large part of the portion reserved for additional variable capital (a_v) and is still not sufficient to continue the expansion of constant capital at the postulated rate of 10 per cent a year. In year 1 the accumulated constant capital (a_c) amounts to 20 per cent of the disposable surplus value of 100 000. By year 35 it climbs to 510 563, or to over 97 per cent of the disposable surplus value. Full employment requires a residue of surplus value amounting to 26 265. But only 14 756 survives as a residue to cover wages. For the capitalists' consumption nothing remains. The disposable mass of surplus value does not suffice to secure the valorisation of the swollen capital. Because 11 509 workers remain unemployed in the following year, the expanded capital now operates on a reduced valorisation base.

Long before this final point is reached, already from year 21 onwards when capitalist consumption begins to decline absolutely, accumulation will have lost all meaning for the capitalist. Each further advance in accumulation means a further absolute reduction in capitalist consumption. The vital importance of capitalist consumption to the continued existence of capitalism is evident only at this point. For accumulation to occur, surplus value must be deployable in a threefold direction and must be divided into three corresponding fractions:

i)   additional constant capital (a_c)
ii) additional variable capital (a_v) or additional means of subsistence for workers
iii) a consumption fund for the capitalists (k)

Each of these three fractions is equally essential to the further expansion of production on a capitalist basis. If the available surplus value could cover only the first two, accumulation would be impossible. For the question necessarily arises – why do capitalists accumulate? To provide additional employment to workers? From the point of view of capitalists that would make no sense once they themselves get nothing out of employing more workers.

From the point of view of the distribution of income, such a mode of production would end up losing its private capitalist character. Once the k portion of surplus value vanishes, surplus value in the specific sense of an income obtained without labour would have disappeared. The other two fractions of surplus value, the additional constant capital (a_c) and the additional variable capital (a_v), retain their character of surplus value only so long as they are means for the production of the consumption fund of the capitalist class. Once this portion disappears, not an atom of unpaid labour falls to the share of the capitalists. For the entire variable capital falls to the share of the working class, once the means of production have been replaced out of it. Surplus value in the sense of unpaid labour, of surplus labour over and above the time required to produce essential means of subsistence, would have vanished. All means of consumption would now form necessary means of consumption. So it follows that the k portion is an essential characteristic condition of the accumulation of capital.

The vacuous and scholastic manner in which Luxemburg argues is apparent now. Contemptuously she dismisses this element from her analysis:

> And yet, the growing consumption of the capitalists can certainly not be regarded as the ultimate purpose of accumulation; on the contrary, there is no accumulation in as much as this consumption takes place

and increases; the personal consumption of the capitalists must be regarded as simple reproduction. (1968, p. 334)

Luxemburg does not bother to explain how under simple reproduction the consumption of the capitalists can actually grow in the long run. Regarding the purpose of accumulation Marx tells us that the aim of the entire process 'does not by any means exclude increasing consumption on the part of the capitalist as his surplus value ... increases; on the contrary, it emphatically includes it' (1956, p. 70). But to Luxemburg accumulation only seems to make sense if the consumption of capitalist commodities is left to the non-capitalist countries. This belongs completely in the tradition of mercantilism:

> we find that certain exponents of the mercantile system ... deliver lengthy sermons to the effect that the individual capitalist should consume only as much as the labourer, that the nation of capitalists should leave the consumption of their own commodities, and the consumption process in general, to the other, less intelligent nations. (Marx, 1956, p. 60)

Obviously Marx had anticipated the whole of Luxemburg's theory.

We should not suppose, however, that the capitalist simply waits passively until the entire k portion has been swallowed up. Long before any such time (at latest from in the scheme when the k portion begins to decline absolutely) he will do his utmost to halt the tendency. In order to do this he must either cut the wages of the working class or cease to observe the conditions postulated for accumulation, that is, the condition that constant capital must expand by 10 per cent annually to absorb the annual increase in the working population at the given technological level. This would mean that from now on accumulation would proceed at a slower rate, say 9.5 or 8 per cent. The tempo of accumulation would have to be slowed down, and that, too, permanently and to an increasing degree. In that case accumulation would fail to keep step with the growth of the population. Fewer machines and so on would be required or installed, and this only means that the productive forces would be constrained from developing.

It also follows that from this point in time on a growing reserve army would necessarily form. The slowing down of accumulation and the formation of the industrial reserve army must necessarily follow even if wages are assumed to be constant throughout this period. At any rate, it would not be the result of an increase in wages, as Bauer supposes.

Marx's theory of breakdown is also a theory of crises

The Marxist theory of accumulation described here comprises not only a theory of breakdown but also a theory of crises. Previous writings on Marx could not come to terms with the essence of his theory due to their lack of understanding of the method that underlies Marx's analysis and the structure of his magnum opus. The objection has repeatedly been made that, despite its crucial role in his system, Marx nowhere ever produced a comprehensive description of his theory of crisis, that he made scattered conflicting attempts at an explanation in various passages of the book. This objection rests on a crude misunderstanding. The object of Marx's analysis is not crisis, but the capitalist process of reproduction in its totality. Given his method of investigation Marx examines the unending circuit of capital and its functions through all the phases of the process of reproduction. Expressed in a formula this would mean:

$$\text{Circuit one:} \quad M - C \overset{\displaystyle mp}{\underset{\displaystyle l}{\big\langle}} \ldots P \ldots C + c - M + m = M'$$

$$\text{Circuit two:} \quad M' - C \overset{\displaystyle mp}{\underset{\displaystyle l}{\big\langle}} \ldots \text{etc}$$

Analysing each of the phases of capital in its circuit as money capital, productive capital and commodity capital, Marx asks: what impact do they have on the process of production, can this process advance smoothly, or does the normal course of reproduction encounter disruptions in its various phases? If so what sort of obstacles, and what are the factors that hinder the reproduction process in a given phase?

One consequence of this method of investigation is that Marx is compelled to return to the problem of crises at various places in his work, in order to assess the specific impact of each of the individual factors that come into play in the different phases of the circuit. A systematic description of the role of all these factors will have to be reserved for my major study. Given the specific object of this investigation I shall examine the impact of one factor alone, even if it is the decisively important one – the accumulation of capital from the standpoint of crises. I shall be looking at the effects of the fact that a given capital which began its first circuit as M (money capital), opens up its second circuit as M' (expanded money capital).

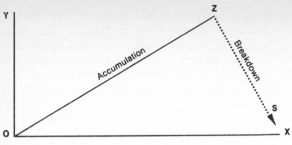

Figure 1

I have shown that as long as no counteracting or modifying tendencies intervene, the effects are such that from certain exactly determinable level of capital accumulation they have to lead to a breakdown of the system. In the coordinate system OX and OY (Figure 1), if the line OX represents a condition of 'normal valorisation' and OZ the line of accumulation in accordance with this equilibrium condition, then the crisis of valorisation can be expressed as a deviation of the line of accumulation in the direction ZS. This would be the tendency towards breakdown, the basic tendency of the system or its 'trend'.

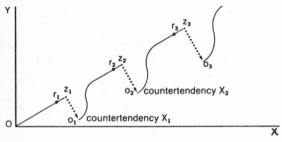

Figure 2

Let us suppose that in our coordinate system the breakdown sets in at point z_1 (Figure 2) and manifests itself in the form of an enormous devaluation of capital whose overaccumulation starts at r_1 (this is represented graphically by the punctuated line $z_1 - o_1$). In that case the overaccumulated capital will be reduced back to the magnitude required for its normal valorisation, and the system will be brought back to a new state of equilibrium at the higher level $o_1 - x_1$.

We know that in Marx's conception crises are simply a healing process of the system, a form in which equilibrium is again re-established, even if forcibly and with huge losses. From the standpoint of capital every crisis is a 'crisis of purification'. Soon the accumulation process picks up again, on an expanded basis, and within certain limits (for instance, $o_1 - r_2$) it can proceed without any disruption of equilibrium. But 'beyond certain limits', from point r_2 on, the accumulated capital again grows too large. The mass of surplus value starts to decline, valorisation begins to slacken until finally, at point z_2, it evaporates completely in the way described earlier. The breakdown sets in again and is followed by devaluation of capital, $z_2 - o_2$, and so on.

If we can show that due to various counteracting tendencies the unfettered operation of the breakdown tendency is repeatedly constrained and interrupted (at points z_1, z_2, z_3 ...) then the breakdown tendency will not work itself out completely and is, therefore, no longer describable in terms of an uninterrupted straight line ZS. Instead it will break up into a series of fragmented lines ($O - z_1 - o_1$, $o_1 - z_2 - o_2$, $o_2 - z_3 - o_3$ ...) all tending to the same final point. In this way the breakdown tendency, as the fundamental tendency of capitalism, splits up into a series of apparently independent cycles which are only the form of its constant, periodic reassertion. Marx's theory of breakdown is thus the necessary basis and presupposition of his theory of crisis, because according to Marx crises are only the form in which the breakdown tendency is temporarily interrupted and restrained from realising itself completely. In this sense every crisis is a passing deviation from the trend of capitalism.

Despite the periodic interruptions that repeatedly defuse the tendency towards breakdown, the mechanism as a whole tends relentlessly towards its final end with the general process of accumulation. As the accumulation of capital grows absolutely, the valorisation of this expanded capital becomes progressively more difficult. Once these countertendencies are themselves defused or simply cease to operate, the breakdown tendency gains the upper hand and asserts itself in the absolute form as the final crisis.[6]

An anti-critical interlude

The passing of booms and the turn to depression is frequently explained in terms of a series of factors that push costs of production up, reduce profitability and dampen business activity. This is the view of G Cassel who gets stuck at the surface level and cannot grasp the deeper connections, the essence underlying the appearances. It is obvious that increases in costs of production do threaten profitability and can intensify the crisis. But this factor only accelerates the formation of a crisis, it does not produce the crisis itself.

The methodological significance of the analysis proposed here is that it forestalls any such attempt to displace the problem or to drive it into secondary issues. Interest and its fluctuations are excluded from the analysis;

we are concerned with a total surplus value that has not yet split into its several portions. Rising prices are likewise excluded; by assumption commodities sell at value. The same is true of the commodity labour power; by assumption workers receive only the value of their labour power in the course of accumulation. And in spite of all this the process of capital accumulation grinds to a halt. The crisis ensues. Its formation is thus independent of the various price movements.

The real problem, the essence of the appearances, emerges in its pure form only through abstraction from all these subsidiary moments. The accumulation of capital is too large – there is absolute overaccumulation – because valorisation is insufficient. Is such a description only correct from a purely abstract logical point of view; is it reconcilable with the facts of experience? Does the accumulation process really come to an end due to overaccumulation of capital? Cassel assures us that even in the final stages of the business cycle there is never a superfluity of fixed capital (1923, p. 579). There is no overaccumulation of capital but rather a capital shortage, an insufficient supply of capital. So does our theory of accumulation contradict the facts of experience?

Cassel argues that the origin of crises lies in a 'wrong calculation' by businessmen of the future state of the capital market or of the supply of savings that will be forthcoming to match their investment schedules. Apart from the purely psychological character of this theory, it simply obscures matters. The supply of capital is too small. But what capital is Cassel talking about? Obviously not about the already accumulated and functioning capital. Since he refers to a future supply of savings, he can only be meaning the additional capital that has still to be accumulated and which is symbolised in the scheme by the magnitudes a_c and a_v.

What is the source of the supply of this capital? Why is there a shortage of this capital? Instead of pursuing the formation of this capital to its birthplace – the sphere of production – Cassel gets bogged down in the sphere of circulation. Before it is saved it has to be produced. It is produced by the workers and appropriated by the capitalist as surplus value. This future capital forms only a portion of the surplus value, the portion that is not consumed but destined for accumulation. To say that this additional capital is increasingly in short supply as accumulation progresses only means that in the course of accumulation the primordial source of this capital, surplus value, becomes progressively more scarce, too small, in relation to the already accumulated mass of capital. If the mass of surplus value is too small then so is the portion destined for purposes of accumulation.

Cassel simply mixes up concepts. He speaks of a capital shortage, an insufficient supply of capital. In the language of the banker everything is capital. But Cassel is not talking about capital, but about a part of surplus value that still has to be accumulated, a part that represents capital only potentially and becomes capital only through its function in the valorisation process. So really there is not a shortage of capital, but a shortage of surplus value. In contrast, there is an overaccumulation of the already functioning capital. Overproduction of capital and imperfect valorisation are correlative concepts each of which determines the other.

A capital that fails to fulfil its function of valorisation ceases to be capital; hence its devaluation. The devaluation of capital is here a necessary, logical consequence of its insufficient valorisation. It is otherwise with Cassel. He too refers to a 'sudden devaluation of fixed capital' due to capital shortage. He speaks of devaluation because in reality such a phenomenon exists, and theory must take some stand in relation to it. But Cassel cannot account for the fact of devaluation in terms of his theory. It bears no logically necessary connection with it. From Cassel's theory of crises it is in fact impossible to derive an explanation of the devaluation of capital. Given his subjective theory of prices how can capital be 'devalued' if it is in short supply? On the other hand, in Marx's theory imperfect valorisation and devaluation of the original capital stand in a close logical connection.

A definitive answer to the question raised by Diehl is also possible only now. He asked if there was any necessary relationship between Marx's theory of value and surplus value and socialism. He argued no, despite conceding that profit, ground-rent, etc, are rooted in the surplus value extorted from workers. But no socialist conclusions necessarily follow as long as we suppose that surplus value is indispensable to technical and economic progress.

What a fantastic misunderstanding. Surely it is not a question of moral assessment of surplus value but of the variations in its magnitude that decide what civilising role it plays. As the possibility of valorisation disappears surplus value ceases to play any such role; it ceases to develop the productive forces of society and capitalism must necessarily make way for a higher form of production. Marx showed that given its dynamic basis in the law of value, capital accumulation runs up against definite limits, that is, it bears a transitory character because in the long run the surplus value does not suffice for the valorisation of c and v.

Oppenheimer is one of the sharpest and best known recent critics of Marx's law of accumulation. He says: 'Honestly speaking it can no longer be disputed that ... Marx's law of capitalist accumulation and his deduction of the reserve army are logically erroneous and that therefore his definition of the tendency of capitalist development is false' (1923, p. 1098).

But Oppenheimer's mistakes are strikingly obvious when we compare what he means by the Marxist theory of accumulation with the one presented here. The elegant deductions characteristic of a sharp thinker fail completely here.

He vacillates in his characterisation of the theory of accumulation. Sometimes he sees it purely as a product of Hegel's dialectic of contradiction: 'The solution Marx proposed flowed from his application of the "dialectical method"' (Oppenheimer, 1919, p. 115). According to him the theory of breakdown, which he agrees is the 'pillar of Marx's whole economics and sociology' (p. 137), flows not from an analysis of capitalism but from an application of Hegel's dialectical method. But elsewhere Oppenheimer states that the problem Marx was concerned with was not resolvable purely by deduction. Marx's theory of the inevitable growth of a reserve army was, according to Oppenheimer, based on a purely empirical 'impression' that he gained from a study of British capitalism (Oppenheimer, 1903, p. 56). Yet the Marxist theory of accumulation was established by way of a deduction which he calls 'an imposing deduction' (1919, p. 144), a 'gigantic effort' (p. 146), a 'solution attempted in the grand style' (p. 135). All of this only shows that Oppenheimer has overlooked the real content of Marx's theory.

The imperfect valorisation of the accumulated capital, in Marx the decisive phenomenon that destroys the capitalist mechanism from the inside, is not mentioned by Oppenheimer even once. Instead Oppenheimer brings in two elements that have nothing to do with Marx's theory of accumulation.[7]

The first is 'that machinery sets free workers' (1919, p. 137). I have already drawn out the difference between the displacement of workers by machinery and their being set free in the very process of accumulation. Oppenheimer confuses these phenomena. Machinery displaces the worker. Hence Marx supposedly argues that the productive process creates 'a chronic relative overpopulation', which leads to a permanent oversupply of labour power that pins wages down to the minimum.

The process of setting free that Marx discusses in the chapter on accumulation is something quite different from displacement by machinery. Its cause is the accumulation of capital; that is, insufficient valorisation at a definite, advanced stage of accumulation. Down to this point the number of workers grows absolutely: 'With the growth of the total capital, its variable constituent or the labour incorporated in it, also does increase' (Marx, 1954, p. 590). But with accumulation it increases 'in a constantly diminishing proportion' (p. 590) until at a specific level of accumulation its growth ceases completely and turns into 'a relatively redundant working population, ie, a population of a greater extent than suffices for the average needs of the self expansion of capital, and therefore of surplus population' (p. 590).

Oppenheimer misses the point completely because he ignores the basic difference between the technical labour process and the capitalist valorisation process. Machinery in relation to labour power ($M:L$) and constant capital in relation to variable ($c:v$) represent two absolutely different categories and to confuse them is to end up in serious mistakes. It was from the 'social form' and not from the technical application of the real means of production that Marx deduced the necessary end of the accumulation process.

Oppenheimer's interpretation of the theory of the reserve army in the sense of a chronic overpopulation is quite false. What prevails instead is the law of the alternative attraction and repulsion of workers, so that the absolute number of workers who find employment and are later thrown off can, and does, increase: 'in all spheres, the increase of the variable part of capital, and therefore of the number of labourers employed by it, is always connected with violent fluctuations and transitory production of a surplus population' (Marx, 1954, pp. 590–1). So it is not a question of chronic overpopulation, as Oppenheimer supposes, but of the periodic reforming and reabsorption of the reserve army within the production cycle: 'The course characteristic of modern industry, namely, a decennial cycle ... depends on the constant formation, the greater or less absorption, and the re-formation of the industrial reserve army or surplus population' (Marx, 1954, pp. 592–3). It follows that the absolute number of workers can grow and indeed must grow if accumulation or expanded reproduction is to occur.

The second so-called premise of Marx's deduction is the classical wages fund theory (Oppenheimer, 1919, p. 138). According to Oppenheimer, Marx 'took over this theory in its decisive aspects' (p. 141). 'The classical theory derived all prices from supply–demand relations, and resolved the problem of wages, ie, of the price of labour on the same basis' (p. 138).

So Marx is supposed to have resolved the problem of wages in terms of supply and demand. I have shown the complete untenability of this view elsewhere (Grossmann, 1926, p. 180). Marx's theory of wages is only a special case of the theory of value applied to the commodity labour power. Just as in value theory the determination of the magnitude of value proceeds quite independently of competition, or supply and demand, the same is true for Marx's theory of wages.

In Marx the wage is determined by the reproduction costs or value of labour power which is independent of competition. Because Oppenheimer fails to understand this determination of wages in terms of value, the factor which, according to Marx, exerts an upward pressure on real wages in the course of capitalist development – namely, the growing intensity of labour – likewise escapes him. This is why he can arrive at the patently false conclusion that in the Marxist system wages 'can never rise above their lowest point' (1919, p. 149).

Since Oppenheimer's description of Marx's theory of wages as a wage fund theory is absolutely false, the criticisms he develops of Marx's theory of accumulation from this particular aspect also crumble. To demonstrate the inevitable formation of a reserve army Marx hardly needed to refer to supply and demand relations. In his system the reserve army of labour is a result of the process of reproduction at a late stage of accumulation not, as Oppenheimer supposes, a permanent precondition for the reproduction of the capital relationship. Given the nature of Marx's simplifying assumptions, the reserve army can be deduced as a necessary consequence of 'accumulation or of the development of wealth on a capitalist basis' (1954, p. 592). Once it has come into being this surplus population 'becomes, conversely, the lever of capitalist accumulation, nay, a condition of existence of the capitalist mode of production' (p. 592).

The existence of the reserve army is a vital condition for empirically given capitalism, but not by way of reproducing the capital relationship so much as to make possible sudden expansions of production, because: 'In all such cases, there must be the possibility of throwing great masses of men suddenly on the decisive points without injury to the scale of production in other spheres. Overpopulation supplies these masses' (p. 592). Initially, however, Marx takes as the object of his analysis not this empirically real capitalism with its sudden expansions, but the ideal trajectory of capitalist production, and so he is perfectly justified in excluding the reserve army from his analysis in the initial stages.

Now we come to Oppenheimer's description of Marx's 'proof procedure'. What is the basic meaning of Chapter 25 of *Capital Volume One* on 'the general law of capitalist accumulation'? Oppenheimer takes it to mean that the existence of a reserve army is a crucial precondition of the reproduction of the capitalist relationship. This is completely wrong. The existence of capital itself – of the separation of the worker from the means of production – is quite sufficient for the reproduction of the capitalist relationship. A reserve army is not crucial in this respect.

Oppenheimer is preoccupied with the problem of the setting free of workers through machinery and misses the basic point in Chapter 25. His myopic concentration on machinery precludes him from ever tackling the problem of insufficient valorisation due to accumulation. He deals with the latter only in passing, and even then entirely from the standpoint of the subjective experience of the individual capitalist. Again Oppenheimer overlooks the fact that Marx does not directly analyse empirical reality; in the chapter on accumulation the object of his analysis is surplus value and its variations of magnitude, whereas reality only confronts us with the individual parts into which surplus value splits up (interest, profit, rent, commercial profit, etc). Surplus value is only a theoretical form of totalising these individual parts that confront us in reality.

Marx's proof procedure has the character of a deduction. With respect to deductions of this nature Oppenheimer makes an excellent comment: 'Any appeal to experience is quite inadmissible. A deduction is not validated because its results conform to experience' (1919, p. 150). But in his critique of Marx's deduction Oppenheimer appeals precisely to experience. Marx has to deduce a specific phenomenon, the imperfect valorisation of the total social capital, from the very conditions of accumulation. Against Marx's demonstration that in the course of accumulation the shortage of surplus value brings accumulation to a standstill, Oppenheimer replies that 'experience teaches us that as interest declines accumulation proceeds all the more vehemently' (p. 149). Oppenheimer equates the shortage of surplus value, or imperfect valorisation, with a declining rate of interest. The rate of interest may decline to any level, but not surplus value. Interest is only an individualised portion of profit. Thus if interest falls, the entrepreneur's profit rises.

Suppose interest were to fall due to an oversupply of loan capital. What would be the result? Loan capital would flow into production, and the money capitalist would be transformed into an industrial capitalist. All that would result is a redistribution of capital. The matter is quite different when we look at the total surplus value, and total social capital. Once surplus value declines below certain exactly calculable limits capital accumulation necessarily breaks down, due to the defective valorisation of capital. The result would be an extraordinary devaluation of capital. Oppenheimer presents matters as if accumulation and its scale depend solely on the good will and psychology of the saver. He ignores the objective conditions – the magnitude of the disposable surplus value – which determine the limits of the scale of accumulation. Oppenheimer knows no such limits to the accumulation of capital. He supposes that workers displaced by machinery can be reabsorbed as long as accumulation is sufficiently rapid.

Oppenheimer overlooks the essential question – that for a given size of population and rate of surplus value is the requisite scale and tempo of accumulation possible in the long run? I would say 'no' and I have tried to demonstrate this exactly as is possible within the limits of deduction. Oppenheimer cites three possible forms through which the accumulation of capital can compensate for the retrenchments.

i) Partial compensation where there is more retrenchment in certain industries than redeployment in others.
ii) Full compensation where retrenchment and redeployment are equal.
iii) Overcompensation where redeployment is greater.

Oppenheimer then asks:

Which of these three cases is the actual one? This problem cannot be resolved through more deduction: it is an equation with several unknowns. It can only be solved with figures: one would have to compare the number of unemployed at different points in time. (1903, p. 56)

He adds that there was hardly any statistical data available to Marx to decide the question. As neither deduction nor empirical proof was possible he was left with an impression that the reserve army tends to increase.

So according to Oppenheimer the fundamental law of the Marxist system was an illicit generalisation of vague empirical impressions. The entire argument is untenable. Marx's theory of breakdown was neither a generalisation from purely empirical observations nor an elaboration of Hegel's dialectic of contradiction. It was derived through deduction as a self-evident consequence of the accumulation of capital on the basis of the law of value. Oppenheimer's statement that the problem is not soluble by deduction is contradicted by the fact that I have used a concrete numerical example to provide an actual solution and, as we shall see, this is also possible mathematically. As far as empirical relationships are concerned there may very well be a difficulty of an equation with several unknowns. But no such difficulty exists for theory. Through the simple procedure of making certain assumptions theory can transform all unknown variables into known quantities which are also measurable.

The scheme developed earlier proceeds from a state of equilibrium where despite a rising organic composition of capital, the retrenchment of workers is cancelled by their redeployment. And yet this state is only possible for a certain period of time. At a certain point accumulation becomes impossible on the basis assumed because it runs up against limits to valorisation; Oppenheimer's second case is transformed into his first case. At this late stage of accumulation the retrenchment of workers dominates over their redeployment not due to the action of machinery, but due to imperfect valorisation. The available surplus value does not suffice to keep accumulation going on the necessary scale.

Oppenheimer abstains from presenting any deductive counterproof against Marx and relies purely on empirical facts. But Oppenheimer himself knows that we cannot arrive at a theory through simple experience. Marx could quite easily agree that from time to time overcompensation has occurred in industry. But this would not in the least affect the Marxist law of accumulation and breakdown. Indeed additional labour power is a necessary constitutive part of the very concept of accumulation. The entire system is constructed on the notion of surplus value, on the greatest possible intensive and extensive exploitation of labour power. By its very nature capital strives to employ the largest number of workers. Marx himself notes that, on the whole, the number of workers employed in industry grows not only absolutely but as a ratio of the total population. As the population base expands the upper limits of capital accumulation are pushed back. This is one form in which the breakdown tendency is defused and postponed to the future (See Chapter 3, section 13). Nevertheless it follows from the law of accumulation that for a given size of working population capital accumulation encounters insuperable limits, beyond which any further accumulation is pointless.

Naturally the internal consequences of accumulation are always interrupted and neutralised by modifying circumstances. Hence the periodic, cyclical alteration of phases of expansion and breakdown. However if we abstract from the alternating attraction and repulsion of workers in the course of the industrial cycle, and follow through only the secular tendency of development, we shall have to conclude that in the initial stage of capital accumulation population was, on the whole, too large in relation to the existing scale of accumulation. Hence Malthus and Malthusianism. In the late stage of accumulation the inverse relationship dominates. In relation to the enormous accumulation of capital, population – the base for valorisation – becomes increasingly smaller. Hence the sharpening tensions in the advanced capitalist countries in the course of accumulation, the increasing role of capital exports, the ever more brutal expansionist tendencies of capital to secure the largest possible reserves of human labour power. But here capitalism runs into obstacles. The world is already divided up. The economic displacement of large masses of people encounters difficulties. And so the very tendencies that defuse the breakdown are themselves defused, and the breakdown intensifies.

K Muhs's critique of Marx (1927) shows not the slightest trace of originality. He simply draws together the arguments developed by others. Like them he ignores the decisively important passages of *Capital Volume Three* on the falling rate of profit. With Oppenheimer he agrees that Marx's theory of accumulation has an empirical basis. This is then criticised empirically. The superficiality of this method is perfectly obvious. Totally incapable of mobilising a single theoretical argument to launch a frontal attack on the law of accumulation, Muhs tries to finish off the theory through an empirico-statistical detour. The expansion of population in industrialised countries is supposed to refute the theory that workers are set free in the course of accumulation. But theory? There is not the least trace of any theory in Muhs.

On the other hand the process of breakdown described above should not be confused either with the limits to accumulation that Bauer talks about. So as not to be taken for an apologist of capital, Bauer claims that he has discovered a limit to the accumulation of capital. This limit is set by: (i) the proportionality between the two departments of the reproduction scheme and (ii) the rate of growth of population at a given level of productivity. Variable capital has to be accumulated in a specific proportion to increases in population. This prescribes the limits to the growth of constant capital since there is likewise a specific proportionality between constant and variable capital. The proportionality $c:v$ is the limit Bauer discusses. If the constant capital expands at a faster rate than that required in terms of its proportional relation to variable capital the result will be overaccumulation of capital. A slower rate means underaccumulation.

Crises arise only because the necessary proportionality between accumulation and population is not maintained. As long as accumulation proceeds within these limits, it can advance indefinitely under the assumptions made. Bauer speaks of 'overaccumulation'. But this occurs only because the conditions specified by him are violated. In fact he argues that these conditions can be maintained even in the long run and the very mechanism of capital ensures that all disturbances of equilibrium are automatically corrected: 'Like underaccumulation, overaccumulation is only a passing phase of the industrial cycle' (Bauer, 1913, p. 870).

In my description the process is totally different. I have shown that even if all conditions of proportionality are maintained and accumulation occurs within the limits imposed by population, the further preservation of these limits is objectively impossible. The system of production described in Bauer's own scheme has to breakdown or the conditions specified for the system have to be violated. Beyond a definite point of time the system cannot survive at the postulated rate of surplus value of 100 per cent. There is a growing shortage of surplus value and, under the given conditions, a continuous overaccumulation. The only alternative is to violate the conditions postulated. Wages have to be cut in order to push the rate of surplus value even higher. This cut in wages would not be a purely temporary phenomenon that vanishes once equilibrium is re-established; it will have to be continuous. After year 36 either wages have to be cut continually and periodically or a reserve army must come into being.

This would not be one of those periodic crises within the system that Bauer refers to, for a crisis of this sort could always be surmounted by adjusting the scale of the productive apparatus to the available population. Here there is no more room for adjustments. The proportionality conditions required by Bauer have been preserved throughout and still after year 35 a crisis, a tendency towards breakdown, sets in. The real dynamic of the capitalist system is quite different from what Bauer supposes. He maintains that capitalism is characterised by a 'tendency for the accumulation of capital to adjust to the growth of population' (p. 871). I have shown the opposite – there is a tendency towards an absolute overaccumulation of capital that outstrips the limits imposed by population.

The same hold for Tugan-Baranovsky. He believes that:

If social production were organised according to a plan, if those in charge of it had a perfect knowledge of demand and the power to shift labour and capital freely from one branch of production to another, the supply of commodities would never exceed the demand (Tugan-Baranovsky, 1901, p. 33).

Bauer's scheme represents precisely this kind of planned, organised production in which the managers know all they need to about demand and have the power to adapt production to demand. In spite of this a tendency towards breakdown emerges, valorisation declines absolutely and a reserve army forms. This only shows that the problem is not whether there is a surplus of commodities or not. In fact we have assumed a state of equilibrium where, by definition, there can be no unsaleable residue of commodities. Yet still the system must break down. The real problem lies in the valorisation of capital; there is not enough surplus value to continue accumulation at the postulated rate. Hence the catastrophe.

Obviously, as Lenin correctly remarks, there are no absolutely hopeless situations. In the description I have proposed the breakdown does not necessarily have to work itself out directly. Its absolute realisation may be interrupted by counteracting tendencies. In that case the absolute breakdown would be converted into a temporary crisis, after which the accumulation process picks up again on a new basis. In other words the valorisation of the overaccumulated capital can be met through capital exports to countries at a lower stage of accumulation. Or a sharp devaluation of the constant capital during the crisis might improve the prospects for valorisation. Or wage cuts could have the same effect in terms of warding off the catastrophe. But quite apart from the fact that all these situations violate the assumptions postulated in Bauer's scheme, these solutions would have a purely temporary impact. Restored accumulation will again generate the very same phenomena of overaccumulation and imperfect valorisation.

The logical and mathematical basis of the law of breakdown

In year 1 of Bauer's reproduction scheme the amount due for capitalisation constitutes 25 per cent of a surplus value of 100 000 (20 000 a_c + 5 000 a_v = 25 000). In year 2 the capitalised conponent increases to 25.95 per cent of an expanded surplus value of 105 000 (22 000 a_c + 5 250 a_v = 27 250). [The actual ratio should be 25.95 per cent – J Banaji]. Under these conditions the reservoir of surplus value is progressively exhausted and the accumulated capital can only be valorised at an increasingly unfavourable rate. After some time the reservoir dries up completely – the quotas due for capitalisation turn out to be far in excess of the available mass of surplus value even though notionally they are only fractions of this surplus value. This is the contradiction; at the hypothesised rate of accumulation the mass of surplus value is no longer sufficient. The breakdown of the system is the inevitable consequence.

Apart from the arithmetical and logical proofs that we have been given already, mathematicians may prefer the following more general form of presentation which avoids the purely arbitrary values of a concrete numerical example.

Meaning of the symbols

c = constant capital. Initial value = c_o. Value after j years = c_j
v = variable capital. Initial value = v_o. Value after j years = v_j
s = rate of surplus value (written as a percentage of v)
a_c = rate of accumulation of constant capital c
a_v = rate of accumulation of variable capital v
k = consumption share of the capitalists
S = mass of surplus value = $k + \dfrac{a_c.c}{100} + \dfrac{a_v.v}{100}$

Ω = organic composition of capital, or $c{:}v$
j = number of years

Further let $r = 1 + \dfrac{a_c}{100}$; $w = 1 + \dfrac{a_v}{100}$

The formula

After j years, at the assumed rate of accumulation a_c, the constant capital c reaches the level $c_j = c_o.r^j$. At the assumed rate of accumulation a_v, the variable capital v reaches the level $v_j = v_o.w^j$. The year after $(j + 1)$ accumulation is continued as usual, according to the formula:

$$S = k + \frac{c_o.r^j.a_c}{100} + \frac{v_o.w^j.a_v}{100} = \frac{s.v_o.w^j}{100}.$$

whence

$$k = v_o.w^j\,\frac{(s - a_v)}{100} - \frac{c_o.r^j.a_c}{100}$$

For k to be greater than 0, it is necessary that

$$\frac{v_o.w^j\,(s - a_v)}{100} > \frac{c_o.r^j.a_c}{100}$$

$k = 0$ for a year n, if $\dfrac{v_o.s^n\,(s - a_v)}{100} = \dfrac{c_o.r^n.a_c}{100}$

The timing of the absolute crisis is given by the point at which the consumption share of the entrepreneur vanishes completely, long after it has already started to decline. This means:

$$\frac{(r)^n}{s} = \frac{s - a_v}{\Omega.a_c}$$

whence

$$n = \frac{\log \left(\dfrac{s - a_v}{\Omega . a_c} \right)}{\log \left(\dfrac{100 + a_c}{100 + a_v} \right)}$$

This is a real number as long as $s > a_v$. But this is what we assume anyway throughout our investigation.

Starting from time-point n, the mass of surplus value S is not sufficient to ensure the valorisation of c and v under the conditions postulated.

Discussion of the formula

The number of years n down to the absolute crisis thus depends on four conditions:

i)   The level of the organic composition Ω. The higher this is the smaller the number of years. The crisis is accelerated.
ii) The rate of accumulation of the constant capital a_c, which works in the same direction as the level of the organic composition of capital.
iii) The rate of accumulation of the variable capital a_v which can work in either direction, sharpening the crisis or defusing it, and whose impact is therefore ambivalent.
iv) The level of the rate of surplus value s which has a defusing impact; that is, the greater is s, the greater is the number of years n, so that the breakdown tendency is postponed.

The accumulation process could be continued if the earlier assumptions were modified:

i)   the rate of accumulation a_c is reduced, and the tempo of accumulation slowed down;
ii) the constant capital is devalued which again reduces the rate of accumulation a_c;
iii) labour power is devalued, hence wages cut, so that the rate of accumulation of variable capital a_v is reduced and the rate of surplus value s enhanced;
iv) finally, capital is exported, so that again the rate of accumulation a_c is reduced.

These four major cases allow us to deduce all the variations that are actually to be found in reality and which impart to the capitalist mode of production a certain elasticity.

In reality we find that once the given level of valorisation collapses and the accumulation process stagnates, sooner or later counteracting tendencies come into play. The capitalist attempts to restore the valorisation of his capital. In the crisis capital is devalued and this is followed by a reorganisation and concentration process in which the rate of profit is increased through higher productivity and rationalisation; the same effect is achieved through direct wage cuts. We shall get to know these counteracting tendencies a bit more in Chapter 3.

Through the impact of these processes the breakdown tendency is interrupted, accumulation can restart on a new level, and the absolute collapse is transformed into a temporary crisis. This is the simple explanation of what Spiethoff falsely regards as Marx's confusion of the long-term and general tendencies that drive towards breakdown with conjunctural shifts of a short-term character.

The crisis is therefore, from the standpoint of capitalist production, a healing process through which the valorisation of capital is restored; 'crises are always but momentary and forcible solutions of the existing contradictions. They are violent eruptions which for a while restore the disturbed equilibrium' (Marx, 1959, p. 249). By its very nature the duration of this process of recovery is indeterminable. Whereas the time-span of accumulation can be calculated down to its maximal point z – so that the length of the upswing is determinate – an exact determination of the length of the crisis is not possible. By one means or another the entrepreneur strives to restore valorisation until sooner or later he succeeds in doing so. The crisis is only a more or less prolonged interval between two phases of accumulation.

Once counteracting tendencies come into play, the assumptions under which the analysis was worked out necessarily change. A modification to these assumptions along the lines suggested above would mean that for a period of time the process continues on a new basis, up until a new absolute crisis which can be exactly determined under the new set of assumptions and calculated according to the same formula. The crisis can likewise be surmounted by changing the conditions postulated yet again – for instance if the entrepreneur enforces a renewed cut in wages. Yet quite apart from the fact that a wage cut would disrupt the initial assumption of the expansion of variable capital corresponding to increases in the working population, the further continuation of accumulation would still prove untenable after a certain lapse of time. Despite the cut in wages it would again run up against the limits of valorisation and thus necessitate further wage cuts, and so on and so forth.

These underlying connections enable us to draw out the true meaning of Marx's statement that it lies in the essence of capitalism to push wages not simply down to the minimum necessary for subsistence, but even lower than this minimum:

> The zero of their [the labourers'] cost is therefore a limit in a mathematical sense, always beyond reach, although we can always approximate more and more nearly to it. The constant tendency of capital is to force the cost of labour back towards this zero. (1954, p. 562)

Later Marx states that:

> The greater the social wealth, the functioning capital, the extent and energy of its growth, and, therefore, also the absolute mass of the proletariat and the productiveness of its labour, the greater is the industrial reserve army. The same causes which develop the expansive power of capital, develop also the labour power at its disposal. The relative mass of the industrial reserve army increases therefore with the potential energy of wealth. But the greater this reserve army in proportion to the active labour army ... the greater is official pauperism. *This is the absolute general law of capitalist accumulation.* Like all other laws it is modified in its workings by many circumstances, the analysis of which does not concern us here. (p. 603)

Marx goes on to argue that 'in proportion as capital accumulates, the lot of the labourer, be his payment high or low, must grow worse' (p. 604).

People have tried to challenge this absolutely necessary general tendency which is inherent in pure capitalism by reference to the actual level of real wages in this or that period. As if Marx ever denied that it was possible for real wages to increase in specific phases of capitalist accumulation. The fact remains that at a late stage of accumulation this general tendency towards the depression of real wages emerges inexorably from the very process of capital accumulation on the basis of a rising organic composition. It follows that this tendency can be delayed for some time; it can be slowed down by the action of specific counteracting tendencies, but it cannot be abolished. Abstracting from such purely temporary phases, we see that from a certain point of accumulation onwards wages must decline continuously under pure capitalism, despite any initial increases. After this point the tempo of accumulation and technological advance slows down and the reserve army grows.

Obviously such a process cannot last indefinitely. A continuous deterioration of wages is only possible theoretically; it is a purely abstract possibility. In reality the constant devaluation of labour power accomplished by continual cuts in wages runs up against insuperable barriers. Every major cut in its conditions of life would inevitably drive the working class to rebellion. In this way, and through the very mechanism that is internal to it, the capitalist system moves incessantly towards its final end, dominated by the 'law of entropy of capitalist accumulation'.

Why the Marxist theory of accumulation and breakdown was misunderstood

There are specific reasons why the compelling logic of Marx's theory of accumulation was never followed through consistently to its proper conclusion, even by Marxists themselves. From his correspondence it is possible to see how painful it was for Marx to find that even in party circles in Germany there was an almost unbelievable indifference to *Capital*. The immaturity of the German workers' movement of that time corresponds better to Lassalle's pamphlets than to the massive and brilliant structure of Marx's theory. Even the leading thinkers of the workers' movement were incapable of grasping the decisive aspects of Marx's theory. It is quite typical that W Liebknecht in 1868 requested Engels 'to clarify where the real difference lies between Marx and Lassalle'. So it is not difficult to understand why, as M Beer tells us today, that:

> down to 1882 and for some years afterwards, there was practically no trace of Marxism in Germany. The writings of Lassalle, the recollections of 1848 and French literature formed the real sources from which the movement drew for its theories, ideas and feelings. Many socialists had been trained by Rodbertus or Duhring, others were at best acquainted with the publications of the International Working Men's Association, and still others founded their demands on appeals to morality and humanity. Kautsky was the first to get through, little by little, with his popularisation of Marx's ideas. (1923, p. 77)

Precisely when the publication of Marx's *Capital* was finally complete with the appearance of *Volume Three*, the rapid flowering of German capitalism doomed any deeper understanding of Marx's theory. The general feeling was that Marx's theory flatly contradicted the real tendencies of capitalism. Far from any further deepening of Marxist theory, it was an epoch characterised by a drift away from it. It was this period of vigorous capital accumulation (1890–1913) that gave birth to revisionism and to those notions of an unfettered, equilibrated capitalism which would recur later even in the writings of the official spokesmen of theory, like Hilferding and Bauer. The case of Hilferding shows how deeply the fear of catastrophe characteristic of bourgeois economists penetrated into this tendency of Marxism.

In historical retrospect such an attitude to Marx's *Capital* is understandable. The great popularity of the book was initially due to the parts which describe the immediate process of production within the factory. Its description of the labour process, which is simultaneously a process of producing value and surplus value, focused sharply on the position of the working class and its exploitation by capital and made the day-to-day class struggle something entirely comprehensible. So *Volume One* became the 'bible' of the working class for decades to come.

Those parts of the work which describe the historical tendencies of capital accumulation suffered an entirely different fate. However brilliantly they handled the question of capitalist breakdown, they were doomed to remain unintelligible. Capitalism had still to reach a maturity where the question of breakdown and the problem of realising socialism could possess an immediate reality. Marx was so far ahead of his own time that these portions of his work were bound to remain incomprehensible at first, and in this sense Marx's own life work only went to confirm even further the truth of the materialist conception of history.

Two whole generations had to pass, following the appearance of *Capital*, before the general advance of accumulation ripened capitalism to its present imperialist stage and generated the conflicts that would find an ephemeral solution in the massive convulsions of war. Only now did the question of achieving socialism gradually descend from the nebulous world of the socialist programme to the reality of day-to-day practice. Today we turn to *Capital* in search of answers to questions that are no longer purely academic, no longer simply problems of theory, but problems rooted in the needs of daily life. The historical situation has changed and this change tears aside the veils that concealed entire words and meanings from previous generations. The time has come for a reconstruction of Marx's theory of breakdown.

'Rate of profit' and 'mass of profit' have entirely different meanings for theory, despite the close connection between them. Several writers like Charasoff, Boudin and others felt that the central point of Marx's theory was contained here. But they could not demonstrate the necessary breakdown of capitalism because they confined their attention to the fall in the rate of profit. Breakdown cannot be derived from this. How could a percentage, a pure number such as the rate of profit produce the breakdown of a real system? Table 2 showed that the capitalist system can survive despite the fall in the rate of profit and that the final breakdown in year 35 has nothing to do with the falling rate of profit as such. We cannot explain why in year 34, with a rate of profit of 9.7 per cent, the system survives and why in the next year, with a rate of profit of 9.3 per cent, it breaks down. An explanation is only possible when we relate the breakdown not to the rate of profit, but to its mass: 'accumulation depends not only on the rate of profit but on the amount of profit' (Marx, 1969, p. 536).

If we accept the view of Sombart and Bauer that value in Marx is in no sense a real phenomenon but merely an idea, a 'mental fact' or an aid to thought, then the breakdown of capitalism due to a relative decline in the mass of profits (a decline in the rate of profit is simply the external expression of this fact) becomes an inexplicable mystery. Ideas can scarcely destroy a real system. This is why Sombart and Bauer could never come to terms with the Marxian theory of breakdown. But matters are quite different if value and therefore the mass of profit is conceived as a real magnitude. In this case the system has to break down due to a relative fall in the mass of profit, even if the latter can increase, or does increase, absolutely. A falling rate of profit is thus only an index that reveals the relative fall in the mass of profit. The falling rate of profit is, moreover, only important for Marx in so far as it is identical with a relative decline in the mass of surplus value.

Only in this sense is it possible to state that with a falling rate of profit the system breaks down. The rate of profit falls because the mass of profit declines relatively: 'The drop in the rate of profit ... expresses the falling relation of surplus value to advanced total capital' (Marx, 1959, p. 214). It is this relative decline in the mass of profits (or of surplus value) conceived as a real magnitude that accounts for the 'conflict between the expansion of production and production of surplus value' (p. 247). Beyond a certain limit to accumulation there is too little surplus value to secure the normal valorisation of the constantly expanding capital.

The factors of the breakdown and the business cycle

Writers like O Morgenstern (1928) simply reject the notion that there are any regular or systematic economic fluctuations. They ascribe to crises a purely contingent character in the sense that phases of expansion and decline succeed one another purely accidentally. H Dietzel saw purely random fluctuations of the harvest as the basic determinant of conjunctural oscillations (1909). Bohm-Bawerk thought a theory of the economic cycle could only form the concluding chapter of a logically complete economic theory. In that case, when it asserts that a theory of economic cycles is impossible, bourgeois economics only ends by confessing the bankruptcy of its own economic science.

No representative of bourgeois economics could give even a moderately exact causal explanation of the periodicity of crises. At best they could give only a partial explanation of this or that phase of the economic cycle. This failure to account for the periodicity of crises obviously also removes any theoretical basis for establishing the length of the individual phases or the amplitude of the cyclical movements.

When it comes down to determining the span of the individual phases commentators have plunged straight into empiricism. The fantastic uproar created recently by the 'exact' results attained by the various business cycle schools only goes to hide the state of theoretical bankruptcy and hopeless empiricism that lurks behind the mathematical disguises of these schools. In the United States observations led to the conclusion that there has been a tendency for the phases of the cycle to become shorter. In contrast Tugan-Baranovsky, from his own survey of the British data, came to the conclusion that the cyclical crises have become more prolonged (1901, p. 166). The 'debate on method' fought out over the last four decades between the historical and the deductive schools, regarding the way a theory is constructed, has simply passed over bourgeois economists without any deeper traces.

Today, in the field of business cycle studies, the hopeless empiricism of the historical school of Schmoller is again dominant. What was the old historical school if not an attempt to establish a preparatory basis for the construction of theories in the form of the richest possible historical evidence? The whole orientation of the modern business schools in the United States and Europe is characterised by the compilation of data of this kind, with only this difference, that the data is perhaps more contemporary. The basic concern of all their work is the selection of appropriate indicators. If in America these relate chiefly to circulation, prices, markets, in Germany production is also considered. Yet the basic point is that in either case causal explanation is displaced by description. Bourgeois economics is today tired of theory. A Lowe is therefore quite right in saying that: 'Basically over the last decade business cycle theory has not advanced a single step forward' (1926, p. 166).[8]

Yet even among Marxists there is no less confusion in this field. Marx referred to the factors that prolonged or abbreviate the length of the cycle, and for his period assumed that 'in the essential branches of modern industry this life-cycle now averages ten years. However, we are not concerned here with the exact figure' (1956, pp. 188–9). The amplitude of the cyclical movements, or of the varying phases of the industrial cycle could be greater or smaller. Yet this would not abolish the periodicity of the movement.

Kautsky feels that despite his basic disagreement with Tugan-Baranovsky's theory of crisis, he agrees with him on several points. One of these is 'Tugan-Baranovsky's remarks on the causes that determine the periodicity of crises'(1901, p. 133). That this is logically untenable should be obvious. How can one disagree with a theory of crisis and yet accept the causes of periodicity proposed by this theory? And what is Tugan-Baranovsky's epoch-making discovery which impressed Kautsky so much?

> Like Tugan I would identify the fitful international expansion of railways as one the basic factors behind the alternation of prosperity and crisis. In the nineteenth century the expansion of the world market and the extension of the railways went hand in hand. (p. 137)

This is how Kautsky distorted and vulgarised the Marxian theory of crisis. It is quite natural that Lederer then supposed that the labour theory of value is quite incapable of tackling dynamic phenomena and that apart from Luxemburg's theory 'the whole question of booms and slumps can only be viewed as one of disproportionality.' (1925, p. 359)

Lederer argues that:

> Within the labour theory of value crises are explained either in terms of the contradiction between increases in productivity and the lagging capacity of the market, or from a wrong distribution of means of production in the individual spheres. But if these are really the causes of crisis there is no reason why an understanding of these causes should not eliminate crises altogether. Moreover, the periodic character of the crisis is not explained by these theories. (p. 360)

In other words given a labour theory of value we end up either with an underconsumption theory or with a disproportionality theory, and neither of these can account for periodicity.[9]

I have shown that given the labour theory of value Marx's theory of accumulation does lead to a theory of breakdown and crises, but for quite different reasons to those listed by Lederer. The theory of overaccumulation explains why the reproduction process necessarily takes a cyclical form and it is the only theory that allows us to establish the length of the individual phases of the cycle.[10]

Given the method underlying this book, the procedure by which we seek to establish the duration of the phases cannot be an empirical or a statistical one. Even if a firm statistical relationship could be established between certain economic phenomena and the duration of the cycle, this would not by itself show the logically necessary character of the relationship. By means of statistics one can never show why variations in one factor should necessarily cause variations in another. Hayek is quite right in saying that empirically ascertainable relationships among economic facts remain theoretically problematic as long as they are not reducible to underlying patterns 'whose logically necessary character emerges independently of their statistical determination' (1928, p. 251). He goes on to state that:

> As with any economic theory there are basically only two criteria of validity for a theory of business cycles. Such a theory has to be deducible in a logically rigorous way, from the basic principles of the given system of theory, and secondly, it has to be able to generate a purely deductive explanation of the various phenomena one actually observes in the course of the cycle. (p. 252)

Obviously this also holds for the duration of its specific phases. Therefore in the following I want to derive the amplitude of cyclical movements in a purely deductive manner, as a necessary consequence of the basic elements of the mechanism of reproduction.

The formula proposed earlier gives an exact specification of the factors that determine the duration of the phase of expansion; the length of the phase can be calculated under the conditions specified in the scheme, even if in actual reality the pure movement of this scheme is intersected by circumstances of the most varied kind. I shall use Bauer's reproduction scheme to show how the length of the phase of expansion is abbreviated or prolonged depending on the variations of these factors.

First, if Bauer had assumed a higher initial organic composition of capital (for instance, $200\,000\,c + 25\,000\,v$) and thus a smaller reservoir of surplus value, the system would break down much earlier because the consumption of the capitalists, the k portion, would already start declining from year 1. This is shown in Table 2.3:

Table 2.3

	c	v	k	a_c	a_v	
Year 1	200 000 +	25 000 +	3 750 +	20 000 +	1 250 =	250 000
2	220 000 +	26 250 +	2 938 +	22 000 +	1 312 =	272 500
3	242 000 +	27 562 +	1 984 +	24 200 +	1 378 =	297 124
4	266 000 +	28 940 +	893 +	26 600 +	1 447 =	323 880
5	292 600 +	30 387 +	0 +	29 260 +	1 519 =	

Deficit = 392

With a higher organic composition the system has to break down earlier, in year 5. Either the surplus value due for capitalisation will show a deficit or the rate of surplus value, and thus the degree of exploitation, has to be increased – wages have to be cut.

Thus the level of the organic composition of capital has enormous significance for the breakdown tendency and explains why Marx should have said, at the very start of the chapter on the general law of capitalist accumulation, that the 'most important factor in this inquiry is the composition of capital and the changes it undergoes in the course of the process of accumulation' (1954, p. 574).

Secondly an increase in this rate of accumulation of constant capital will likewise accelerate the breakdown. Table 2.4 assumes the rate of accumulation of constant capital (a_c) to be 20 per cent instead of 10 per cent.

Table 2.4

	c	v	k	a_c	a_v	
Year 1	200 000 +	100 000 +	55 000 +	40 000 +	5 000 =	400 000
Year 2	240 000 +	105 000 +	51 750 +	48 000 +	5 250 =	450 000
Year 7	597 196 +	134 008 +	7 870 +	119 438 +	6 700 =	865 220
Year 8	716 634 +	140 078 +	0 +	143 326 +	0 =	

If the rate of accumulation were doubled to 20 per cent the breakdown would follow in year 8. Already by this year the additional constant capital required would be larger than the total surplus value available. Nothing would be left for additions to variable capital (a_v) or for capitalist consumption.

So far we have looked at the rate of accumulation of constant capital purely from the side of its value magnitude. But what would this factor mean if we were to look at it not from its value aspect, but from the aspect of its natural form or its material content? It represents the means of production which are necessary for expanding the productive apparatus. Now what influence does the physical and 'moral' life cycle of this element have on the course of accumulation? Sismondi had already claimed that crises are closely connected with the life cycle of fixed capital:

> It has been remarked that the violent shocks by which manufacturing industry is convulsed nowadays are related to the rapidity with which scientific discoveries are following one another ... Not only are the values of existing commodities thereby diminished, but the entire fixed capital and all the machinery ... is rendered useless. (Grossmann, 1924, p. 45)

However no one before Marx explained what exactly the connection was.

The reproduction scheme has so far assumed, for the sake of simplification, that the life cycle of fixed capital equals one period of reproduction; that fixed capital is completely used up in each cycle of production and therefore has to be renewed from the year's product. This assumption has a merely fictitious character and it has to be modified. It is more realistic to suppose that the fixed component of constant capital operates over several cycles of production and does not need to be renewed annually. Its participation in the production of value and surplus value is extended over several years. In this case even if the value of the fixed capital is transferred to the product in a smaller annual rate of depreciation, it nevertheless helps in creating a growing mass of value, and therefore of surplus value, in proportion to its actual durability. The valorisation of the given capital is thereby improved, so that the breakdown tendency is weakened – the duration of the phase of expansion is prolonged. Because technological improvements progressively consolidate the physical durability of fixed capital, we have here a factor that tends to prolong the business cycle.

The 'moral' depreciation of fixed capital had precisely the opposite effect. By shortening the time during which the fixed capital functions and thereby reducing the total mass of value and surplus value which it forms, it only makes the valorisation of the given capital worse and cuts short the period of accumulation, or the upswing. About this Marx says:

> As the magnitude of the value and the durability of the applied fixed capital develop with the general development of the capitalist mode of production, the lifetime of industry and of industrial capital lengthens in each particular field of investment to a period of many years ... Whereas the development of fixed capital extends this life on the one hand it is shortened on the other by the continuous revolution in the

means of production, which likewise incessantly gains momentum with the development of the capitalist mode of production. This involves a change in the means of production and the necessity of their constant replacement, on account of moral depreciation, long before they expire physically. One may assume that in the essential branches of modern industry this life-cycle now averages ten years. However we are not concerned here with the exact figure. This much is evident: the cycle of interconnected turnovers embracing a number of years, in which is held fast by its fixed constituent part, furnishes a material basis for the periodic crises. During this cycle business undergoes successive periods of depression, medium activity, precipitancy, crisis. (1956, pp. 188–9)

Thirdly an increase in the accumulation of variable capital has the same effect as the rate of accumulation of constant capital if the population remains constant or grows at the assumed rate of 5 per cent. On this assumption variable capital can accumulate more rapidly than it does in the scheme only if wages are rising from one year to the next. Consequently annual increases in variable capital stem from two causes: (i) because the number of workers is growing; (ii) because wages are rising. Under the circumstances higher wages mean a fall in the rate of surplus value. Suppose the working population increases by 5 per cent every year, whereas wages rise by 20 per cent. Other conditions being equal, we get the result shown in Table 2.5:

Table 2.5

	c	v	a_c	a_v	k	
Year 1	200 000 +	100 000 +	20 000 +	26 000 +	54 000 =	400 000
Year 2	220 000 +	105 000 +	22 000 +	32 300 +	50 700 =	430 000
Year 5	292 600 +	121 550 +	29 260 +	53 151 +	39 139 =	535 700
Year 11	518 357 +	162 886 +	51 835 +	105 236 +	5 815 =	1 154 791
Year 12	570 192 +	171 030 +	57 019 +	115 497 +	0	
Year 13	627 211 +	179 581 +	172 516 =	Deficit 1 486		

[Note that the variable capital column (v) reflects only the annual rise of 5 per cent in the working population. The column for accumulated variable capital (a_v) meanwhile reveals the sum required to pay the growing number of workers a cumulative annual wage increase of 20 per cent – TK]

An increase in the rate of accumulation of variable capital accelerates the breakdown enormously. If wages were to rise by 20 per cent there would be a shortage of surplus value by year 12.

This case where the rate of accumulation of variable capital rises simply because wages are increasing, while the rate of growth of population remains constant at 5 per cent, must be distinguished from the case where the rate rises because the population itself is expanding at over 5 per cent. If all other conditions are the same such an expansion of the valorisation base would necessarily weaken the breakdown tendency. If the working population grows by 8 per cent a year, and consequently the mass of surplus value grows at 8 per cent, then under the conditions assumed in Table 2.4 the breakdown would be postponed by one year, as shown in Table 2.6.

Table 2.6

	c	v	k	a_c	a_v	
Year 1	200 000 +	100 000 +	52 000 +	40 000 +	8 000 =	400 000
Year 2	240 000 +	108 000 +	51 360 +	48 000 +	8 640 =	456 000
Year 7	597 196 +	158 685 +	26 553 +	119 438 +	12 694 =	914 566
Year 8	716 634 +	171 379 +	14 334 +	143 326 +	13 709 =	1 059 392
Year 9	859 960 +	185 088 +	0 +	171 992 +	14 806	
				186 798 =	Deficit 1 710	

Fourthly, a higher rate of surplus value will slow down the breakdown tendency. Table 2.7 shows the result with a lower rate – it will be speeded up based on a rate of accumulation of constant capital of 20 per cent, variable capital of 5 per cent, and the rate of surplus value only 50 per cent.

Table 2.7

	c	v	k	a_c	a_v	
Year 1	200 000 +	100 000 +	5 000 +	40 000 +	5.000 =	350 000
Year 2	240 000 +	105 000 +	0 +	48 000 +	5 250	
				53 250 =	Deficit 750	

In this example the extremely rapid onset of breakdown is due to the coupling of a higher rate of accumulation with a lower rate of surplus value. Conversely the breakdown would be postponed if the rate of surplus value were, for example, 150 per cent.

In short, the duration of the upswing or the point at which the breakdown, and thus the downturn into crisis, intervenes is a function of four variable but compatible elements: the level of the organic composition of capital; the rate of surplus value; the rate of accumulation of constant capital; and the rate of accumulation of variable capital.

Crises and the theory of underconsumption

Once we have grasped the causes of the boom it becomes possible to explain a series of empirical phenomena which the existing theories of crisis explain only inadequately. It is said that inflation creates an 'artificial' boom. But what is artificial about a boom of this kind? How is a so-called artificial boom different from a real one? For instance if the underconsumption of the masses is the basic cause of crises then inflation should occasion a massive crisis because wages will lag behind commodity prices; real wages will fall and the underconsumption of the working class will increase sharply. But if inflation means an upswing in the economic cycle this only shows that the underconsumption of the masses cannot be a sufficient explanation of crises. According to this inflationist theory the appearance of a boom is something quite self-evident – as real wages fall the rate of profit rises and valorisation is improved.

The necessity of the cyclical process has already been shown despite the abstraction from any consideration of variations in commodity prices, wages and the rate of interest. In fact their movements are only a consequence of the underlying cyclical movements. Therefore to presuppose them is to fall into the error of logical circularity.

We started by assuming complete equilibrium where, despite a continuously rising technological level, the accumulation of capital can keep the entire working population employed. In this state, defined by proportional increases in capital and labour power, accumulation can proceed without any changes in the structure of prices. I have shown that even assuming these favourable conditions, there must come a point at which accumulation necessarily breaks down.

However, a proportional accumulation of this kind is quite unrealistic. The capitalist mechanism contains no regulator that could consciously adapt the scale of accumulation to the requisite state of equilibrium. The actual scale of accumulation will tend to deviate from the equilibrium positions specified in the reproduction scheme. The magnitude of accumulation depends on how much of the surplus value is accumulated as constant and variable capital and how much goes into the personal consumption of the capitalist.

In principle two cases are possible: accumulation may either surpass the equilibrium level or fall short of it. In practice however, only the second case is possible in which only a part of the surplus value is earmarked for purposes of accumulation – for instance, constant capital grows by just 5 per cent a year instead of the 10 per cent assumed by the scheme. In that case not all of the new workers will be absorbed into the productive process and a reserve army will be formed year by year. Part of the remaining, uncapitalised surplus value will enter capitalist consumption. The remainder will be kept in reserve for investment purposes in the form of loan capital.

So far we have taken the total social capital that is productively absorbed into the process of reproduction as a single unit and assumed that the industrial capitalist deploys his own capital. This assumption is purely fictitious and only justifiable methodologically for purposes of simplification. It excludes the monied capitalist or rentier from the scope of the analysis: 'If all capital were in the hands of the industrial capitalists there would be no such thing as interest and the rate of interest' (Marx, 1959, p. 377). But interest exists and our fictitious assumption therefore has to be dropped. In reality only a minor proportion of capitalists operate exclusively with their own capital. The 'majority of industrial capitalists, even if in different numerical proportions, work with their own and borrowed capital' (p. 376). Therefore credit in the sense of the portion of surplus value that is saved has to be reintroduced into the analysis. The abstract reproduction scheme is thus enriched by a further empirical moment and the analysis comes a step closer to actual reality.

Marx states that:

> For the productive capitalist who works on borrowed capital, the gross profit falls into two parts – the interest, which he is to pay the lender, and the surplus over and above the interest, which makes up his own share of the profit. (1959, pp. 372–3)

It follows that the magnitude of the profit that actually falls to the industrial capital 'is determined by the interest, since this is fixed by the general rate of interest … and assumed to be given beforehand, before the process of production begins' (p. 373). Even if there is no law which determines this general rate of interest there is still an 'average level' of the rate of interest corresponding to an equilibrium state of production in a given country at a given period of time. When the productive apparatus is in this state of equilibrium, the entire social surplus value will be used for accumulation, in so far as it is not personally consumed. Yet one group of capitalists – monied capitalists and rentiers – do not function directly in the productive process; they transfer their capital to capitalists who do. The interest that this group receives from its capital can be regarded as a 'normal interest' determined by the number of these capitalists, the size of their capital and so on.

However, we are not dealing with a case of equilibrium but one in which part of the surplus value due for accumulation cannot find productive employment. This loanable portion of capital, which is neither consumed nor directly capitalised, but appears in the money market in search of investment, stimulates business activity by depressing the rate of interest below its 'normal level' in the sense just defined. Accumulation is thus speeded up. Marx states that 'the expansion of the actual process of accumulation is promoted by the fact that the low interest ... increases that portion of the profit which is transformed into profit of enterprise' (1959, p. 495).

An analogous process occurs on the labour market. Originally the entire working population was absorbed into the process of production whereas now, in the case where the constant capital expands at a lower than equilibrium rate, a reserve army begins to form. This in turn depresses the level of wages and again stimulates business activity. The rate of surplus value exceeds 100 per cent because of both factors and the growing profitability on capital produced by a cheapening of the elements of production accelerates the tempo of accumulation. The rate of accumulation would again approximate to its equilibrium rate. Table 2.8 shows that even if we were to assume that constant capital expands at the low rate of 5 per cent a year, the available loan capital would tend to run dry in the course of accumulation.

Table 2.8

	c	v	reserve army	k^*	L	a_c	a_v
Year 1	200 000 +	25 000 +	0 +	2 500 +	12 444 +	10 000 +	56
Year 2	210 000 +	25 056 +	1 194 +	2 505 +	11 994 +	10 500 +	57
Year 3	220 000 +	25 113 +	2 449 +	2 115 +	11 516 +	11 025 +	61
Year 7	268 018 +	24 842 +	7 974 +	2 484 +	9 211 +	13 201 +	38
Year 8	281 219 +	24 880 +	9 576 +	2 488 +	8 386 +	14 060 +	0

* $k = 10$ per cent of the annual surplus value $(s = k + L + a_c + a_v)$

If on the other hand, increased profitability forces up the rate of accumulation of constant capital to over 5 per cent the mass of loan capital would dry up sooner. Suppose that starting from a rate of expansion of 5 per cent the constant capital grows by an additional 2 per cent every year (5 per cent in the second year, seven in the third, nine in the fourth ...) while all other conditions are equal.

Table 2.9

	c	v	reserve	k	a_c	a_v	L
Year 1	200 000 +	25 000 +	0 +	2 500 +	10 000 +	56 +	12 444
Year 2	210 000 +	25 056 +	1 194 +	2 505 +	14 700 +	535 +	7 316
							19 760
Year 3	224 700 +	25 591 +	1 917 +	2 559 +	20 223 +	1 056 +	1 753
							21 513
Year 4	244 923 +	26 647 +	2 293 +	2 664 +	26 941 +	1 565 -	4 523
							16 990
Year 5	271 864 +	28 212 +	2 175 +	2 821 +	35 320 +	2 238 -	12 167
							4 823
Year 6	307 184 +	30 450 +	1 456 +	3 045 +	44 077 +	2 477 -	19 245
							- 14 426
Year 7	(253 361)+	(32 927)+	(74)+	0			

Table 2.9 shows that the course of accumulation breaks up into two distinct phases. In the first, extending over three years, there is a growing mass of loan capital which reaches its maximum point at the end of the third year. Obviously this expansion of loan capital depresses the rate of interest below its normal level and incites the capitalist to expand the scale of production further. The fourth year is the turning point. Due to accumulation the scale of production reaches a level where there is not enough surplus value to valorise the accumulated capital. The accumulation fund $(a_c + a_v)$ shows a deficit of 4 523 which is initially covered by borrowings. This in turn reduces the total mass of available loan capital. Such reductions persist until in the sixth year the loan is completely exhausted. Year 6 is the starting point of the crisis because there is not enough surplus value to continue accumulation, even after borrowings. This means that the already functioning capital has been overaccumulated – there is too much of it. Marx characterises the process in the following way:

> The interest now rises to its average level. It reaches its maximum again as soon as the new crisis sets in. Credit suddenly stops then, payments are suspended, the reproduction process is paralysed ... a superabundance of idle industrial capital appears side by side with an almost absolute absence of loan capital. On the whole, then, the movement of loan capital, as expressed in the rate of interest, is in the opposite direction to that of industrial capital.(1959, pp. 488–9)

Underaccumulation [accumulation below our original equilibrium – TK] expands the volume of loan capital and thereby depresses the rate of interest and enhances the rate of profit. An abnormal upswing follows. Figure 3 shows that the upswing is not a simple straight line but takes the shape of a curve that rises steeply upwards from a low start. The gradual pace of accumulation at the start of this upswing increases progressively under the stimulus of a low rate of interest. When the reserves of loan capital have run dry, accumulation comes to a standstill, or the crisis starts.

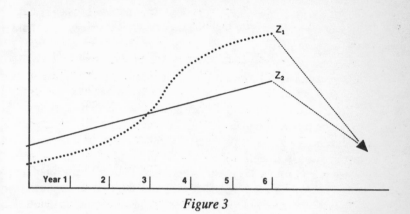

Figure 3

A similar movement is discernible on the labour market. Underaccumulation – which is what we are assuming – means that unused labour powers are available. The depression of wages below the value of labour power enhances the rate of profit. This incites capital to extend the scale of production and because the first half of the expansion phase is characterised by a growing reserve army, this impulse is even more powerful. But the number of unemployed starts to decline and wages begin to rise.

It follows that through the introduction of credit into the analysis the process of accumulation acquires a more realistic character. But no new moments are introduced in terms of our basic explanation of the industrial cycle and of the causes of crisis. If we view the expansion phase as a whole we return to the methodological starting point of the analysis, in the sense that the converse deviations of the rate of interest or of wages cancel out one another to yield an average or normal level.

As against Bauer I have shown that the very mechanism of accumulation leads to an overaccumulation of capital and thus to crisis. Even a cut in wages can only proceed within definite insuperable limits. Thus accumulation necessarily comes to a standstill or the system collapses. At the moment of crisis capital – in the form of the portions of surplus value previously destined for accumulation – are excluded from the process of production. Absolute overproduction begins as unsold stocks accumulate. Money capital in search of investment can no longer be applied profitably in production and turns to the stock exchange.

The activity of the stock exchange is insuperably bound up with the movement of interest on the money-market: 'the price of these securities rises and falls inversely as the rate of interest' (Marx, 1959, p. 467). As the rate of interest jerks upward at the start of every crisis the price of these securities registers a precipitous fall: 'when the money market is tight securities fall for two reasons: first, because the rate of interest rises, and secondly, because they are thrown on the market in large quantities in order to convert them into cash' (p. 467).

The depreciation of securities in times of crisis initiates a massive drive for speculation which is why the end of the crisis, or the phase of depression, goes together with feverish activity on the stock exchange. At Z point (Figure 3) there is overaccumulation, a shortage of investment opportunities, in short, large amounts of disposable capital. This capital turns to the exchange. Lederer's argument that 'even in times of depression savings find investment' (1925, p. 377) ignores the purely illusory character of this investment. From the banker's point of view the stock exchange might be as profitable as any other type of investment. But investments on the stock exchange create neither value nor surplus value. Capital simply shifts according to the stock market quotations. After its dramatic rise during the crisis the rate of interest falls in the depression and the early stages of the period of expansion and so the value of securities start appreciating: 'As soon as the storm is over, this paper again rises to its former level' (Marx, 1959, pp. 467–8). In this way its 'depreciation in times of crisis serves as a potent means of centralising fortunes' (p. 468). Some pages later Marx states:

> Gains and losses through fluctuations in the price of these titles of ownership, and their centralisation in the hands of the railway kings, etc., become, by their very nature, more and more a matter of gamble, which appears to take the place of labour as the original method of acquiring capital wealth. (p. 478)

This completes the causal chain. Starting from the sphere of production I have shown that the very laws of capitalist accumulation impart to accumulation a cyclical form and this cyclical movement impinges on the sphere of circulation (money market and stock exchange). The former is the independent variable, the latter the dependent variable. Once counteracting tendencies begin to operate and valorisation of productive capital is again restored a further period of accumulation sets in. The rate of profit climbs upwards. As soon as it exceeds the income of fixed interest securities money is again channelled from the stock exchange back into the sphere of production. The rate of interest starts rising and with the gradual fall in the price of securities they are transferred to the 'public' which only looks for a long term investment. But this 'long-term' lasts only down to the next crisis or the next wave of speculative buying. Throughout all this there is a growing centralisation of money wealth which in turn accounts for the increasing power of finance capital.

The elasticity of accumulation

Luxemburg criticises Marx's scheme of expanded reproduction in the following terms: 'The limits of this expansion are each time determined in advance by the amount of surplus value which is to be capitalised in any given case' (1968, p. 330). She goes on to state that:

> The diagram thus precludes the expansion of production by leaps and bounds. It only allows of a gradual expansion which keeps strictly in step with the formation of surplus value ... For the same reason, the diagram presumes an accumulation which affects both departments equally and therefore all branches of capitalist production. It precludes expansion of the demand by leaps and bounds just as much as it prevents a one-sided or precocious development of individual branches of capitalist production. Thus the diagram assumes a movement of the aggregate capital which flies in the face of the actual course of capitalist development. (p. 342)

This criticism has generated a whole school. A series of Marxist writers have repeated Luxemburg's objections assuring us that Lenin was the first to formulate the law of the uneven development of capitalism. Evgeny Varga tells us that in '*Capital* Marx did not give a purely economic foundation to the law of the uneven development of capitalism. He took the totality of phenomena as his starting point' (1926, 'Der uberimperialismus', p. 246). Apparently 'Lenin was the first to propose the law of uneven development' (p. 248). Likewise Nikolai Bukharin refers to the 'Leninist law of the unevenness of capitalist development' (1926, p. 9). As always Sternberg blindly follows whatever Luxemburg has to say: 'in a rigid schema of exchange under pure capitalism the sporadic development of individual industries would be inconceivable'(1926, p. 153).

The falsehood of this view is perfectly obvious. Marx ridiculed the harmonist theory of a balanced proportional accumulation in all spheres of production. If this sort of accumulation were possible crises would not exist. This is why Marx says:

> there would be no overproduction, if demand and supply corresponded to each other, if the capital were distributed in such proportions in all spheres of production, that the production of one article involved the consumption of the other, and thus its own consumption. There would be no overproduction, if there were no overproduction. Since, however, capitalist production can allow itself free rein only in certain spheres, under certain conditions, there would be no capitalist production at all if it had to develop *simultaneously* and *evenly* in all spheres. (1969, p. 532)

Luxemburg's criticisms could only have arisen through a failure to grasp the basic aspects of Marx's methodological procedure. Marx's reproduction scheme represents the average line of accumulation, that is the ideal normal trajectory in which accumulation occurs proportionally in both departments. In reality there are deviations from this average line – Marx himself repeatedly draws attention to the elastic power of capital – but these deviations are only explicable in terms of the average line. Luxemburg's mistake is that a model that represents only the ideal trajectory in a range of possibilities is taken for an exact description of the actual trajectory of capital.

The same is true of Bauer. He imagines that the magnitudes of his production scheme are the only possible form in which the process of production can advance without breaks. For each year of production in Bauer's scheme it would be possible to generate a series of variants, each of which would represent a distinct configuration of the departmental distribution of capital without altering the scale of total social production. For the given social scale of production various equilibrium positions are conceivable. For instance accumulation may be totally confined to *Department I*, in which case for several years it would show a powerful development by leaps and bounds, while *Department II* simply stagnates.

Nothing is more characteristic of Luxemburg's scholasticism than the way she criticises Marx's reproduction schemes. Where Marx analyses a case of proportional accumulation Luxemburg objects that he 'precludes the expansion of production by leaps and bounds'. Yet if Marx proceeds to the opposite case, she says:

Marx enables accumulation to continue by broadening the basis of production in Department I. Accumulation in Department II appears only as a condition and consequence of accumulation in Department I ... Department I retains the initiative all the time, Department II being merely a passive follower. Thus the capitalists of Department II are only allowed to accumulate just as much as ... is needed for the accumulation of Department I. (p. 122).

This only shows how completely Luxemburg has misunderstood the significance of Marx's methodological procedure. For who could ensure that accumulation takes place proportionally in the two departments? No such regulator exists under capitalism or can exist. It follows that proportional accumulation is a purely ideal case; a fiction that could actually prevail only accidentally. As a rule the actual process of accumulation is quite unequal in the various branches.

The restricted development of productive forces under capitalism

If the capitalist system inevitably breaks down due to the relative decline in the mass of profit we can understand why Marx ascribed such enormous importance to the tendential fall in the rate of profit, which is simply the expression of this breakdown. It is also clear what it means to say: 'The *real barrier* of capitalist production is *capital itself*. It is that capital and its self expansion appear as the starting and closing point, the motive and purpose of production' (Marx, 1959, p. 250).

Marx criticises Ricardo for confusing the production of use values with the production of value, the labour process with the valorisation process: 'He cannot therefore admit that the bourgeois mode of production contains within itself a barrier to the free development of productive forces, a barrier which comes to the surface in crises' (1969, pp. 527–8). From a purely technological aspect, as a labour process for the production of use values, nothing could impede the expansion of the forces of production. This expansion encounters a barrier in the shape of the valorisation process, the fact that the elements of production figure as capital which must be valorised. If profit disappears the labour process is interrupted. The greatest possible valorisation forms the specific aim of the capitalist process of production.

The barrier to the development of the forces of production of capitalism is of a twofold nature. In the first place the level of technological perfection attainable under capitalism is far lower than it could otherwise be from a social standpoint. Marx was the first to show that under capitalism there is far less scope for the application of improved means of production. From the standpoint of capital what matters is economies in the use of paid labour, and not labour as such. For example, if the production of a commodity costs society 10 hours of labour time, it would make use of any machine that could economise on the labour time – even if 9.5 hours were still needed to produce that commodity. But if a capitalist pays the worker the equivalent of say, 5 hours of labour, he will only find the use of machinery to his advantage if it costs him less than 5 hours.

Quite apart from Asia and Africa, there are large parts of eastern and south-eastern Europe today where living labour is so cheap that it does not pay the capitalist to use machinery. Thus although human labour could be replaced by machinery it is in fact massively wasted. Even in the more advanced capitalist countries like Germany and the United States advanced technology is confined to a relatively small group of capitalists, next to whom there is a large mass of technically backward enterprises which squander human labour by using outdated machinery and manual labour. Even the best technology that is used is not identical with the best that is available. Of course a fantastic number of inventions and patents are bought up by the cartels and trusts, but they do not use them until forced to do so under the pressure of competition.

Secondly competition entails an enormous squandering of the productive forces through the struggle for sales outlets, the overproduction of commodities on one side and unemployment on the other. According to R Liefmann 'this competitive struggle ... is terribly uneconomical, and often represents a huge waste of capital' (1918, p. 50). But are things any better in the epoch of monopoly capitalism? Liefmann argues that as far as cartels are concerned we cannot speak of a conscious regulation of production based on foresight. In fact it turns out that while 'cartel formation gives a powerful impetus to expanding the scale of production of the enterprise ... the cartels often find the greatest difficulties in disposing of the enormously expanded production.' Liefmann maintained that: ' As a rule they [the cartels] have no means of preventing an excessive expansion of enterprises' (pp. 69–70). Liefmann refers to the 'huge overcapitalisation' that characterises the cartels.

After the War underutilisation of capacity became a general phenomenon in the leading capitalist countries. This is the celebrated 'regulation' of production by the cartels and trusts – not a planned calculation and distribution of production according to needs, but restrictions on the utilisation of productive capacity in order to push up the level of prices and profits. Marx states that:

capitalist production meets in the development of its productive forces a barrier which has nothing to do with the production of wealth as such; and this peculiar barrier testifies to the limitations and to the merely historical, transitory character of the capitalist mode of production; testifies that for the production of wealth, it is not an absolute mode, moreover, that at a certain stage it rather conflicts with its further development. (1959, p. 242)

After 1815 English capitalism revolutionised her industry through technological changes in iron production starting with the puddling process. But as the accumulation of capital advanced the rate of technological progress slowed down in Britain. In 1856 the Englishman Bessemer reported the discovery of a new process that was destined to revolutionise the metal working industries and to replace the dominance of iron by steel. But for 20 years Britain ignored the discovery of the Bessemer process and stuck to the puddling process until the competition of Germany, France and Belgium forced her to take it over and refine it. This was repeated again when in 1879 Thomas discovered the basic process named after him. Britain received the finding with pure indifference and let foreigners buy it until, in three years, it revolutionised all the plants on the Continent. The British monopoly was a thing of the past as the leadership in iron and steel production gradually passed into other hands.

At the end of the nineteenth century we find the same picture in the field of electrical technology. British capitalism simply ignored it at a time when there was practically no city in Germany which did not have its 'electricity society'. By 1906 G Schulze-Gaevernitz could refer to the 'technological conservatism' of Britain and list a whole series of industries like iron and steel, machine building, shipbuilding, chemicals and others in which America and Germany had either displaced or were threatening British dominance. However Schulze-Gaevernitz does not accept economic causes as the explanation of British conservatism and prefers to trace this to 'processes of spiritual decay' (1906, p. 212). But if so why did the progressive, in fact revolutionary, character of British economic development change so completely in a few decades? I have shown that under capitalism, at a definite level of the accumulation of capital, technological development has to slow down because the valorisation of capital can no longer sustain it.

This way of posing the problem shows that it is misleading to speak about the stagnation of productive forces under capitalism in general. This is precisely why Kautsky can deny the possibility of an economic breakdown of capitalism, because in his understanding capitalism has proved its capacity to develop the forces of production. But the problem is not one of some abstract capitalism outside space and time but of the actual development of particular historical capitalist countries, each of which lies at a specific stage of capital accumulation. It is a fact that the oldest capitalist country of Europe, which for more than a century played the leading role in industry and which had the greatest accumulation of capital prior to the War, 'has lost its dominance to other nations in several of the most important industries' (Schulze-Gaevernitz, 1906, p. 334). The technological stagnation of Britain and her loss of industrial leadership were rooted in the faltering of her rate of accumulation due to the already huge accumulation of capital.

Once the accumulation of capital increases in countries like Germany and America, there too the process of valorisation will necessarily run into limits that will slow down their technological advance. The law of accumulation expounded above explains the phenomenon already noted by Adam Smith that in the younger countries at an early stage of capitalist development the tempo of accumulation is more rapid than in the wealthier, advanced capitalist countries.

Lenin was right in saying that highly developed capitalism is characterised by an inherent 'tendency to stagnation and decay'. But Lenin linked this tendency to the growth of monopolies. That there is such a connection is indisputable, but a mere statement is not enough. After all one is not dealing simply with phenomena of stagnation. The very same British capitalism that has reached a state of decay economically, shows an extremely aggressive character in other aspects. It is this aggressive character or unusual energy that gives to it the peculiar stamp of so-called 'imperialism'.

Imperialism is characterised both by stagnation and by aggressiveness. These tendencies have to be explained in their unity; if monopolisation causes stagnation, then how can we explain the aggressive character of imperialism? In fact both phenomena are ultimately rooted in the tendency towards breakdown, in imperfect valorisation due to overaccumulation. The growth of monopoly is a means of enhancing profitability by raising prices and, in this sense, it is only a surface appearance whose inner structure is insufficient valorisation linked to capital accumulation.

The aggressive character of imperialism likewise necessarily flows from a crisis of valorisation. Imperialism is a striving to restore the valorisation of capital at any cost, to weaken or eliminate the breakdown tendency. This explains its aggressive policies at home (an intensified attack on the working class) and abroad (a drive to transform foreign nations into tributaries). This is the hidden basis of the bourgeois rentier state, of the parasitic character of capitalism at an advanced stage of accumulation. Because the valorisation of capital fails in countries at a given, higher stage of accumulation, the tribute that flows in from abroad assumes ever increasing importance. Parasitism becomes a method of prolonging the life of capitalism.

The opposition between capitalism and its forces of production is an opposition between value and use value, between the tendency to an unlimited production of use value and a production of values constrained by the limits to valorisation. Marx writes:

> The contradiction to put it in a very general way, consists in that the capitalist mode of production involves a tendency towards absolute development of the productive forces, regardless of the value and surplus value it contains ... while, on the other hand, its aim is to preserve the value of the existing capital and promote its self expansion to the highest limit. (1959, p. 249)

Capital accomplishes this twofold objective through technological advance; by the development of a progressively higher organic composition of capital which, however, entails the consequences we know already:

> The methods by which it accomplishes this include the fall of the rate of profit, depreciation of the existing capital and development of the productive forces of labour at the expense of already created productive forces ... The periodical depreciation of existing capital ... disturbs the given conditions, within which the process of circulation and reproduction of capital takes place, and is therefore accompanied by sudden stoppages and crises in the production process. (Marx, 1959, p. 249)

Surveying the process as a whole we get the following picture. The accumulation process is a movement that proceeds through the opposition between use value and value. From the use value aspect the forces of production are developed absolutely ruthlessly. This accumulation of use values (which is simultaneously an accumulation of values) leads to a fall in the rate of profit, which in turn means that valorisation of the advanced capital is no longer possible at the given rate. This means a crisis, a devaluation of the existing capital. Yet this reanimates the accumulation of capital from its value side: 'The accumulation of capital in terms of value is slowed down by the falling rate of profit, only to hasten still more the accumulation of use values, while this, in its turn, adds new momentum to accumulation in terms of value' (Marx, 1959, p. 250). The entire process moves by fits and starts, through crises and their attendant devaluation of capital, so that the forces of production find their limit in the possibilities of valorisation. Marx writes:

> The limits within which the preservation and self expansion of the value of capital resting on the expropriation and pauperisation of the great can alone move – these limits come continually into conflict with the methods of production employed by capital for its purposes, which drive development of the social productivity of labour. The means – unconditional development of the productive forces of society – comes continually into conflict with the limited purpose, the self expansion of the existing capital. The capitalist mode of production is, for this reason, a historical means of developing the material forces of production and creating an appropriate world market and is at the same time a continual conflict between this its historical task and its own corresponding relations of social production. (1959, p. 250)

Similarly in a passage some pages later Marx writes:

> Here the capitalist mode of production is beset with another contradiction. Its historical mission is unconstrained development in geometrical progression of the productivity of human labour. It goes back on its mission whenever, as here, it checks the development of productivity. It thus demonstrates again that it is becoming senile and that it is more and more outlived itself. (p. 262)

The ideas developed here were already proposed in *Capital Volume One* in a more general form. But in these passages from *Volume Three* Marx shows concretely – through an analysis of the capitalist process of accumulation – that capitalism, though historically necessary for the expansion of productivity, becomes in the course of time a fetter on this expansion.

The Marxist theory of imperfect valorisation

Let us suppose with Luxemburg that capitalism is not the exclusively prevalent mode of production but has to rely on a non-capitalist sector. In that case, on the periphery of Bauer's scheme there are non-capitalist markets that buy up the surplus value produced capitalistically within the scheme, but otherwise unsaleable. Let us suppose that only after this transaction is the surplus value convertible into a usable natural form and earmarked for accumulation in the capitalist country. In short we assume that Bauer's scheme now represents an accumulation whose elements have returned from the non-capitalist countries after being realised there. But what follows? Even if the surplus value were realised in the non-capitalist countries the breakdown of capitalism would still be inevitable due to the causes mentioned.

This only shows that Luxemburg's entire hypothesis is totally irrelevant to the problem concerned and therefore quite superfluous. Whether surplus value is realised internally or in a non-capitalist sector has no bearing either on the life span of capitalism or on the timing and inevitability of its final collapse. In both cases the breakdown would be inevitable and its timing would be the same. This flows from the fact of capitalist accumulation on the basis of a progressively rising organic composition of capital; from the fact that c grows faster than v. The question of where the surplus value is realised is quite irrelevant. All that matters is the magnitude of the surplus value.

The first two decades of discussions around Marx were dominated by the idea of the breakdown of capitalism. Then, around the turn of the century, Tugan-Baranovsky came up with his theory of a possible unlimited development of capitalism. He was soon followed by Hilferding and Bauer and finally Kautsky. So it was entirely natural that Luxemburg should defend the fundamental conception of the inevitable breakdown of capitalism against the distortions of Marx's epigones. But instead of testing Marx's reproduction scheme within the framework of his total system and especially of the theory of accumulation, instead of asking what role it plays methodologically in the structure of his theory, instead of analysing the schema of accumulation down to its ultimate conclusion, Luxemburg was unconsciously influenced by them. She came around to believing that Marx's schemes really do allow for an unlimited accumulation:

> We are running in circles, quite in accordance with the theory of Tugan-Baranovsky. Considered in isolation, Marx's diagram does indeed permit of such an interpretation since he himself explicitly states time and again that he aims at presenting the process of accumulation of the aggregate capital in a society consisting solely of capitalists and workers. (Luxemburg, 1968, pp. 330–1)

Luxemburg was of the opinion that Marx 'does not go any further into the question of accumulation than to devise a few models and suggest an analysis. This is where my critique begins' (1972, p. 48).

We could scarcely imagine a worse distortion of Marx's methodological principles. Because Luxemburg took the schemes as implying the possibility of unfettered accumulation she was forced to abandon them in order to salvage the notion of breakdown flowing from *Capital Volume One*. In her own words:

> Assuming the accumulation of capital to be without limits, one has obviously proved the unlimited capacity of capitalism to survive! ... If the capitalist mode of production can ensure boundless expansion of the productive forces, of economic progress, it is invincible indeed. (1968, p. 325)

With her ad hoc model of the need for non-capitalist markets Luxemburg thought she was killing two birds with one stone – refuting the equilibrium dreams of the neo-harmonist writers by showing that there is an inexorable economic limit to capitalism and simultaneously explaining imperialism.

Capitalism is dominated by a blind, unlimited thirst for surplus value. According to the interpretation that Luxemburg gives it would appear as if the system suffers from an excess of surplus value, that it contains an unsaleable residue of surplus value and in this sense possesses too much surplus value. Such a theory is quite illogical and self contradictory in terms of trying to understand the most important and peculiar function of capital, the function of valorisation.

The whole matter is quite different in the interpretation I have given. The capitalist mechanism falls sick not because it contains too much surplus value but because it contains too little. The valorisation of capital is its basic function and the system dies because this function cannot be fulfilled. In explaining how this happens the logical unity and consistency of Marx's system finds its most powerful expression. Unless we are going to overthrow the logical unity of the system we have to be able to demonstrate the necessary breakdown of capitalism in terms of the theory itself – that is, on the basis of the law of value without recourse to unnecessary and complicating auxiliary hypotheses. The Marxian theory of crises can account for recessions and their necessary periodic recurrence without having to invoke special causes. This illustrates the essential character of the logical structure of Marx's theory of breakdown and its difference from all other theories of the business cycle.

The latter are theories of equilibrium. They bear a static character. They cannot deduce the general crisis – seen as a discrepancy between demand and supply – from the system itself because in equilibrium theory prices represent an automatic mechanism for adjusting one to the other.

Disruptions of equilibrium can only be explained in terms of exogenous factors.

There is no such defect in Marx's theory of crises. True, Marx's proof procedure starts from the assumption of equilibrium. But equilibrium forms only a tentative methodological fiction with which Marx shows that in the long run equilibrium is impossible under capitalism; by its very nature capitalism is not static but dynamic. All the requirements placed on any theory with respect to its logical unity are satisfied, if purely deductively, proceeding from the inner course of capitalist accumulation itself. Keeping with the logic of the total system we can show the possibility and necessity of economic movements that lead to the periodic disruption of the system's equilibrium and to its final destruction.

This enables us to clarify the basic differences between the outlook of classical economy and that of Marx. Adam Smith had already discerned a threat to capitalism in the falling rate of profit because profit is the motor force of production. But Smith accounts for declining profitability in terms of growing competition of capitals. Ricardo grounds the law of the falling rate of profit in terms of natural factors related to the declining productivity of the soil. By contrast Marx deduces the breakdown of the capitalist system quite independently of competition. His starting point is a state of equilibrium. Because valorisation falters at a specific level of accumulation, the struggle for markets and for spheres of investment must begin. Competition is a consequence of imperfect valorisation, not its cause.

As against Ricardo, Marx roots the breakdown in the social form of production; in the fact that the capitalist mechanism is regulated by profit and at a certain level of capitalist accumulation there is not enough profit to ensure valorisation of the accumulated capital. The law of breakdown is the fundamental law that governs and supports the entire structure of Marx's thought.

Notes

1. Oppenheimer, who is otherwise a sharp thinker, fails to notice the methodological significance of Marx's reproduction schemes. He argues that Marx's division of the annual product into $c + v + s$ 'was simply a device for the deduction of surplus value. The deduction failed' (1928, p. 311). But Marx did not need any device for the deduction of surplus value because the latter is a fact and facts do not need any proofs. The methodological construction was not designed to prove the fact of surplus value but to establish exactly the variations in the magnitude of surplus value in the course of accumulation.

2. The basic mistake is Bauer's assumption that the rate of surplus value is constant despite the assumed rising organic composition of capital. Bauer's other mistakes relate not so much to the construction of his scheme as to his underlying lack of methodological clarity. He confuses the purely fictitious trajectory of accumulation represented by the scheme with the actual trajectory of accumulation.

3. The same holds for Tugan-Baranovsky who followed through the development of his system for only three years and claimed that it 'is quite unnecessary to continue with the analysis into the fourth and fifth and following years' (1901, p. 24).

4. To think as Boudin that a fall in the rate of profit 'naturally interrupts the advance of the accumulation process and acts like an automatic brake'(1909, p. 169) is to understand nothing of Marx's system. I have shown that it is not only not natural that accumulation should slow down with a fall in the rate of profit but that, on the contrary, it can proceed at an accelerated pace.

5. According to Marx there is too much capital and too many workers with respect to valorisation. Rosa Luxemburg shatters the clear sense of this passage by forcibly interjecting her theory of insufficient market outlets, of which there is no trace in Marx. After quoting the passage concerned she asks 'In relation to what is there too much of both? In relation to the market under normal conditions. As the market for capitalist commodities periodically grows too small, capital must remain unemployed and consequently part of the labour force as well' (1972, p. 126). Yet Marx says not a single word about the lack of markets. On the contrary, he says that the very causes that expanded markets and accelerated accumulation have also lowered the rate of profit. Hence he says the precise opposite of what Luxemburg supposes: not a decline in profitability due to lack of markets and the impossibility of accumulating but a decline in profitability due to accelerated accumulation and expansion of markets. Moreover Luxemburg states that the market for capitalist commodities periodically grows too small. But she herself makes not the slightest effort to show why there is this periodic shortage of outlets and from her standpoint the periodicity of crises simply cannot be explained.

6. This exposition suggests that capital accumulation forms the decisive element in Marx's theory of crises. Nevertheless, the influence of other factors is of great significance for the actual course of crises, especially the role of fixed capital as the factor which governs the periodicity of the crisis. I cannot go into this in more detail because this factor comes under simple reproduction and is therefore outside the framework of my analysis. Here I merely say that in contrast to the prevalent conception, even in Marxist writings, that there is no problem of a business cycle under simple reproduction, Marx demonstrates that even in simple reproduction crises must periodically burst forth due to the impact of fixed capital.

7. Oppenheimer drags in a third kind of setting free, arguing that more labour is displaced in the countryside than in industry and concludes that 'the process

of setting free can have nothing to do with changes in the organic composition of capital' (1913, p. 105). Oppenheimer overlooks something quite elementary: the basis of Marx's analysis is capitalism in its pure form. Marx is concerned with the condition of workers who already function as wage labourers. In the countryside the setting free is a setting free of small producers; it is their proletarianisation and conversion into wage labour.

8. No earlier epoch has come even vaguely close to ours in the abundance of data at its disposal. Yet what theoretical results can these writings lay claim to? The limited significance of this entire direction of research for theory is admitted by the chief statistician of the Federal Reserve Bank of New York, Carl Snyder: 'If we were to ask what is the sum total of theorems to flow from these detailed and penetrating studies the answer would have to be that their yield in terms of forecasts or controls, both hallmarks of any real scientific knowledge, is truly low' (1928, p. 27). To expect the construction of theory to be directly promoted by expanding empirical insights is a complete misunderstanding of the logical relationship of theory and empirical research.

9. Lederer's critique of disproportionality theory is the best thing that has been written on the subject. However it does not affect the Marxist theory of crisis because the latter traces crises to the periodically recurring shortage of surplus value. Any theory of disproportionality implies a theory of partial overproduction. Yet Marx deduces the inner crisis of capitalism from a generalised overproduction arising from a complete proportionality.

10. In the following description of the cycle I can only go into the essential causal relationships. Therefore I shall have to refrain from a more detailed treatment of credit and of its impact on the reproductive process, reserving this for my major study. The Marxist position has to show why crises are inevitable quite irrespective of credit and of the circulation process and how they are rooted in causes within production.

3   Modifying Countertendencies

Introduction

An abstract deductively elaborated theory never coincides directly with appearances. In this sense the theory of accumulation and breakdown expounded above does not directly correspond with the appearances of bourgeois society in its day to day life. The conditions of capitalism conceived in its pure form (which we have analysed so far) and those of the system in its empirical manifestations (which we have to analyse now) are by no means identical. This is because a theoretical deduction involves working with simplifications; many real factors pertaining to the world of appearances are consciously excluded from the analysis.

So far we have assumed:

  i)   that the capitalist system exists in isolation – that there is no foreign trade;
 ii)   that there are only two classes – capitalists and workers;
iii)   that there are no landowners, hence no groundrent;
 iv)   that commodities exchange without the mediation of merchants;
  v)   that the rate of surplus value is constant and corresponds to the magnitude of the wage – that is a rate of surplus value of 100 per cent;
 vi)   that there are only two spheres of production, producing means of production and means of consumption;
vii)   that the rate of growth of population is a constant magnitude;
viii)   that the value of labour power is constant; and
 ix)   that in all branches of production capital turns over once a year.

Any theory has to work with such provisional assumptions which are a potential source of mistakes. But these assumptions have allowed us to determine the direction in which the accumulation of capital works, even if the results of this analysis have a provisional character.

130

Marx was perfectly conscious of the abstract, provisional nature of his law of accumulation and breakdown. Having presented *'the absolute general law of capitalist accumulation'*, he says that: 'Like all other laws it is modified in its working by many circumstances, the analysis of which does not concern us here' (1954, p. 603). Elsewhere, in describing the process of accumulation, he writes: 'This process would soon bring about the collapse of the capitalist production were it not for counteracting tendencies' (1959, p. 246). Marx gave an analysis of these counteracting tendencies in various places in *Capital Volume Three* as well as in *Theories of Surplus Value*.

Once we have shown the tendency of accumulation in its pure form we have to examine the concrete circumstances under which the accumulation of capital proceeds, in order to see how far the tendency of the pure law is modified in its realisation. We are asking whether, and if so in what direction, the tendencies of development of the pure system are changed once this system reincorporates, by degrees, foreign trade, landowners who live off groundrent, merchants and the middle classes – and once the rate of surplus value or the level of wages are allowed to vary. These considerations mean that the abstract analysis comes closer to the world of real appearances. It enables us to verify the law of breakdown: to see to what extent the results of the abstract theoretical analysis are confirmed by concrete reality.

Considering the gigantic increases in productivity and the enormous accumulation of capital of the last several decades the question arises – why has capitalism not already broken down? This is the problem that interests Marx:

> the same influences which produce a tendency in the general rate of profit to fall, also call forth counter-effects, which hamper, retard, and partly paralyse this fall. The latter do not do away with the law, but impair its effect. Otherwise, it would not be the fall of the general rate of profit, but rather its relative slowness, that would be incomprehensible. Thus, the law acts only as a tendency. And it is only under certain circumstances and only after long periods that its effects become strikingly pronounced. (1959, p. 239)

Once these counteracting influences begin to operate, the valorisation of capital is reestablished and the accumulation of capital can resume on an expanded basis. In this case the breakdown tendency is interrupted and manifests itself in the form of a temporary crisis. Crisis is thus a tendency towards breakdown which has been interrupted and restrained from realising itself completely.

Return for a moment to the illustration of the cyclical process of accumulation in Figure 2. (See p. 84)

Due to the very nature of the accumulation process there is a basic difference between the two phases of the cycle with respect to their duration and their character. We have seen that only the phase of accumulation is defined by a specific regularity; that only the length of the expansion phase $(0 - z1, 0 - z2 \ldots)$ and the timing of the downturn into a crisis are open to exact calculation. No such calculation is possible with respect to the duration of the crisis $(z1 - o1, z2 - o2 \ldots)$. At $z1$, $z2$, and so on valorisation collapses. The ensuing overproduction of commodities is a consequence of imperfect valorisation due to overaccumulation. The crisis is not caused by disproportionality between expansion of production and lack of purchasing power – that is, by a shortage of consumers. The crisis intervenes because no use is made of the purchasing power that exists. This is because it does not pay to expand production any further since the scale of production makes no difference to the amount of surplus value now obtainable. So on the one hand purchasing power remains idle. On the other, the elements of production lie unsold.

At first only further expansion of production becomes unprofitable; reproduction on the existing scale is not affected. But with each cycle of production this changes. The portion of the surplus value earmarked for accumulation each year goes unsold. As inventories build up the capitalist is forced to sell at any price to obtain the resources to keep the enterprise going on its existing scale. He is compelled to reduce prices and cut back on his scale of production. The scale of operations is reduced or they shut down completely. Many firms declare bankruptcy and are devalued. Huge amounts of capital are written off as losses. Unemployment grows.

This sickness leads in one of two directions. Either there is nothing to stop the breakdown tendency from working itself out and the economy simply ceases to function; or specific measures are undertaken to counteract the sickness so that the sickness is stopped and turns into a healing process. The question arises: how is a crisis surmounted? How is a new period of upswing initiated? The mere statement that crises are a form of sickness is quite useless if we have no conception of what this sickness is caused by. The specific means by which a crisis is surmounted are obviously closely related to the diagnosis of the sickness. The remedies prescribed would vary according to whether the underlying cause of crises is seen as the underconsumption of the masses, as disproportions between branches of production or as a shortage of capital.

There are, of course, cases where the boom has been precipitated by a massive flow of funds from abroad – for instance, the huge imports of

American capital into Germany over 1926–7. But in numerous instances – and this is the general rule – crises have been surmounted without any flow of foreign funds. And just as crises have been surmounted while many of its so-called causes (for instance, underconsumption of the masses) are still present, so we find that all the factors generally cited to explain the boom turn out to be quite useless in explaining how the depression itself is overcome. The remedies proposed are not logically connected with the diagnosis of industrial sickness.

In contrast to these various theories, our theory shows that the means actually enforced to surmount a crisis correspond perfectly to the actual causes of industrial sickness in our analysis. In this sense the theory provides a consistent explanation of the two phases of the industrial cycle, both of the turn from expansion to crisis and of the process through which the crisis is later surmounted. From the argument that crises are caused by an imperfect valorisation of capital it follows that they can only be overcome if the valorisation of capital is restored. But this cannot come about by itself, merely in the course of time. It presupposes a series of organisational measures. Crises are only surmounted through such a structural reorganisation of the economy.

The capitalist mechanism is not something left to itself. It contains within itself living social forces: on one side the working class, on the other the class of industrialists. The latter is directly interested in preserving the existing economic order and tries, in every conceivable way, to find means of 'boosting' the economy, of bringing it back into motion through restoring profitability.

The circumstances through which the crises can be overcome vary enormously. Ultimately however, they are all reducible to the fact that they either reduce the value of the constant capital or increase the rate of surplus value. In both cases the valorisation of capital is enhanced – the rate of profit rises. Such circumstances lie both within production and in the sphere of circulation, and pertain both to the inner mechanism of capital as well as to its external relations to the world market.

The capitalist's continual efforts to restore profitability might take the form of reorganising the mechanism of capital internally (for instance, by cutting costs of production, or effecting economies in the use of energy, raw materials and labour power) or of recasting trade relations on the world market (international cartels, cheaper sources of raw material supply and so on). This involves groping attempts at a complete rationalisation of all spheres of economic life. Many of these measures fail while the programme of reorganisation is often completely beyond the reach of the smaller enterprises, which are thus wiped out. In the end capital finds suitable means of raising profitability and a reorganisation is gradually enforced. By its very nature the duration of this reorganisation and economic restructuring process is something purely contingent and therefore impossible to calculate.

In the pages that follow I shall not go into a detailed description of all the several countertendencies that hinder the complete working out of the breakdown. I shall confine myself to presenting only the most important of them and to showing how the operation of these countertendencies transforms the breakdown into a temporary crisis so that the movement of the accumulation process is not something continuous but takes the form of periodic cycles. We shall also see how, as these countertendencies are gradually emasculated, the antagonisms of world capitalism become progressively sharper and the tendency towards breakdown increasingly approaches its final form of an absolute collapse.

Part 1: Countertendencies Internal to the Mechanism of Capital

Increases in the rate of profit through the expansion of productivity

In Chapter 2 I outlined the methodological considerations which prompted Marx to analyse the problem of accumulation and crisis on the assumption of constant prices. This assumption made it possible to prove that the cyclical movements of expansion and decline are independent of fluctuations in the level of commodity prices and wages. Here I want to show that the opposite assumption of the bourgeois economists, who take the price fluctuations as their starting point, simply confuses the issue.

We have already seen that in analysing the business cycle Lederer starts from rising prices as the decisive factor: 'If we look at periods of boom, then we find that in such periods all prices rise' (1925, p. 387). According to Lederer, expansions in the scale of production which characterise periods of boom are a result of rising prices. But how is the general increase in prices possible? Lederer argues that if the value of money is held constant a general increase in prices can only flow from changes on the commodity supply side. 'However', Lederer continues, 'such changes in the volume of production are only consequent on changes in the level of prices' (p. 388). So Lederer sees a vicious circle which can only be broken by new purchasing power being injected into the process of circulation by the expansion of credit. 'Only credit creates the boom or makes it possible' (p. 391) by raising the level of demand and therefore of prices. 'Only through additional credit and thus newly created purchasing power is any significant expansion of the productive process possible' (p. 387).

Lederer's argument is unconvincing. Apart from its defective methodological starting point, it is both logically contradictory and contradicts the actual course of the boom. Firstly a general increase in prices is something meaningless apart from the case where the value of money falls. Yet such a general price increase is purely nominal – it has no impact on the mass of profit. Bearing this in mind the whole basis of Lederer's deductions simply falls. Secondly the most important renovations and expansions in the productive apparatus occur in periods of depression when commodity prices are low. It is the demand generated by these programmes of expansion that raises the level of prices, assuming that this demand exceeds the supply.

In principle rising prices are by no means necessary in surmounting crises. They are only a consequence, not a cause, of booms. Extensions in the scale of production can, and do, occur without rising prices and even if the level of prices is low. This is basic to any understanding of the problem. According to Lederer rising prices and the programmes of expansion supposedly linked to them are a result of credit expansion. In which case it follows that credit is released when prices are still low. So Lederer has to be able to tell us who will take the credit to extend the scale of production when prices are low? Lederer is simply running in circles.

The fact remains that programmes of expansion are undertaken in periods of depression when prices are low. Any deeper analysis has to start here if we are going to understand the process in its pure form. At a certain level of the accumulation of capital there is an overproduction of capital or a shortage of surplus value. Overproduction does not mean that there is not enough purchasing power to buy up commodities, but that it does not pay to buy commodities for programmes of expansion because it is not profitable to extend the scale of production: 'In times of crisis … the rate of profit, and with it the demand for industrial capital has to all extents and purposes disappeared' (Marx 1959, p. 513). Due to lack of profitability, accumulation is interrupted and production is carried out on the existing scale. Prices are bound to fall. The fall in prices is only a consequence of stagnation not its cause.

Because commodities are unsaleable when the crisis starts, competition sets in. Each individual capital tries to secure for itself, at the cost of other capitals, that which is unattainable by the totality of capitals. From a scientific point of view, this proves that competition is necessary under capitalism. We started by assuming the most favourable condition for capital, a state of equilibrium in which supply and demand coincide. Yet at a certain level of the accumulation of capital competition must necessarily arise. Earlier we looked at the capitalist class as a single entity. But in examining the crisis we must take account of the mutual competition of the individual capitalists.

Let us go back to the question posed earlier – how is the crisis surmounted? How does a renewed expansion of production come about? The answer is: through the reorganisation and rationalisation of production by which profitability is again restored even at the depressed level of prices prevailing. Figure 4 is a schematic illustration of the entire movement.

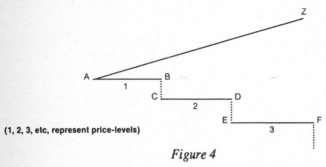

(1, 2, 3, etc, represent price-levels)

Figure 4

The crisis started at the prices prevailing at level 1. As a result the price level fell from *B* to *C* until they stabilised at their new and lower level 2 (line *C–D*). Taking all the capitals in their totality, further accumulation was quite pointless on the prevailing basis. Suppose there are four enterprises, of equal size but different organic compositions, in a particular branch of industry:

1) $50c : 50v$
2) $40c : 60v$
3) $35c : 65v$
4) $25c : 75v$

  $150c : 250v$

Assume that $150c$ represent the absolute limit of accumulation on the existing basis. At this point a crisis ensues and the companies are forced to reorganise, that is to rationalise their plants. For example companies 1 and 2 decide to merge so that the organic composition expands, say in the ratio of $7c : 3v$. In the new enterprise with $90c$ only $38v$ (instead of 110) is thus used. Labour power to the value of $72v$ is set free; rationalisation leads to the formation of a reserve army. Once the merger is complete we have three enterprises as a result of the concentration process and a reserve army of $72v$.

$$
\begin{array}{lrcl}
1) & 90c & : & 38v \\
2) & 35c & : & 65v \\
3) & 25c & : & 75v \\
\hline
 & 150c & : & 178v
\end{array}
$$

For the new enterprise resulting from the merger, the higher organic composition entails a restoration of its profitability even at the lower price level 2. Firstly because the higher organic composition of capital means an increase in the productivity of labour and thus a reduction in unit costs. Secondly because an increase in the productivity of labour also means a higher rate of surplus value. This increase in the rate of surplus value implies that as the other companies also decide to rationalise the total surplus value obtainable expands proportionately, quite irrespective of the fact that every year a new generation of workers is appearing on the labour market. It follows that the maximum possible limit to the accumulation of capital is pushed further back beyond the level $150c$.

During the crisis there was overproduction. How was the upturn produced? Was the scale of operations reduced? On the contrary, it was expanded even further. And yet the crisis was surmounted.

That crises are surmounted although the scale of operations is extended even further is the best proof that crises do not stem from a lack of purchasing power, a shortage of consumers, or from disproportions in the individual spheres of industry. Because the crisis is rooted in a lack of valorisation it necessarily disappears once profitability is improved even if prices remain low.

The empirical evidence for this view confirms it word for word. Take the example of German shipping where, due to massive overproduction of tonnage and the ruinously low freight charges that followed, the biggest shipping companies incurred consistently heavy losses throughout the depression years 1892–4. How was this severe crisis overcome? R Schachner tells us that the depression in freight charges stimulated important changes in the technological structure of shipping. In 1894 and 1895, 'encouraged by low construction costs, all the big companies went in for the large scale steamer' (1903, p. 5). Due to this revolution in shipping enterprise, world shipping statistics show an increasing average size of ships: in 1893 the average was 1 418 gross register tons, in 1894 1 457 grt, in 1895 1 499 grt, in 1896 1 532 grt. The smaller companies could no longer compete on the freight market with these giant steamers and were forced to sell off their steamers at enormous losses. The position of the big shipping companies was entirely different, despite their intense competition with England. In 1895 the Hamburg–America line stated in its annual report: 'Despite miserable freight charges, our new steamers were able to operate at a profit due to their large tonnage and their savings in (fuel) costs' (p. 7). To overcome the crisis of overproduction of tonnage the tonnage was expanded even further, despite low prices.

The same process was repeated when, after the boom years of 1897–1900, a new crisis started in 1901. Again there was an attempt to relieve the impact of the depression through a general drive to cut costs in shipping by expanding the individual scale of operations still further (Schachner, p. 96). This happened a third time after the War. In spite of the huge losses due to the War, world shipping was afflicted by an over-supply of loading capacity. By 1926 world tonnage had increased by 31.7 per cent compared to its pre-war level.

Yet world trade had still to recover its pre-war levels, so it is not surprising that there was a state of severe depression in the world freight market. Rates declined steeply to rockbottom levels of profitability. How was this crisis overcome? Despite the massive oversupply of tonnage, international shipping converted to the latest type of vessels with a still larger scale of operations. As against an average capacity of 1 857 grt in 1914, the figure was 2 136 grt in 1925. Loading capacities increased even more sharply. Today a modern 8 000 ton steamer with a 10-knot speed consumes only 30 tons of coal per day. Prior to the War it consumed 35–6 tons per day. Yet the most significant technological change, decisive to the whole question of profitability, was the introduction of a new type of propulsion. In 1914 mechanised vessels formed just 3.1 per cent of the total world tonnage. By the end of 1924 their share was 37.6 per cent. As against the old coal-run steamers, the new mechanised ships were characterised by much higher loading capacities relative to size, by lower fuel costs and by savings in manpower. For instance on English vessels, despite a shorter working day, average crew size declined from 2.58 per grt in 1920 to 2.41 per grt in 1923.

In short, despite the trough in freight rates, the technological rationalisation of shipping restored profit levels and enabled the industry to overcome its crisis.

Because it is so recent, we hardly need to substantiate the fact that the last great depression following the German stabilisation of 1924–6 was overcome by the same methods of rationalisation – by a process of fusion and concentration, and increases in the productivity of labour through technological renovations. Profitability was revived and the crisis surmounted through increases in productivity and extensions in the scale of production. If we survey the process in its pure form over a longer period of several cycles and in abstraction from various countertendencies, it follows that prices show a declining tendency from one crisis to the next (in Figure 4, from level 1 to level 2 and so on), whereas the scale of production undergoes continuous expansion. In reality the process does not take this pure form due to the intervention of various subsidiary factors.

In a given branch of production the crisis is never overcome purely through the technological improvements within the branch itself. The capitalists also gain from the technological and organisational changes accomplished in other spheres of industry, either because these changes reduce their investment costs by cheapening basic elements of the reproductive process or because improvements in transport or monetary circulation shorten the turnover time of capital and thus increase the rate of surplus value. The more a movement of rationalisation spreads and penetrates into a whole series of new industries, the more the boom gains in intensity because improvements in one sphere of industry mean an expanding mass of surplus value in others.

Reducing the costs of variable capital through increases in productivity

a) Starting from a dynamic equilibrium the previous analysis assumed a constant rate of surplus value of 100 per cent throughout the course of accumulation. This conflicts with reality and has a purely fictitious, tentative character. It has to be modified.[1] Rising productivity cheapens commodities; in so far as this includes commodities that go into workers' consumption, the elements of variable capital are thereby cheapened, the value of labour power therefore declines and surplus value and the rate of surplus value increase. Marx says:

> hand in hand with the increasing productivity of labour, goes ... the cheapening of the labourer, therefore a higher rate of surplus value, even when the real wages are rising. The latter never rise proportionally to the productive power of labour. (1954, p. 566)

A further factor in enhancing the rate of surplus value is the rising intensity of labour that goes together with general increases in productivity. The increasing degree of exploitation of labour that flows from the general course of capitalist production constitutes a factor that weakens the breakdown tendency.

b) The 'depression of wages below the value of labour power' (Marx, 1959, p. 235) works in the same direction. Obviously, since the efficiency of work is going to fall, this can only be a temporary step.

Throughout the analysis we have assumed, in keeping with the hypothetical state of equilibrium, that the commodity labour power is fully employed – that there is no reserve army to begin with and consequently, like all other commodities, labour power is sold at its value. However I have shown that even on this assumption, a reserve army of labour necessarily forms at a certain level of capital accumulation due to insufficient valorisation. Beyond this point the mass of the unemployed exert a downward pressure on the level of wages so that wages fall below the value of labour power and the rate of surplus value rises. This forms a further source of increases in valorisation, and so another means of surmounting the breakdown tendency. The depression of wages below the value of labour power creates new sources of accumulation: 'It ... transforms, within certain limits, the labourer's necessary consumption fund into a fund for the accumulation of capital' (Marx, 1954, p. 562).

Once this connection is clear, we have a means of gauging the complete superficiality of those theoreticians in the trade unions who argue for wage increases as a means of surmounting the crisis by expanding the internal market. As if the capitalist class is mainly interested in selling its commodities rather than the valorisation of its capital. The same holds for F Sternberg. He cites the low wages prevalent in England in the early nineteenth century as one reason 'why the crises of this period caused far deeper convulsions in English capitalism than those of the late nineteenth century' (1926, p. 407). Low wages, and therefore a high rate of surplus value, form one of the circumstances that mitigate crises.

Shortening the turnover time and its impact on the rate of surplus value

In the reproduction schemes a period of production lasts one year and the working period and period of production are identical. There is no period of circulation and the working periods follow one another immediately. The duration of the production period is the same in all spheres of production and the assumption is made that in all branches capital turns over once every year. None of these several assumptions corresponds to reality and they are intended purely for simplification. First the working period and production time are not identical in reality. Secondly, apart from the production time, there must also be a circulation time. And finally turnover time varies from one branch of production to another and is determined by the material nature of the process of production. If the analysis is to bear any correspondence to the real appearances those assumptions also have to be modified.

According to Marx the 'difference in the period of turnover is in itself of no importance except so far as it affects the mass of surplus labour appropriated and realised by the same capital in a given time' (1959, p. 152). The impact of turnover on the production of surplus value can be summarised by saying that during the period of time required for turnover the whole capital cannot be deployed productively for the creation of surplus value. A portion of the capital always lies fallow in the form of either money capital, commodity capital or productive capital in stock. The capital active in the production of surplus value is always limited by this portion and the mass of surplus value obtained diminished in proportion. Marx says that the 'shorter the period of turnover, the smaller this idle portion of capital as compared with the whole, and the larger, therefore, the appropriated surplus value, provided other conditions remain the same' (1959, p. 70).

The reduction of turnover time means reductions of both production and circulation time. Increases in the productivity of labour are the chief means of reducing the production time. As long as technological advances in industry do not entail a simultaneous considerable enlargement of constant capital, the rate of profit will rise. Meanwhile the 'chief means of reducing the time of circulation is improved communications' (Marx, 1959, p. 71). The technological advances in shipbuilding mentioned above fall into this category.

The rationalisation of German railways with the introduction of the automatic pneumatic brake made possible total savings of around 100 million marks a year, mainly through reductions in personnel and major changes in the speed of freight traffic. Once shunting was mechanised so that trains could be built more quickly and cheaply, and many lines were electrified, the railway system was completely revolutionised.

Apart from improvements in transport, savings are achieved by reducing expenditure on commodity capital. Before commodities are sold they exist in the sphere of production in the shape of stock whose storage constitutes a cost. The producer tries to restrict his inventory to the minimum adequate for his average demand. However this minimum also depends on the periods that different commodities need for their reproduction. With improvements in transport, storage costs can be cut as a proportion of the total volume of sales transactions. In addition such costs tend to fall relative to total output as this output becomes 'more concentrated socially' (Marx, 1956, p. 147).

Every crisis precipitates a general attempt at reorganisation which, among other things, attacks the existing level of storage costs. The time during which capital is confined to the form of commodity capital tends to become progressively shorter. That is, the annual turnover of capital is speeded up. This is a further means of surmounting crises. Marx says that: 'the scale of reproduction will be extended or reduced commensurate with the particular speed with which that capital throws off its commodity form and assumes that of money, or with the rapidity of the sale' (1956, p. 40).

The additional money capital required for an expanded scale of production

Many writers argue that the programmes of expansion characteristic of the boom are impossible without an additional sum of money; that additional credit creates the boom or makes it possible. But the capitalist mechanism and its cyclical fluctuations are governed by quite different forces. I have already shown that production can be extended even if the level of prices remains constant or falls.

Nevertheless assuming a given velocity of circulation of money, additional money is required to extend the scale of production. But this is for quite different reasons than those adduced by supporters of the credit theory. We know from Marx's description of the reproduction process that both the individual and the total social capital must split into three portions if the process of reproduction is to have any continuity. Apart from productive and commodity capital, one portion must stay in circulation in the form of money capital. The size of this money capital is historically variable. Even if it grows absolutely it declines in proportion to the total volume of sales transactions.

At any given point of time however, it is a given magnitude which can be calculated according to the law of circulation. If production is expanded then, other things being equal, the mass of money capital also has to be expanded. What is the source of this additional money capital required for expansions in the scale of reproduction?

In Chapter 15 of *Capital Volume Two* Marx showed how through the very mechanism of the turnover money capital is always periodically set free. While one portion of capital is tied up in production during the working period another portion is in active circulation. If the working period were equal to the circulation period the money flowing back out of circulation would be constantly redeployed in each successive working period, and vice versa, so that in this case no part of the capital successively advanced would be set free. However in all cases where the circulation period and the working period are not equal 'a portion of the total circulating capital is set free continually and periodically at the close of each working period' (Marx, 1956, p. 283). As the case of equality is only exceptional it follows that 'for the aggregate social capital, so far as its circulating part is concerned, the release of capital must be the rule' (p. 284). Thus a 'very considerable portion of the social circulating capital, which is turned over several times a year, will therefore exist in the form of released capital during the annual turnover cycle which is set free ... the magnitude of this capital set free will grow with the scale of production ... the magnitude of the released capital grows with the volume of the labour process or with the scale of production' (p. 284).

Engels thought that Marx had attached 'unwarranted importance to a circumstance, which, in my opinion, has actually little significance. I refer to what he calls the "release" of money capital' (1956, p. 288). This assessment of Engels appears to me to be completely off the mark. Through his analysis Marx did not merely show that large masses of money capital are periodically set free through the very mechanism of the turnover. He also explicitly refers to the fact that due to the curtailment of the periods of turnover as well as to technical changes in production and circulation – as we have seen, carried through chiefly in periods of depression – a 'portion of the capital value advanced becomes superfluous for the operation of the entire process of social reproduction ... while the scale of production and prices remain the same' (p. 287). This superfluous part 'enters the money market and forms an additional portion of the capitals functioning here' (p. 287). It follows that after every period of depression a new disposable capital stands available. This setting free of a part of the money capital also affects the valorisation of the total capital; it increases the rate of profit in the sense that the same surplus value is calculated on a reduced total capital. The setting free of a part of the money-capital is thus a further means of surmounting the crisis. Marx thus shows that despite the assumption of equilibrium:

> a plethora of money capital may arise ... in the sense that a definite portion of the capital value advanced becomes superfluous for the operation of the entire process of social reproduction ... and is therefore eliminated in the form of money capital – a plethora brought about by

the mere contraction of the period of turnover, while the scale of production and prices remain the same. (p. 287)

The reduction in the turnover period generates an additional mass of money capital which is used to expand the scale of reproduction further whenever a period of boom is beginning. Marx has this function in mind when he states that the 'money capital thus released by the mere mechanism of the turnover movement ... must play an important role as soon as the credit system develops and must at the same time form one of the latter's foundations' (p. 286).

The conflict between use value and exchange value

Up to now Marxists have drawn attention to the fact that with the general progress of capital accumulation the value of constant capital increases absolutely and relative to variable capital. Yet this phenomenon forms only one side of the accumulation process; it examines the process from its value side. However – and this cannot be emphasised enough – the reproduction process is not simply a valorisation process; it is also a labour process, producing not only values but also use values. Considered from the side of use value, increases in the productivity of labour represent not merely a devaluation of the existing capital, but also a quantitative expansion of useful things.

Earlier I referred to how rising productivity cheapens the use values consumed by workers and, as a result, raises the rate of surplus value. Now we shall examine the impact of increases in the mass of use values, through rising productivity, on the fund for accumulation. Marx proceeds from the empirical fact that:

with the development of social productivity of labour the mass of produced use values, of which the means of production form a part, grows still more. And the additional labour, through whose appropriation this additional wealth can be reconverted into capital, does not depend on the value, but on the mass of these means of production (including means of subsistence), because in the production process the labourers have nothing to do with the value, but with the use value, of the means of production. (1959, p. 218)

Increases in productivity that impinge on the material elements of productive capital, especially fixed capital, mean a higher profitability for individual capitals. The same mechanism operates when we look at the process of reproduction in its totality. Marx writes:

> with respect to the total capital ... the value of the constant capital does not increase in the same proportion as its material volume. For instance, the quantity of cotton worked up by a single European spinner in a modern factory has grown tremendously compared to the quantity formerly worked up by a European spinner with a spinning wheel. Yet the value of the worked up cotton has not grown in the same proportion as its mass. The same applies to machinery and other fixed capital ... In isolated cases the mass of the elements of constant capital may even increase, while its value remains the same, or falls. (1959, p. 236)

The expansion in the mass of use values in which a given sum of value is represented is of great indirect significance for the valorisation process. With an expanded mass of the elements of production, even if their value is the same, more workers can be introduced into the productive process and in the next cycle of production these workers will be producing more value. Marx writes that as a consequence of growing productivity:

> More products which may be converted into capital, whatever their exchange value, are created with the same capital and the same labour. These products may serve to absorb additional labour, hence also additional surplus labour, and therefore create additional capital. The amount of labour which a capital can command does not depend on its value, but on the mass of raw and auxiliary materials, machinery and elements of fixed capital and necessities of life, all of which it comprises, whatever their value may be. As the mass of the labour employed, and thus of surplus labour increases, there is also a growth in the value of the reproduced capital and in the surplus value newly added to it. (p. 248)

Elsewhere Marx says:

> the most important thing for the direct exploitation of labour itself is not the value of the employed means of exploitation, be they fixed capital, raw materials or auxiliary substances. In so far as they serve as means of absorbing labour, as media in or by which labour and, hence, surplus labour are materialised, the exchange value of machinery, buildings, raw materials, etc, is quite immaterial. What is ultimately essential is, on the one hand, the quantity of them technically required

for combination with a certain quantity of living labour, and, on the other, their suitability, ie, not only good machinery, but also good raw and auxiliary materials. (1959, pp. 82–3)

With increases in productivity and the mass of use values, the mass of means of production (and of subsistence) which can function as means of absorbing labour expands more rapidly than the value of the accumulated capital. The means of production can therefore employ more labour and extort more surplus labour than would otherwise correspond to the accumulation of value as such. Marx says that with increases in productivity and a cheapening of labour power the:

> same value in variable capital therefore sets in movement more labour power, and, therefore, more labour. The same value in constant capital is embodied in more means of production, ie, in more instruments of labour, materials of labour and auxiliary materials; it therefore also supplies more elements for the production both of use value and of value, and with these more absorbers of labour. The value of the additional capital, therefore, remaining the same or even diminishing, accelerated accumulation still takes place. Not only does the scale of reproduction materially extend, but the production of surplus value increases more rapidly than the value of the additional capital. (1954, p. 566)

This tendency for the mass of use values to expand runs parallel with the opposite tendency for constant capital to increase in relation to variable – and hence for the number of workers to decline. However these 'two elements embraced by the process of accumulation … are not to be regarded merely as existing side by side in repose … They contain a contradiction which manifests itself in contradictory tendencies and phenomena. These antagonistic agencies counteract each other simultaneously' (Marx, 1959, pp. 248–9). 'The accumulation of capital in terms of value is slowed down by the falling rate of profit, to hasten still more the accumulation of use values, while this, in its turn, adds new momentum to accumulation in terms of value' (p. 250).

In Table 2.2 we saw that with an increase in working population of 5 per cent a year and an expansion of constant capital of 10 per cent, the system would have to collapse in year 35. But because the mass of capital grows more rapidly in use value than in value terms, and because the employment of living labour depends not on the value but on the mass of the elements of production, it follows that to employ the working population at a given level a much smaller capital would actually suffice than shown in the table itself. Increases in productivity and the expansion of use values bound up with them react as if the accumulation of values were at a lower or more initial stage. They represent a process of economic rejuvenation. The life span of accumulation is thus prolonged. But this only means that the breakdown is postponed, which, 'again shows that the same influences which tend to make the rate of profit fall, also moderate the effects of this tendency' (p. 236).

It is thus completely inadequate to examine the process of reproduction purely from the side of value. We can see what an important role use value plays in this process. Marx himself always tackled the capitalist mechanism from both sides – value as well as use value.

The emergence of new spheres of production with a lower organic composition of capital

Critics have often pointed out that according to Marx's prognosis 'competition rages like a plague among the capitalists themselves, eliminates them on a massive scale until eventually only a tiny number of capitalist magnates survive' (Oppenheimer, 1927, p. 499). Sternberg repeats the same point. Having portrayed Marx's argument in this fashion it is easy to pronounce that it is not substantiated by the concrete tendencies of historical development.

But this overlooks the essential point of Marx's methodological procedure. Marx's schemes deliberately simplify – they show only two spheres of production within which individual capitals progressively succumb to concentration. On this assumption the number of capitalists progressively declines. But the assumption that there are only two spheres of production is fictitious and it has to be modified so as to correspond with empirical reality. Marx shows that there is a continual penetration by capital into new spheres in which:

> portions of the original capitals disengage themselves and function as new and independent capitals. Besides other causes, the division of property, within capitalist families, plays a great part in this. With the accumulation of capital, therefore, the number of capitalists grows to a greater or lesser extent. (1954, p. 586)

The concentration of capital is thus supplemented by the opposite tendency of its fragmentation. In this way 'the increase of each functioning capital is thwarted by the formation of new and the sub-division of old capitals' (p. 586). Because the minimum amount of capital required for business in spheres with a higher organic composition is very high and is growing continuously, smaller capitals 'crowd into spheres of production which Modern Industry has only sporadically or incompletely got hold of' (p. 587). These are naturally spheres with a lower organic composition where a relatively larger mass of workers is employed.

If a new branch of production comes into being employing a relatively large mass of living labour – in which therefore the composition of capital is far below the average composition which governs the average profit – a larger mass of surplus value will be produced in this branch. Marx says that competition 'can level this out, only through the raising of the *general level* (of profit), because capital on the whole realises, sets in motion, a greater quantity of unpaid surplus labour' (1969, p. 435). Obviously this must also restrain the breakdown tendency. On the one hand the lower organic composition of capital raises the rate of profit, on the other the formation of new spheres of production makes possible further investment of capital.

In this way a cyclical movement evolves – the self-expanding capital searches out new investment possibilities while new inventions create such possibilities, new spheres of industry develop suddenly, superfluous capital is reabsorbed, and gradually there is a new accumulation of capital which is destined to become superfluous on an ever larger scale, and so on. This accounts for the importance of:

> new offshoots of capital seeking to find an independent place for themselves ... as soon as formation of capital were to fall into the hands of a few established big capitals, for which the mass of profits compensates for the falling rate of profit, the vital flame of production would be altogether extinguished. It would die out. (Marx,1959, p. 259)

British capitalism is deeply symptomatic of these processes. While the traditional industrial centres of the North, of Scotland and Wales have been in a chronic crisis, a whole series of new industries have begun to spring up in the South, in the Midlands and in the areas surrounding London. A report published by the inspector-general of factories shows that these industries have a much lower organic composition of capital. For example around London, apart from a few car-assembly plants, there are factories producing bandages, minor electrical fittings, bedsteads, bedspreads, ice-creams, mixed pickles, cardboard boxes and pencils. Among the few newer industries with a fairly high organic composition are rayon and automobiles. The latter involves some 14 500 units, over half of which are repair shops scattered across the country. According to data released by the Ministry of Labour (1926) the number of workers employed in the new industries increased by 14 per cent in the space of three years (1923–6), while those employed in the older industries like coalmining and shipbuilding declined by 7.5 per cent.

Earlier Britain could afford to import small-scale stuff from the Continent and Japan, whereas now it has to produce it itself. Even if the development of such industries does relieve the general impact of the economic depression it cannot compensate for the catastrophic consequences of the decline of the older branches which formed the basis of Britain's domination. In fact the new industries employ a total of only 700 000 workers, whereas the majority are still in the traditional branches like coal, textiles, shipbuilding and so on.

The struggle to abolish groundrent

A model of pure capitalism where there are only two classes, capitalists and workers, assumes that agriculture forms only a branch of industry completely under the sway of capital. In other words we abstract from the category of groundrent, from the existence of landlords. But how are the results of this analysis modified once this assumption is dropped?

Modern, purely capitalist, groundrent is simply a tax levied on the profits of capital by the landlord. To the landlord 'the land merely represents a certain money assessment which he collects by virtue of his monopoly from the industrial capitalist' (Marx, 1959, p. 618). When Marx refers to the levelling of surplus value to average profit he says:

> This appropriation and distribution of surplus value, or surplus product, on the part of capital, however, has its barrier in landed property. Just as the operating capitalist pumps surplus labour, and thereby surplus value and surplus product in the form of profit, out of the labourer, so the landlord in turn pumps a portion of this surplus value ... out of the capitalist in the form of rent. (p. 820)

Rent thus plays a role in depressing the level of the average rate of profit; it speeds up the breakdown tendency of capitalism. Spokesmen of capitalism have always been hostile to groundrent because 'landed property differs from other kinds of property in that it appears superfluous and harmful at a certain stage of development, even from the point of view of capitalism' (p. 622). Ricardo's writings were directed against the interests of the landlords and their supporters. The land reform movements of the latter part of the nineteenth century sprang fundamentally from the same source.

The struggle to eliminate commercial profit

Commercial profit has the same impact on the breakdown of capitalism as groundrent. Earlier we assumed that merchant's capital does not intervene in the formation of the general rate of profit. Again, this assumption has a purely methodological value; it has to be modified. Marx says that 'in the case of merchant's capital we are dealing with a capital which shares in the profit without participating in its production. Hence, it is now necessary to supplement our earlier exposition' (1959, p. 284). Commercial profit is a 'deduction from the profit of industrial capital. It follows [that] the larger the merchant's capital in proportion to the industrial capital, the smaller the rate of industrial profit, and vice versa' (p. 286). Clearly this will intensify and speed up the breakdown of capitalism.

In periods of crisis this struggle against traders is a means of improving the conditions of valorisation capital. In his report on the American crisis, Professor Hirsch has shown that in America the elimination of large-scale traders by rural cooperatives in grain, fruit and milk has assumed massive proportions, with cooperative sales accounting for as much as 20 per cent of the total sales of US agricultural produce. The cotton farmers of the north are likewise engaged in a struggle to eliminate intermediaries and supply the spinners directly.

This movement acquires its most powerful expression in the drive by the modern cartels and trusts to increase profitability by reducing the costs of sales and import transactions through a centralisation and elimination of intermediary trade. According to Hilferding its capacity to wipe out the trader is one of the basic reasons for the superiority of the combined enterprise. With the rapid advance of cartelisation in the iron and steel industry, the significance of commercial capital has declined. There is a striking tendency to wipe out intermediary trade as the mining and production stages are integrated vertically into a single enterprise, so that no profit is diverted to commercial capital at any single stage of the process. This is the realisation of Rockefeller's maxim; 'pay a profit to nobody'. Commercial capital is either left to supplying small customers or forced into a position of dependence on industrial capital. 'The development of large-scale industrial concerns, or the formation of monopolies', says T Vogelstein:

has dethroned the princely merchant and transformed him into a pure agent or stipendiary of the monopolies ... This world of monopolies is ridding itself of every vestige of commerce ... By transferring sales transactions to the syndicates ... the industrial concern reduces purely commercial activity to a minimum and leaves this to a few people in the head office or to individual trading concerns affiliated to itself. (1914, p. 243)

The formation of their own export organisations by the larger associations and concerns is yet another example of the tendency to wipe out independent large-scale trade. In copper a system of trading survives but no longer as an independent function; the system is intricately connected with the producers. Dyestuffs and electricals are two industries with their own sales organisations abroad. According to the calculations made by E Rosenbaum of Germany's total imports in 1926, around 48.3 per cent were direct, that is, transacted without the mediation of any trading concerns. In the case of textile raw materials the figure was 50 per cent and in ores and metals as high as 90 per cent (1928, pp. 130 and 146).

The squeeze on commercial profit to enhance the average rate of profit on industrial capital is a product of the growing barriers to valorisation that arise in the course of capital accumulation. Therefore as the level of accumulation advances, the tendency to eliminate commercial capital intensifies.

However the squeeze on commercial profit is not tantamount to a cessation of commercial activity. The latter cannot be done away with under capitalism because commercial agents fulfil basic functions of industrial capital in the process of its circulation, namely, its function of realising values. In this respect they are simply representatives of the industrial capitalist. Marx says that:

In the production of commodities, circulation is just as necessary as production itself, so that circulation agents are just as much needed as production agents. The process of reproduction includes both functions of capital, therefore it includes the necessity of having representatives of these functions, either in the person of the capitalist himself or of wage labourers, his agents. (1956, pp. 129–30)

Despite the tendency for commercial profit to be eliminated, commercial functions gain in importance as capitalism develops. This is regardless of whether they are represented by individual merchants, trade organisations, cooperatives or industrial trusts and concerns. Prior to capitalism there was no large-scale commercialisation of the product of labour: 'The extent to which products enter trade and go through the merchants' hands depends on the mode of production, and reaches its maximum in the ultimate development of capitalist production, where the product is produced solely as a commodity' (Marx, 1959, p. 325). It follows that the share of commerce in the overall occupational structure must expand. There is a growing number of commercial businesses and commercial employees. A new middle stratum of commercial agents, commercial employees, secretaries, accountants, cashiers emerges.

The question arises – what impact does the existence of this new middle stratum have on the course of the capitalist reproduction process? Can it reduce the severity of capitalist crises and weaken the breakdown tendency, as the reformists have argued ever since Bernstein? Marx points to the different character of this middle stratum which arises on the foundations of capitalist production:

> The outlay for these [commercial wage-workers], although made in the form of wages, differs from the variable capital laid out in purchasing productive labour. It increases the outlay of the industrial capitalist, the mass of the capital to be advanced, without directly increasing surplus value. Because it is an outlay for labour employed solely in realising value already created. Like every other outlay of this kind, it reduces the rate of profit because the advanced capital increases, but not the surplus value. (1959, p. 299)

Due to the variable capital expended on these commercial wage workers, the accumulation fund available for the employment of more productive workers is reduced.

> A part of the variable capital must be laid out in the purchase of this labour power functioning only in circulation. This advance of capital creates neither product nor value. It proportionately reduces the dimensions in which the advanced capital functions productively. (Marx, 1956, p. 136)

The rate of valorisation of the total social capital is thereby diminished and the breakdown tendency intensified, quite regardless of the fact that these middle strata may initially consolidate the political domination of capital. As these middle strata grow the breakdown is speeded up. As long as the mass of surplus value is growing absolutely this is not visible. But once there is a lack of valorisation due to the advance of accumulation this fact is shown all the more sharply.

The economic function of 'third persons'

The term third persons is used by Marx in a double sense. Sometimes he refers to the independent, small-scale producers who are remnants of earlier forms of production. They are not intrinsically connected with capitalism as such and so must be excluded from any analysis of its inner nature. We shall see later (pp. 169–73) how far these elements can and do affect capitalist production through the mediation of the world market. Secondly Marx understands by third persons bureaucrats, the professional strata, rent receivers and so on, who exist on the foundations of capitalism but do not participate in material production either directly or indirectly and are therefore unproductive from the standpoint of such production. They do not enlarge the mass of actual products but, on the contrary, reduce it by their consumption, even if they perform various valuable and necessary services by way of repayment. The income of these people is not obtained by virtue of their control of capital, so it is not an income got without work.

However important these services may be they are not embodied in products or values. In so far as the performers of these sevices consume commodities they depend on those persons who participate in material production. From the standpoint of material production their incomes are derivative. Marx writes:

> All members of society not directly engaged in reproduction, with or without labour, can obtain their share of the annual commodity product – in other words, their articles of consumption – primarily out of the hands of those classes to which the product first accrues – productive workers, industrial capitalists and landlords. To that extent their revenues are materially derived from wages (of the productive labourers), profit and rent, and appear therefore as derivative vis-a-vis those primary revenues. (1956, p. 376)

This group of third persons which was initially excluded from the analysis of pure capitalism has to be reintroduced at a later stage. Marx points out that society 'by no means consists of only two classes, workers and industrial capitalists, and ... therefore consumers and producers are not identical categories' (1969, p. 493). The:

> first category, that of the consumers ... is much broader than the second category [producers], and therefore the way in which they spend their revenue, and the very size of the revenue give rise to very considerable

modifications in the economy and particularly in the circulation and reproduction process of capital. (p. 493)

What significance does the existence of these people have for the reproduction and accumulation of capital? In so far as their material incomes are dependent incomes – that is, drawn from the capitalists – we are dealing with groups which are, from the standpoint of production, pure consumers. As long as this consumption by third persons is not sustained directly at the cost of the working class, surplus value or the fund for accumulation is reduced. Of course these groups perform various services in return, but the non-material character of such services makes it impossible for them to be used for the accumulation of capital. The physical nature of the commodity is a necessary precondition of its accumulation. Values enter the circulation of commodities, and thereby represent an accumulation of capital, only insofar as they acquire a materialised form.

Because the services of third persons are of a non-material character, they contribute nothing to the accumulation of capital. However their consumption reduces the accumulation fund. The larger this class the greater the deduction from the fund for accumulation. In Germany in 1925 the services of such groups were valued at six billion marks, which amounts to 11 per cent of the total national income. In Britain, where there is a large number of such persons, the tempo of accumulation will have to be slower. In America, where their proportion is low, it can be much more rapid. If the number of these third persons were cut down, the breakdown of capitalism could be postponed. But there are several limits to any such process, in the sense that it would entail a cut in the standard of living of the wealthier classes.

Expanding the scale of production on the existing technological basis: simple accumulation

Along with Bauer we assumed that each year there are technological changes going on which mean that constant capital is expanding more rapidly than variable capital. However production is not always expanded on the basis of a higher organic composition. Capitalists may expand production on the existing technological basis for an extended period of time. In such cases we are dealing with simple accumulation where the growth of constant capital proceeds in step with variable capital – the expansion of capital exerts a proportional attraction on workers. Of course, the technological foundations of capitalism are being constantly improved and the organic composition is always changing. Nevertheless these changes are 'continually interrupted by periods of rest, during which there is a mere quantitative extension of factories on the existing technical basis' (Marx, 1954, p. 423).

As the accumulation of capital advances these periods of rest become progressively shorter. However to the extent that such periods of rest occur, they imply a weakening of the breakdown tendency. Marx writes:

> This constant expansion of capital, hence also an expansion of production, on the basis of the old method of production which goes quietly on while new methods are already being introduced at its side, is another reason why the rate of profit does not fall as much as the total capital of society grows. (1959, p. 263)

We shall see that as world market antagonisms intensify, technological superiority is the sole means of surviving on the world market. The sharper the struggle on the world market the greater the compulsion behind technological changes, so that the intermediate pauses are shortened. Gradually this counteracting factor becomes less and less important.

The periodic devaluation of capital on the accumulation process

The assumption of constant values is one of the many underlying the reproduction scheme of Marx. Bauer adopts this assumption in two senses: (i) the value of the constant capital used up in the process of production is transferred intact to the product; (ii) the values created in each cycle of production are accumulated in the next cycle without undergoing any quantitative changes. (Some values are of course destroyed in consumption.) This constancy is postulated although Bauer's scheme presupposes continuous technological progress. He does not notice the contradiction.

Technological progress means that since commodities are created with a smaller expenditure of labour their value falls. This is not only true of the newly produced commodities. The fall in value reacts back on the commodities that are still on the market but which were produced under the older methods, involving a greater expenditure of labour time. These commodities are devalued.

There is no trace of this phenomenon in Bauer's scheme. He refers to devaluations but this is only due to periodic overproduction. The implication is that if the system were in equilibrium there would be no devaluations

– the value relations of any given point of time would survive indefinitely. Things are quite different in Marx. Devaluation necessarily flows out of the mechanism of capital even in its ideal or normal course. It is a necessary consequence of continual improvements in technology, of the fact that labour time is the measure of exchange value.

It follows that the assumption of constant values has a purely provisional character. The question arises – how is the law of accumulation and breakdown modified in its workings when the assumption is dropped? Until now this problem has never been posed. Both Bauer and Tugan realised that holding values constant is a simplifying assumption. But neither modified this assumption. For this reason their models of reproduction are completely unrealistic fictions which cannot reflect or explain the actual course of capitalist reproduction.

Devaluation of capital goes hand in hand with the fall in the rate of profit and is crucial for explaining the concentration and centralisation of capital that accompanies this fall.

We have seen how the accumulation process encounters its ultimate limits in insufficient valorisation. The further continuation of capital depends on restoring the conditions of valorisation. These conditions can only be secured if a) relative surplus value is increased or b) the value of the constant capital is reduced 'so that the commodities which enter either the reproduction of labour-power, or into the elements of constant capital, are cheapened. Both imply a depreciation of the existing capital' (Marx, 1959, p. 248). This depreciation does not come about as a consequence of over-production but in the normal course of capitalist accumulation – as a result of constant improvements in technology. Advances in technology thus entail 'periodical depreciation of existing capital – one of the means immanent in capitalist production to check the fall of the rate of profit and hasten accumulation of capital value through formation of new capital' (p. 249).

The result of the devaluation of capital is reflected in the fact that a given mass of means of production represents a smaller value. The result is analogous to that which arises from growing productivity – cheapening of the elements of production and a faster growth of the mass of use values as compared with the mass of value. However in the case of rising productivity the elements of production actually start off cheaper whereas here we are dealing with a case where the elements of production produced at a given value are only subsequently devalued.

With devaluation the technological composition of capital remains the same while its value composition declines. Both before and after devaluation the same quantity of labour is required to set in motion the same mass of means of production and to produce the same quantity of surplus value.

But because the value of the constant capital has declined this quantity of surplus value is calculated on a reduced capital value. The rate of valorisation is thereby increased and so the breakdown is postponed for some time. In terms of Bauer's scheme, periodic devaluation of capital would mean that the accumulated capital represents a smaller value magnitude than shown by the figures there and would, for example, only reach the level of year 20 as late as year 36.

In other words, however much devaluation of capital may devastate the individual capitalist in periods of crisis, they are a safety valve for the capitalist class as a whole. For the system devaluation of capital is a means of prolonging its life span, of defusing the dangers that threaten to explode the entire mechanism. The individual is thus sacrificed in the interest of the species.

The devaluation of accumulated capital takes various forms. Initially Marx deals with the case of periodic devaluation due to technological changes. In this case the value of the existing capital is diminished while the mass of production remains the same. The same effect however, is produced when the apparatus of reproduction is used up or destroyed in terms of value as well as use value through wars, revolutions, habitual use without simultaneous reproduction, etc. For a given economy the effect of capital devaluation is the same as if the accumulation of capital were to find itself at a lower stage of development. In this sense it creates a greater scope for the accumulation of capital.

The specific function of wars in the capitalist mechanism is only explicable in these terms. Far from being an obstacle to the development of capitalism or a factor which accelerates the breakdown, as Kautsky and other Marxists have supposed, the destructions and devaluations of war are a means of warding off the imminent collapse, of creating a breathing space for the accumulation of capital. For example it cost Britain £23.5 million to suppress the Indian uprising of 1857–8 and another £77.5 million to fight the Crimean War. These capital losses relieved the overtense situation of British capitalism and opened up new room for her expansion. This is even more true of the capital losses and devaluations to follow in the aftermath of the 1914–18 war. According to W Woytinsky, 'around 35 per cent of the wealth of mankind was destroyed and squandered in the four years' (1925, pp. 197–8). Because the population of the major European countries simultaneously expanded, despite war losses, a larger valorisation base confronted a reduced capital, and this created new scope for accumulation.

Kautsky was completely wrong to have supposed that the catastrophe of the world war would inevitably lead to the breakdown of capitalism and then, when no such thing happened, to have gone on to deny the inevitability of the breakdown as such. From the Marxist theory of accumulation it follows that war and the destruction of capital values bound up with it weaken the breakdown and necessarily provide a new impetus to the accumulation of capital. Luxemburg's conception is equally wrong: 'From the purely economic point of view, militarism is a pre-eminent means for the realisation of surplus-value; it is in itself a sphere of accumulation' (1968, p. 454).

This is how things may appear from the standpoint of individual capital as military supplies have always been the occasion for rapid enrichment. But from the standpoint of the total capital, militarism is a sphere of unproductive consumption. Instead of being saved, values are pulverised. Far from being a sphere of accumulation, militarism slows down accumulation. By means of indirect taxation a major share of the income of the working class which might have gone into the hands of the capitalists as surplus value is seized by the state and spent mainly for unproductive purposes.

The expansion of share capital

Among the factors that counteract the breakdown Marx includes the fact that a progressively larger part of social capital takes the form of share capital:

> these capitals, although invested in large productive enterprises, yield only large or small amounts of interest, so-called dividends, once costs have been deducted ... These do not therefore go into levelling the rate of profit, because they yield a lower than average rate of profit. If they did enter into it, the general rate of profit would fall much lower. (1959, p. 240)

In the scheme, where the entire capitalist class is treated as a single entity, the social surplus value is divided among the portions a_c and a_v required for accumulation, and k which is available to the capitalists as consumption. Now suppose there were capitalists (owners of shares, bonds, debentures, etc.) who did not consume the whole of k, but generally only a smaller portion of it, then the amount remaining for accumulation would be larger than the sum $a_c + a_v$. This could then form a reserve fund for the purposes of accumulation, which would make it possible for accumulation to last longer than is the case in the scheme. The fact that many strata of capitalists are confined strictly to this normal interest, or dividend, is thus one of the reasons why the breakdown tendency operates with less force. This is also the basic reason why Germany, following the example of Britain where this happened much earlier, has seen a sharp increase in the bonds of the industrial societies.

The accumulation of capital and the problem of population

Bauer argued that crises only stem from a temporary discrepancy between the scale of the productive apparatus and increases in population. The crisis automatically adjusts the scale of production to the size of population and is then overcome. Luxemburg produced a brilliant refutation of this harmonist theory (1972, pp. 107–39). She showed that in the decades prior to the War the tempo of accumulation was more rapid than the slow rate at which the population increased in various countries. Bauer's observation that 'under capitalism there is a tendency for the accumulation of capital to adjust to the growth of population' (1913, p. 871) is thus incompatible with the facts. In the fifty years from 1870 to 1920, the US population increased by around 172 per cent, while the accumulation of capital in industry expanded by more than 2 600 per cent.

However Luxemburg's critique, which is perfectly valid against Bauer, makes the basic mistake of seeing population only as a market for capitalist commodities: 'It is obvious that the annual increase of 'mankind' is relevant for capitalism only to the extent that mankind consumes capitalist commodities' (1972, p. 111). She sees in population a limit to the accumulation of capital in the sense that it cannot provide a sufficient market for those commodities.

My own view is diametrically opposed to both Bauer's and Luxemburg's. Against Bauer, and using his own reproduction scheme, I have shown that from a certain stage – despite increases in population – an overaccumulation of capital results from the very essence of capital accumulation. Accumulation proceeds, and must proceed, faster than population grows so that the valorisation base grows progressively smaller in relation to the rapidly accumulating capital and finally dries up. From this it follows that if capital succeeds in enlarging the valorisation base, or the number of workers employed, there will be a larger mass of obtainable surplus value – a factor which will weaken the breakdown tendency. Therefore there is a perfectly comprehensible tendency for capital to employ the maximum possible number of workers. This does not in the least contradict the other tendency of capital of 'employing as little labour as possible in proportion to the invested capital' (Marx, 1959, p. 232). This is because the mass of surplus value depends not merely on the number of labourers employed – at a given rate of surplus value – but on raising the rate of surplus value through increases in the amount of means of production relative to living labour applied in the production process.

From this it follows that with 'a sufficient accumulation of capital, the production of surplus value is only limited by the labouring population if the rate of surplus value ... is given' (Marx, 1959, p. 243). Therefore population does form a limit on accumulation, but not in the sense intended by Luxemburg. If population expands the interval prior to absolute overaccumulation is correspondingly longer. This is what Marx means when he writes:

> If accumulation is to be a steady, continuous process, then this absolute growth in population – although it may be decreasing in relation to the capital employed – is a necessary condition. An increasing population appears to be the basis of accumulation as a continuous process (1969, p. 477).

The tendency to employ the largest possible number of productive workers is already contained in the very concept of capital as a production of surplus value and surplus labour.

Oppenheimer's criticism, that Marx was forced to admit that despite the overall displacement of workers their total number grows, is really unfounded and meaningless. Capital accumulation is only possible if it succeeds in creating an expanded valorisation base for the growing capital. For example at the low degree of accumulation which survived in Germany up to the end of the 1880s the nascent large-scale industry failed to absorb the entire working population. Emigration became necessary to contain this situation. In the decade 1871–80 some 622 914 persons emigrated abroad from the country. In the following decade this number rose to 1 342 423. But with the rapid upsurge of industrialisation and the accelerated tempo of accumulation in the 1890s, emigration ceased and even gave way to immigration from Poland and Italy into the industrial areas of the West. The absorption of these additional labour powers provided the basis for producing the surplus value required for the valorisation of the expanded capital.

Natural increases in urban population and migration from the countryside were insufficient. This was the case despite continuous intensification of labour which meant that the mass of exploited labour was growing faster than the number of exploited workers. A shortage of labour power persisted despite the recruitment of new workers and the reabsorption of workers displaced by the increasing mechanisation of work processes and rising organic composition of capital. After the 1907 crisis capital was compelled to seek out an expanded valorisation base by intensifying the incorporation of women workers. This had the additional advantage of being cheaper. In a penetrating account of the German economy A Feiler tells us:

> It became increasingly clear that the rapid expansion of female labour which had characterised the depression years of 1908 and 1909 was not some passing phenomenon that would vanish once the rate of employment restabilised. It survived the depression years into the boom. The number of women workers continued to rise. In the five years from 1905 to 1910 ... the number increased by 33 per cent. This trend intensified in the years that followed. The number of women employed in factories and offices increased much more rapidly than the number of men. This was a revolution pure and simple ... At the end of 1913 there were as many employed women in Germany as employed men. (1914, p. 86)

However, not much more can be drawn out of the disposable mass of labour power. Children and old people cannot be inducted into the production process. The reservoir of human labour is running dry. If there is a declining inflow of labour into production the source of additional surplus value is restricted. This means an intensified struggle on the world market in search of the sources of additional surplus value required for the valorisation of the expanded capital.

But even in countries where population is expanding the danger of overaccumulation is inherent. Given a rising organic composition of capital, every increase in the number of workers implies only a temporary weakening of the breakdown, not its final overcoming. Because constant capital expands much more rapidly than population it follows that after a more or less long period of accumulation a point must come at which the given population is not enough to valorise the swollen mass of capital. At this point capital begins to press against the extreme boundary of valorisation. Population begins to form the limit to the accumulation of capital not because the consumption base of capital is too narrow but because the valorisation base is insufficient. As a result of insufficient valorisation a reserve army is created and there is chronic unemployment. Yet this unemployment has nothing to do with the introduction of machinery: it flows from the accumulation of capital. A working population which is scarce generates a working population which is surplus.

It is not difficult to see why the question of population should have changed so rapidly since Malthus' time. The slow tempo of accumulation characteristic of early capitalism generated a concern about overpopulation and its attendant misery. Today bourgeois writers in both France and Germany are concerned about whether the future accumulation of capital will find adequate reserves of labour power at its disposal. The modern bourgeois economist is characterised by his dread of underpopulation.

It might be argued that the threat is not too serious because there are still hundreds of millions of people in the enormous continents of Asia and Africa who could satisfy capital's insatiable appetite for labour. But the point is not whether there are large masses of people in this or that part of the world, but whether they are available where capitalism needs them. If we look at the matter this way then colonial capitalism and imperialism are characterised by a shortage of labour power. It would be superfluous to go into all the evidence available from various parts of the world. I shall only take a few examples.

Australia is not important as a market for the advanced capitalist economies. Australia's significance lies in its production. Next to Argentina, Australia is the world's most important producer of wool. Broken Hill District alone supplies around 20 per cent of the world's total production of zinc. The copper mines of Mount Morgan are among the world's largest. The immigration of cheap labour power has therefore always played an important role in the various colonisation projects relating to Australia, starting with the famous system devised by Wakefield who established his own companies in Adelaide, South Australia (1836) and Wellington in New Zealand (1839) by importing impoverished immigrant workers whose fares were paid by him.

This drive for labour power has persisted. According to W Pember-Reeves Australia's production could be increased significantly if coloured workers were allowed jobs on the sugar plantations of Queensland (1902, Chapter 4). However capital ran up against the opposition of white workers to the immigration of coloured workers. W Dressler tries to counter this fear of competition from immigrant labour by saying that in the long run the white workers would leave the unhealthy jobs to immigrant workers and would have to take on supervisory functions (1915, pp. 188–9). As recently as 1925 we hear that 'in Australia there is an absolute shortage of labour power' (F Hess, 1925, p. 138).

The picture is the same in all the colonial countries. It is true of the South African mines, the cocoa plantations of Sao Tome, the copper districts of Katanga, the cotton fields of French Cameroon and Equatorial Africa, the sugar plantations of the Dominican Republic and Guyana, the rubber plantations of Sumatra and Borneo. 'In large parts of Africa', according to a report in the *Berliner Borsen Courier* [Berlin Stock Exchange Courier], the black population ... is being pushed back into increasingly smaller reservations ... in Kenya around five million acres have been reserved for settlement by whites.' In this way 'increasingly greater masses of blacks are compelled to sell their labour power to European entrepreneurs at starvation wages' (6 May 1928). In Sumatra and Borneo whatever little labour there is prefers to work on the rubber plantations of the native peasantry than on the large-scale plantations owned by the big European capitalists, who literally treat them like animals.

When Marx described the gruesome exploitation of the British working class in *Capital* bourgeois economists called it a 'one-sided' picture and tried their best to show that the conditions described were characteristic only of the early stages of industrial development, and were bound to be superseded by the gradual progress of social reforms. Yet Marx's description of the conditions of the British working class of the early nineteenth century was an empirical illustration of tendencies which Marx had established through a theoretical analysis of the nature of capital.

Restrained in its wolf-like hunger for labour at home, West European capital celebrates even more unbridled orgies of exploitation in the territories recently opened up to capitalist production. The shameless character of capital's exploitation of the labour of women and children is repeated here on an enormously magnified scale. And the immense squandering of human life that follows only intensifies the shortage of labour.

Part 2: Restoring Profitability through World Market Domination

Introduction: The economic function of imperialism

Among the several simplifying assumptions which underlie Marx's analysis of the reproduction process is the assumption that the capitalist mechanism is an isolated entity without any external relationships: 'The involvement of foreign commerce in analysing the annually reproduced value of products can ... only confuse without contributing any new element of the problem, or of its solution. For this reason it must be entirely discarded' (Marx, 1956, p. 474).

Yet Marx himself repeatedly underlined the colossal importance of foreign trade to the development of capitalism; in 1859 he proposed a six-book structure for his investigations of the capitalist economy and intended the 'world market' to be one of the six. Although the structure of the work was later changed, its object of inquiry remained basically the same. In *Capital* we find the 'creation of the world market' listed as one of the 'three cardinal facts of capitalist production' (1956, p. 266). Elsewhere Marx writes: 'Capitalist production does not exist at all without foreign commerce' (1956, p. 474). And:

> it is only foreign trade, the development of the market to a world market, which causes money to develop into world money and *abstract labour* into social labour ... Capitalist production rests on the *value* or the transformation of the labour embodied in the products into social labour. But this is only [possible] on the basis of foreign trade and of the world market. This is at once the precondition and the result of cap-italist production. (Marx, 1972, p. 253)

So what scientific value can there be in a theoretical system which abstracts from the decisively important factor of foreign trade?

People have tried to escape the problem by postulating a gap in Marx's system; they have argued that after all *Capital* is an unfinished work. Thus A Parvus argues that the founders of scientific socialism 'died much too early' (1901, p. 587) to leave us any analysis of trade policy. Recently A Meusel has argued that Marx was naturally less interested in problems of foreign trade because the only significant foreign trade controversy which he lived to see, the struggle for the abolition of the Corn Laws, appeared to be a conflict between the landed aristocracy and the industrial middle class; 'it was easy to suppose that the working class had no immediate strong interests of its own in policies relating to foreign trade' (Meusel, 1928, p. 79). This distortion explains why Meusel cannot grasp the tremendous importance of foreign trade in Marx's work, even though this is repeatedly and emphatically drawn out in *Capital* and *Theories of Surplus Value*. Luxemburg also starts from the conception that Marx ignored foreign trade in his system, that 'he himself explicitly states time and again that he aims at presenting the process of accumulation of the aggregate capital in a society consisting solely of capitalists and workers' (1968, pp. 330–1). Luxemburg could only explain this by postulating a gap in Marx's work, supposedly due to the fact that 'this second volume [of *Capital*] is not a finished whole but a manuscript that stops short half way through' (pp. 165–6). Luxemburg then constructs a theory to fill in the so-called gap. This may be a convenient way of disposing of theoretical problems but it shatters the underlying unity of the system and creates a hundred new problems.[2]

What Luxemburg sees as a gap in Marx's system is transformed by Sternberg into its basic limitation. Marx turns out to be a builder of completely abstract systems which were bound to lead to untenable conclusions insofar as they ignored the basic aspects of reality. He says that 'Marx analysed capitalism on an assumption that has never corresponded with reality, namely that there is no non-capitalist sector' (1926, p. 303). Whereas Luxemburg at least regarded Marx's whole system as a solid achievement of theory, Sternberg informs us that the whole system is a delapidated structure. He states that Luxemburg 'broke off too soon' in her demolition of Marx's system. She 'failed to see that every stone of the structure is affected by the fact of the existence of a non-capitalist sector, not only the accumulation of capital but crisis, the industrial reserve army, wages, the workers' movement and, above all, the revolution' (p. 9). So all these basic questions of Marxist theory are tackled incorrectly because Marx built his system on the unproven and improbable assumption that there are no non-capitalist countries.

The grotesque character of this entire exposition is obvious. It is the product of a whole generation of theoreticians who go straight for results without any philosophical background, without bothering to ask by what methodological means were those results established and what significance do they contain within the total structure of the system. Sternberg writes a book of over 600 pages simply to register the observation that Marx described only pure capitalism, isolated from external trade relations. Because Marx never ordered the various passages dealing with foreign trade under capitalism into a single, structured chapter, these passages are totally ignored. This is a sad proof of the decline of the capacity to think theoretically.

The function of foreign trade under capitalism

The importance of foreign trade for the increasing multiplicity of use values

The progress of capitalism increases the mass of surplus product accruing to capital. The number of human needs is unlimited and when people have enough of some products there are always others which they can use. Towards the middle of the last century people consumed a greater variety of products than fifty years earlier, and today this variety is greater still.

Foreign trade plays an important role in expanding this multiplicity of products. Here what matters is international exchange as such, regardless of whether it takes place with capitalist or non-capitalist ones. By increasing the multiplicity of products foreign trade has the same impact as product diversification on the home market. An increasing variety of use values facilitates accumulation and weakens the breakdown tendency. Marx says:

> If surplus labour or surplus value were represented only in the national surplus product, then the increase of value for the sake of value and therefore the exaction of surplus labour would be restricted by the limited, narrow circle of use values in which the value of the [national] labour would be represented. But it is foreign trade which develops its [the surplus product's] real nature by developing the labour embodied in it as social labour which manifests itself in an unlimited range of different use values, and this in fact gives meaning to abstract wealth. (1972, p. 253)

Thus the limits on the production of surplus value are extended; the breakdown of capitalism is postponed.

This aspect of the exchange relationship does not exhaust the problem of foreign trade and its impact on the tendencies of capitalism. Looking at the matter from the value side, I have shown that the problem of breakdown by no means lies in an excess of surplus value but in its opposite, a lack of sufficient valorisation. Therefore we have to examine foreign trade from the aspect of its impact on valorisation.

Expansion of the market as a means of reducing the costs of production and circulation

To understand why foreign trade and market expansion are important we do not need to fall back on the metaphysical theory of the realisation of the surplus value. Their importance is more obvious. Hilferding argues:

> the size of the economic territory ... has always been extremely important for the development of capitalist production. The larger and more populous the economic territory, the larger the individual plant can be, the lower the costs of production, and the greater the degree of specialisation within the plant, which also reduces costs of production. The larger the economic territory, the more easily can industry be located where the natural conditions are most favourable and the productivity

of labour its highest. The more extensive the territory, the more diversi-
fied is production and the more probable it is that the various branches
of production will complement one another and that transport costs on
imports from abroad will be saved. (1981, p. 311)

Due to mass production British industry, which was the workshop of
the world down to the 1870s, could carry through a division of labour,
increases in productivity and cost savings to a level that was unattainable
elsewhere. Whereas weaving and spinning were originally combined, later
they were separated. This resulted in geographical specialisation. Burnley
made the traditional calico prints, Blackburn clothed India and China,
Preston manufactured fine cottons. The factory districts lying close to
Manchester concentrated on more complicated fabrics, like the cotton
velvets of Oldham and high quality calicoes of Ashton and Glossop. Only
mass production of this kind made possible the construction of specialised
machines for individual operations, and this meant important savings in
investment and enterprise costs.

Manchester, previously the centre of the industry, more and more specialised as the exclusive base of the export trade. In the basements of the
city's commercial firms, which were often several stories underground,
steam engines and hydraulic presses were reducing cotton yarns and
fabrics to half their thickness.

Such a high level of production specialisation meant huge cost reductions due to savings in non-productive expenses, reduced work interruptions and increases in productivity and the intensity of labour. Economies
in production are supplemented by economies in the sphere of circulation.
The number of importers, brokers and so on is compressed to the absolute
minimum. An intricate system of transport connects supply bases to
centres of production. Special credit organisations emerge with their own
terms of payment. All of this enhances valorisation by reducing the costs
of investment, manufacturing and marketing. This is what accounted for
the competitive superiority of British capitalism.

The compulsion to produce the greatest possible surplus value is
enough to account for the enormous importance of market expansion and
struggles for markets. We do not need to fall back on Luxemburg's notion
of the necessity of non-capitalist markets for realising surplus value. In
fact it is irrelevant whether the markets in question are capitalist or not.
What matters is mass outlets, mass production and the specialisation and
rationalisation of work and circulation which mass production makes possible. It makes no difference whether German chemicals are exported to
Britain or to China.

Finally the specialisation and geographical concentration of production in specific lines contributes to the training of a highly efficient workforce, and therefore to increases in the skill and intensity of labour. A German worker cited by Schulze-Gaevernitz talks of German workers being less efficient than British workers due to lack of tradition, in the sense that in Britain workers have acquired a basic experience in handling machinery through specialised work lasting over generations. The result is that in Britain three or four workers can operate 1 000 spindles whereas in Germany at that time it needed six to ten (1892, p. 109).

We should add that France for example, which possesses an old and flourishing silk industry at Lyons, remained totally dependent on Britain for her imports of raw silk from China and Japan. All attempts to procure Chinese silk directly, with the help of French banks, failed because Britain was able to buy the silk more cheaply due to her extensive trade connections and lower freight costs. In addition despite the double freight costs involved in importing the raw material all the way from Australia and shipping the final product back there, British woollens remain cheaper and more competitive than Australian woollens because the size of the Australian market forces the individual units there to diversify instead of specialising. Domestic prices are higher than world market prices, sales are confined exclusively to the home market and this means that protection is necessary. The same holds for the woollen industries of La Plata (Argentina) and South Africa, although wool is directly available there and this dispenses with double transport costs.

All this explains why the USA has emerged as an increasingly more dangerous competitor on the world market. The enormous advantages of a large and integrated scale of operations, in territorial terms, gives American industry completely different possibilities of expansion than those available in Europe.

Mass production and mass sales have always been basic objectives of capitalist production. But they have become matters of life and death for capitalism only in the late stage of capital accumulation when a purely domestic valorisation of the gigantic mass of capital becomes more and more difficult. Mass production is necessary to obtain the various advantages of specialisation which are inseparable from mass production. It is also necessary for achieving a level of competitive superiority on the world market. Politically mass production means the triumphant domination of the large-scale enterprise over the small and medium enterprises. It explains the tendency to form transnational empires in place of the nation state. The categories in terms of which we think today are no longer those of nation states but of entire continents.

Foreign trade and the sale of commodities at prices of production deviating from values

Among the simplifying assumptions of the reproduction scheme an especially important role is played by the assumption that commodities exchange at value; that is, that their prices coincide with their values. This is only possible if we abstract from competition and suppose that all that happens in circulation is that one commodity of a given value is exchanged against another of the same value. But in reality commodities do not exchange at their values. Such an assumption has to be dropped and the conclusions established on that basis further modified.

What sort of modifications are required? Up to now this problem has always been examined from the standpoint of the transfer of value among capitalists – a social process in which the prices of production of individual commodities differ from their values but on the basis of total price remaining equal to total value. No one has systematically tackled the problem of the deviation of prices from values in international exchange or related this problem to the overall structure of Marx's system. For instance Hilferding and the followers of Kautsky were in no position to grasp the elements of novelty in Marx's treatment of this problem as long as they were mainly interested in rejecting the theory of breakdown. This likewise precluded any deeper analysis of the function of foreign trade under capitalism.

If like Ricardo, we suppose that the law of value is directly applicable to international trade then the question of foreign trade has no bearing on the problem of value and accumulation. On this assumption foreign trade simply mediates the exchange of use values while the magnitude of value and profit remains unaltered. In contrast Marx draws out the role of competition in international exchange.

If we look at the sphere of production it follows that the economically backward countries have a higher rate of profit, due to their lower organic composition of capital, than the advanced countries. This is despite the fact that the rate of surplus value is much higher in the advanced countries and increases even more with the general development of capitalism and the productivity of labour. Marx (1959, pp. 150–1) gives an example where the rate of surplus value is 100 per cent in Europe and 25 per cent in Asia while the composition of the respective national capitals is $84c + 16v$ for Europe and $16c + 84v$ for Asia. We get the following results for the value of the product:

Asia
$16c + 84v + 21s = 121$. Rate of profit $21/100 = 21$ per cent

Europe
$84c + 16v + 16s = 116$. Rate of profit $16/100 = 16$ per cent

International trade is not based on an exchange of equivalents because, as on the national market, there is a tendency for rates of profit to be equalised. The commodities of the advanced capitalist country with the higher organic composition will therefore be sold at prices of production higher than value; those of the backward country at prices of production lower than value. This would mean the formation of an average rate of profit of 18.5 per cent so that European commodities will sell for a price of 118.5 instead of 116. In this way circulation on the world market involves transfers of surplus value from the less developed to the more developed capitalist countries because the distribution of surplus value is determined not by the number of workers employed in each country but by the size of the functioning capital. Marx states that through foreign trade:

> three days of labour of one country can be exchanged against one of another country ... Here the law of value undergoes essential modification ... The relationship between labour days of different countries may be similar to that existing between skilled, complex labour and unskilled simple labour within a country. In this case, the richer country exploits the poorer one, even where the latter gains by the exchange. (1972, pp. 105–6)

In effect price formation on the world market is governed by the same principles that apply under a conceptually isolated capitalism. The latter anyway is merely a theoretical model; the world market, as a unity of specific national economies, is something real and concrete. Today the prices of the most important raw materials and final products are determined internationally, in the world market. We are no longer confronted by a national level of prices but a level determined on the world market. In a conceptually isolated capitalism entrepreneurs with an above average technology make a surplus profit (a rate of profit above the average) when they sell their commodities at socially average prices. Likewise on the world market, the technologically advanced countries make a surplus profit at the cost of the technologically less developed ones. Marx repeatedly draws out the international effects of the law of value. For instance he says, 'most agricultural peoples are forced to sell their product *below* its value whereas in countries with advanced capitalist production the agricultural product rises to its value' (1969, p. 475). In Chapter 22 of *Capital Volume One* entitled 'national differences in wages', Marx writes:

> the law of value in its international application is ... modified by this, that on the world market the more productive national labour reckons also as more intense, so long as the more productive nation is not compelled by competition to lower the selling price of its commodities to the level of their value. (1954, p. 525)

With the development of capitalist production in a given country therefore, the national intensity and productivity of labour rise above the international average level.

> The different quantities of commodities of the same kind, produced in different countries in the same working time, have, therefore, unequal international values, which are expressed in different prices, ie, in sums of money varying according to international values. The relative value of money will, therefore, be less in the nation with a more developed capitalist mode of production, than in the nation with a less developed. (p. 525)

Likewise in Chapter 17:

> the intensity of labour would be different in different countries, and would modify the international application of the law of value. The more intense working day of one nation would be represented by a greater sum of money than the less intense day of another nation. (p. 492)

Finally in *Capital Volume Three*:

> Capitals invested in foreign trade can yield a higher rate of profit, because, in the first place, there is competition with commodities produced in other countries with inferior production facilities, so that the more advanced country sells its goods above their value even though cheaper than the competing countries. In so far as the labour of the more advanced country is here realised as labour of a higher specific weight, the rate of profit rises, because labour which has not been paid as being of a higher quality, is sold as such ... As regards capitals invested in colonies, etc, on the other hand, they may yield higher rates

of profit for the simple reason that the rate of profit there is higher due to backward development, and likewise the exploitation of labour, because of the use of slaves, coolies, etc. (1959, p. 238)

In the examples cited above the gain of the more advanced capitalist countries consists in a transfer of profit from the less developed countries. It is irrelevant whether the latter are capitalist or non-capitalist. It is not a question of the realisation of surplus value but of additional surplus value which is obtained through competition on the world market through unequal exchange, or exchange of non-equivalents.

The enormous significance of this transfer process and the function of imperialist expansion are only explicable in terms of the theory of breakdown developed earlier. I have already shown that capitalism does not suffer from a hyperproduction of surplus value but, on the contrary, from insufficient valorisation. This produces a tendency towards breakdown which is expressed in periodic crises and which in the further course of accumulation necessarily leads to a final collapse.

Under these circumstances an injection of surplus value by means of foreign trade would raise the rate of profit and reduce the severity of the breakdown tendency. According to the conception I have developed and which, I believe, is also Marx's conception, the original surplus value expands by means of transfers from abroad. At advanced stages of accumulation, when it becomes more and more difficult to valorise the enormously accumulated capital, such transfers become a matter of life and death for capitalism. This explains the virulence of imperialist expansion in the late stage of capital accumulation. Because it is irrelevant whether the exploited countries are capitalist or non-capitalist – and because the latter can in turn exploit other less developed countries by means of foreign trade – accumulation of capital at a late stage entails intensified competition of all capitalist countries on the world market. The drive to neutralise the breakdown tendency through increased valorisation takes place at the cost of other capitalist states. The accumulation of capital produces an ever more destructive struggle among capitalist states, a continuous revolutionisation of technology, rationalisation, Taylorisation or Fordisation of the economy – all of which is intended to create the kind of technology and organisation that can preserve competitive superiority on the world market. On the other side accumulation intensifies the drift to protectionism in the economically backward countries.

Kautsky sees the essence of imperialism in a striving to conquer the non-capitalist agrarian parts of the world. He therefore sees imperialism as merely an episode in the history of capitalism that will pass with the industrialisation of those parts of the world. This conception is totally false. Imperialism must be understood in the specific form that Luxemburg gives to it in her theory of the role of the non-capitalist countries. Imperialist antagonisms subsist even among the capitalist states in their relations to one another. Far from being merely an episode that belongs to the past, imperialism is rooted in the essence of capitalism at advanced stages of accumulation. Imperialist tendencies become stronger in the course of accumulation, and only the overthrow of capitalism will abolish them altogether.

The argument developed here shows how foreign trade can function as a means of surmounting crises. While commodity exports are not confined to periods of crisis or depression it is a fact that in boom periods, when the level of domestic prices is high and shows an upward trend, accumulation in individual spheres of industry creates a market for industry as a whole, and industry works mainly for the national market. Foreign trade gains importance in periods of internal saturation, when valorisation disappears due to overaccumulation and there is a declining demand for investment goods. The drive to export in a period of depression acts as a valve for overproduction on the domestic market. In Germany after the boom year of 1927 there was a tapering off early in 1928. Although a depression has still to come there was, in the first four months of 1928, a retreat in domestic demand practically all along the line. At the same time however, exports provided a compensation. From January to April 1928 exports were around 18.5 per cent higher than in the corresponding part of the previous year. Thus here we have a means of partially offsetting a crisis of valorisation in the domestic economy.

The international character of economic cycles

Far from signifying the impending doom of European capitalism, as Hildebrand (1910) and others forecast, the industrialisation of the more backward countries signifies an expansion of world exports. Contrary to Luxemburg's theory the backward countries gain importance as markets for advanced capitalism precisely to the degree that they industrialise. Today the industrialising colonies are much better markets than the purely agricultural colonies, while the advanced capitalist countries are the best markets. In fact the notion that the backward countries, still mainly dependent on agriculture, could produce enough commodities to pay for the colossal wealth of the capitalist nations is something bordering on absurdity.

The fact that the more industrialised a country is the greater its share of industrial imports, or the fact that the industrialised nations form the best markets for each other, helps to explain a phenomenon for which

Luxemburg's theory has no explanation. I mean the international character of the economic cycle. An upswing in production goes together with rising imports of raw materials, semi-finished goods and so on. In periods of boom net exports of raw materials and semi-finished goods exceed net exports of finished commodities, while the ratio is reversed in periods of depression. Thus there is a strong correlation between booms and raw material imports.

A boom in one country is communicated to other countries through the medium of commodity imports. In this way the rhythm of boom movements becomes progressively synchronised, even if international differences in the chronology of the business cycle persist. Even prior to the War we saw the gradual formation of a parallelism in the economic cycles of the most important countries. The crises of 1900, 1907 and 1913 all had an international character. This parallelism was interrupted by the War and the breaking off of mutual economic ties, but after the War it started to crystallise once more.

Table 3.1: German imports 1925–7 (billions of marks)

	1925	1926	1927
Raw materials & semi-finished goods	7.0	5.3	7.7
Finished goods	1.3	1.0	1.8

The minor boom of 1925 was followed by the depression of 1926 when the total volume of imports declined steeply. In the boom year of 1927 imports exceeded the level of 1925. It is easy to see that such a rapid increase of German imports, by 3.2 billion marks, is bound to have an invigorating effect on the world market. As long as it is sufficiently strong the boom in a single country can communicate itself to all its trade partners. For instance the German boom of 1927 drew along with it all the neighbouring countries of central and eastern Europe which have close economic ties to Germany. In that year there was a revival, of varying strength, in Poland, Czechoslovakia, Austria, Hungary, Switzerland, Belgium, Netherlands, Sweden and Finland.

In periods of depression things are reversed. Imports decline and a chain repercussion starts as orders are cancelled.

Foreign trade and world monopolies

The tremendous importance of cheap raw materials to the level of the rate of profit and thus to the valorisation of capital was first established through practical experience. However the classical economists found it difficult to explain the fact theoretically due to their confusion of the rate of profit with the rate of surplus value. Marx was the first to establish the connection clearly through his own exposition of the laws that govern the rate of profit:

> Since the rate of profit is s/C, or $s/c + v$, it is evident that everything causing a variation in the magnitude of c, and thereby of C, must also bring about a variation in the rate of profit, even if s and v, and their mutual relation, remain unaltered. Now, raw materials are one of the principle components of constant capital ... Should the price of raw material fall ... the rate of profit rises ... Other conditions being equal, the rate of profit, therefore, falls and rises inversely to the price of raw material. This shows, among other things, how important the low price of raw material is for the industrial countries. (1959, p. 106)

Marx goes on to point out that the importance of raw materials to the level of profitability is constantly growing with the development of capitalist industry:

> the quantity and value of the employed machinery grows with the development of labour productivity but not in the same proportion as productivity itself, ie, not in the proportion in which this machinery increases its output. In those branches of industry, therefore, which do consume raw materials ... the growing productivity of labour is expressed precisely in the proportion in which a larger quantity of raw material absorbs a definite of labour, hence in the increasing amount of raw material converted in, say, one hour into products ... The value of raw material, therefore, forms an ever-growing component of the value of the commodity product. (1959, p. 108)

The growing importance of raw materials is also obvious in the fact that as industrialisation advances every capitalist country becomes increasingly dependent on raw material imports. For instance in Germany imports of raw materials for industrial purposes increased by between 40 to 55 per cent between the late 1880s and 1912.

A further point is that monopolistic controls in the world market are easier to carry through in the sphere of raw materials where the range of possible applications is very wide. Competition among the capitalist powers first exploded in the struggles to control raw material resources because the chance of monopoly profits were greatest here. Yet this is not the only factor. Control over raw materials leads to control over industry as such. F Kestner says:

> Because only raw materials or means of production are susceptible to long-term monopolisation, which is generally not the case with finished products – unless raw material syndicates intervene – cartellisation necessarily shifts the economic balance in favour of heavy industry, both in terms of price formation, and in terms of the fact that the processing industries fall under the sway of the raw materials industries. (1912, p. 258)

The struggle for control of raw materials is thus a struggle for control over processing industries, which is itself finally reducible to the drive for additional surplus value. Because raw materials are only found at specific points on the globe, capitalism is defined by a tendency to gain access to, and exert domination over, the sources of supply. This can only take the form of a division of the world. A world monopoly in raw materials means that more surplus value can be pumped out of the world market. For competitors who face such a monopoly it means that the breakdown of capitalism is intensified. The economic roots of imperialism, of the incessant drive to dominate territories capitalistically and later politically, lie in imperfect valorisation.

Perhaps the most obvious case of this is the Anglo–American struggle over oil. The struggles for petroleum in the Caucasus, Mesopotamia and Persia are already well known so I shall be brief here. Oil first became a burning issue for Britain when the discovery of the diesel-engine made it possible to substitute liquid fuel for coal in shipping. Yet the biggest reserves of crude oil and the bulk of oil production were concentrated in American hands. Britain saw the American monopoly as a threat. F Delaisi points out that for close to a century the whole power of British trade and industry was founded on her control over coal. Superiority in the coal market, and especially in the production of bunker coal, enabled Britain to consolidate its traditional maritime dominance. Britain could afford to charge cheaper rates on return-freight than her competitors:

> Thus commodities destined for Britain paid lower transport costs than those destined for other countries. Hence British industry enjoyed a real premium on all overseas raw materials. This was an enormous advantage over all competitors in the struggle to win international markets. (Delaisi, 1921, p. 40)

Once shipping converted to oil all this could change. Britain produced no petroleum. British domination over sea transport was seriously threatened. Then there was the experience of the World War which showed the importance of automobiles and aircraft. The decisive strategic significance of allied control over oil reserves became more and more obvious the longer the War lasted. The oil politics of the postwar period was a direct consequence of these experiences.

Britain realised the implications of this situation quite early on and, at the beginning of this century, quietly and unobtrusively started to acquire reserves of oil that were still going. Against Rockefeller's Standard Oil Trust, Britain founded a series of oil trusts: Royal Shell (later expanded into Royal Dutch Shell), Mexican Eagle, Anglo–Persian Oil, etc. Britain even settled down in the USA to take on the competition of Standard Oil. By 1919 *The Times* could report a speech by G Prettyman, a well-known oil expert, who on the inauguration of the new Anglo–Persian refinery was quoted as saying:

At the outbreak of the War the position was such that the British Empire with her enormous worldwide interests controlled only two per cent of world petroleum reserves … On the currently prevalant foundations and methods of work used, about which he would not like to go into detail, he feels that once differences are settled, the British Empire should not be very far from controlling over half the world's known reserves of petroleum. (7 May 1919)

This result could be achieved thanks to a powerful vertical concentration of the entire industry from production down to distribution, and the corresponding conglomeration of capital which could exert fantastic pressure.

The British oil industry was thus welded together into a single block which today embraces 90 per cent of all Britain's oil interests. At the end of 1920 Anglo–Persian Oil [now British Petroleum – TK] unified some 77 companies with a nominal capital of around £120 million, and Royal Dutch Shell 50 firms with £300 million. Apart from these, there were another 177 companies representing a capital of £266 million. Altogether these firms represent a total capital of £686 million; 52 per cent of this is invested in production, 16 per cent in trade, 12 per cent in transport and 11 per cent in refining.

What was the point of this huge effort? Military security is only part of the answer. Delaisi notes that 'Britain no longer needs to fear the American monopoly' (p. 58). Just prior to the War Britain controlled all the most important coal stations. For the future it sought to control the major oil stations through a tightly organised petroleum industry. One of the basic objectives of Britain's oil strategy was to attain a near monopoly over the transportation of oil. How far this succeeded can be gauged from a report in *The Times* of March 1920, cited by Delaisi, which quotes Sir Edgar Mackay as saying:

> I can say that two thirds of the fields in operation in Central and South America are in British hands ... The Shell group controls interests in all the important oilfields on earth, including those in the USA, Russia, Dutch East Indies, Rumania, Egypt, Venezuela, Trinidad, British India, Ceylon, the Malay States, north and south China, Siam, the Straits Settlements and the Philippines. (Delaisi, 1921, p. 64)

The economic significance was drawn out when Mackay said:

> Assuming their current curve of consumption rises further, then after ten years the United States will have to import 500 million barrels a year which makes, even supposing a very low price of $2 per barrel, an annual expenditure of $1 billion, and most of that, if not all, will go into British pockets. (p. 64)

The idea of joint international control over raw material resources has been mooted time and time again. Even the International Congress of Mineworkers, which took place in August 1920, formulated a resolution calling for the creation of a central international office in the League of Nations. Such an office would not only produce a detailed inventory of all existing resources and gather statistics on them; it would also look after the 'distribution of fuels, minerals and other raw materials'. Such proposals are utopian. I have already shown that the antagonisms of world economy find their deepest source in the lack of valorisation which goes together with the general advance of accumulation. A shortage of surplus value in one national economy can only be compensated at the expense of other economies. Even capitalist attempts to create joint world monopolies have ended in failure, due to irreconcilable interests among the various parties.

The conflict of interests remains the basic aspect in the sense that the whole function of world monopolies lies in the national enrichment of some economies at the cost of others. As a result the increasingly frequent projects to evolve joint control and distribution schemes for raw materials remain pious wishes. Marx already pointed out, with prophetic foresight, that the attempts to regulate production that are often discernible in periods of crisis vanish:

as soon as the principle of competition again reigns supreme ... All thought of a common, all-embracing and far-sighted control over the production of raw materials gives way once more to the faith that demand and supply will mutually regulate one another. And it must be admitted that such control is on the whole irreconcilable with the laws of capitalist production and remains for ever a pious wish, or is limited to exceptional cooperation in times of great stress and confusion. (1959, p. 120)

The function of capital exports under capitalism

Earlier presentations of the question

From a scientific point of view we have to explain why capital is exported and what role is played by the export of capital in the productive mechanism of the capitalist economy.

Sombart is the best example of the superficial way in which these problems are handled in the prevailing theories. He tells us: 'No one can doubt that economic imperialism basically means that by enlarging their sphere of political influence, the capitalist powers are enabled to expand the sphere of investment for their superfluous capital' (1927, p. 71). Here the relation between capital expansion and the drive for power is wrongly described; Sombart makes the drive for power the precondition for capital expansion. The opposite is the case – capital expansion is a precursor of the political domination that follows.

Secondly, from a purely economic point of view, Sombart does not explain why there is such a thing as the expansion of capital to foreign territories. This is something self-evident for him. What we have to explain theoretically is simply presupposed as obvious without any analysis or proof. Why are capitals not invested in the home country itself? Because they are superfluous? But what does superfluous mean? Under what conditions can a capital become superfluous? Sombart simply uses phrases without the slightest attempt to clarify things scientifically.

This issue has been debated for a whole century ever since Ricardo argued that when 'merchants engage their capitals in foreign trade, or in the carrying trade, it is always from choice and never from necessity: it is because in that trade their profits will be somewhat greater than in the home trade' (1984, p. 195).

In his book on imperialism J A Hobson maintains that foreign investments form 'the most important factor in the economics of imperialism' (1905, p. 48). He goes on to state that:

Aggressive imperialism ... which is fraught with such grave incalculable peril to the citizen, is a source of great gain to the investor who cannot find at home the profitable use he seeks for his capital, and insists that his government should help him to profitable and secure investments abroad. (p. 50)

But why are profitable investments not to be found at home? Hobson does not refer to this decisive question. In general his study, which is a valuable descriptive work, evades all theoretical issues. A Sartorius von Waltershausen states that 'in today's world economy the agrarian countries are net importers of capital, the industrialised countries net exporters' (1907, p. 52). However he adds that 'even the highly developed countries stand in debtor–creditor relationships to one another' (p. 52). Obviously the agrarian/industrialised distinction cannot account for export of capital. In that case what is the driving force behind this? Sometimes Sartorius refers to 'economic saturation', a superfluity of the available capital in relation to investment possibilities. But this is not explained. Sartorius appears to have a vague feeling that such a state of saturation is linked to a relatively advanced stage of capitalist development. But Sartorius stays at this purely empirical level.

The treatment of this problem by S Nearing and J Freeman is just as unsatisfying. They agree that the industrialised countries of Europe became exporters of capital only at a specific stage in their development. The same is true of America: 'The United States also reached this stage at the start of the present century'(1927, p. 23). The trend was then accelerated by the war – a whole process of development which might otherwise have taken much longer was compacted into a single decade by the events of the war. But what were these events? The war enormously speeded up the transformation of the USA from the position of a debtor to one of a creditor. The USA became a capital exporting nation 'and was bound to remain so as long as there was surplus capital looking for investment' (p. 24). But the authors do not show why such a surplus emerges or why it cannot find investment in the domestic economy.

Even in Marxist writings we search in vain for any explanation of the specific function of capital exports in the capitalist system. Marxists have simply described the surface appearances and made no attempt to build these into Marx's overall system. So Varga says, 'The importance of capital exports to monopoly capitalism was analysed in detail by Lenin in *Imperialism*; hardly anything new can be added' (1928, p. 56). Elsewhere he simply casts aside any attempt to analyse the problem theoretically and simply produces facts about the volume and direction of international capital flows. 'The rate of profit', he says, 'regulates not only the influx of capital into individual branches of industry, but also its geographical migrations. Capital is invested abroad whenever there are prospects of obtaining a higher rate of profit' (1927, p. 363). This conclusion is hardly original.

Varga fails to understand the dimensions of the question when he goes on to say, 'Capital is exported not because it is absolutely impossible for it to accumulate domestically without "thrusts into non-capitalist markets", but because there is the prospect of higher profit elsewhere' (p. 363). In other words Varga starts from the false assumption that whatever its total amount, capital can always find an unlimited range of investment possibilities at home. He overlooks the simple fact that in denying the possibility of an overabundance of capital, he simultaneously denies the possibility of an overproduction of commodities. In addition Varga imagines any argument that there are definite limits to the accumulation of capital, and that capital export necessarily follows, is incompatible with Marx's conception and can only be made from Luxemburg's position.

I shall show that Varga's conception is untenable, that it was precisely Marx who showed that there are definite limits to the volume of capital investments in any single country; that it was Marx who explained the conditions under which there arises an absolute overaccumulation of capital and therefore the compulsion to export capital abroad. Varga does not notice that his conception of unlimited investment possibilities flatly contradicts and is incompatible with any labour theory of value. Investment of capital demands surplus value. But surplus value is labour and in any given country labour is of a given magnitude. From a given working population only a definite mass of surplus labour is extortable. To suppose that capital can expand without limits is to suppose that surplus value can likewise expand without limits, and thus independently of the size of the working population. This means that surplus value does not depend on labour.

Sternberg argues that the export of capital constitutes a powerful factor for generating a surplus population. By reinforcing the reserve army it depresses the level of wages and enables a surplus value to arise(!). The expansion of capital 'is therefore one of the strongest supports of the capitalist relation and its continuity over time' (1926, p. 36) because a surplus value can arise 'only if there is a surplus population' (p. 16).

Export of capital is supposed to be the most powerful factor of surplus population. Yet in Germany in the years 1926–7 we saw the exact opposite: massive inflows of foreign capital were crucial to the general wave of rationalisation and played a major role in displacing workers or creating a surplus population. If it were simply a question of reducing the amount of capital so as to reduce the demand for labour then a simple transfer of capital would be enough to solve this. For instance German capitalists can go to Canada and settle down there. But this is not an export of capital so much as a loss of capital. In fact if it were simply a question of reducing the amount of capital, the essential aspect of capital exports – the drive to improve the conditions for the further expansion of capital – would no longer hold.

Sternberg tries to explain the export of capital, as he does all other phenomena of capitalism, by reference to competition. Yet the problem is to explain capital exports in abstraction from competition and therefore from the existence of a surplus population. The question is, what compels the capitalist to export capital when there is no reserve army and labour power is sold at its value?

Hilferding is not much better. Because he denies the possibility of a generalised overproduction of commodities, there are no limits to the investment of capital in a given country. So capital is exported only because a higher rate of profit can be expected: 'The precondition for the export of capital is the variation in rates of profit, and the export of capital is the means of equalising national rates of profit' (1981, p. 315). The same holds for Bauer. Inequality of profit rates is the sole reason why capital is exported: 'Initially the rate of profit is higher in the more backward countries which are the targets of imperialist expansion ... capital always flows to where the rate of profit is highest' (1924, p. 470).

Capital exports are thus explained in terms of the tendency for the rate of profit to equalise. But Bauer has the feeling that this explanation is quite useless when it comes to understanding modern imperialism. There has always been a tendency for rates of profit to equalise, whereas capital exports from the advanced capitalist countries started with real vigour only recently. Bauer himself says:

> The drive for new spheres of investment and new markets is as old as capitalism itself; it is as true of the capitalist republics of the Italian Renaissance as of Britain or Germany today. But the force of this tendency has increased enormously in the recent decades. (p. 471)

How does he explain this? Ultimately Bauer has to look for an explanation of rising capital exports in the aggressive character of modern imperialism, which is precisely what has to be explained. Apart from this, if higher rates of profit are what account for the flow of capital to the less developed continents of Asia, Africa and elsewhere, then it is impossible to understand why capital should ever be invested in the industries of Europe and the United States. Why is the whole surplus value not earmarked for export as capital?

In fact we have already seen that an average rate of profit forms on the world market. On page 247 of his book Bauer knows this. But when he comes to deal with the roots of export of capital and imperialist expansion (p. 461) he forgets it and falls back onto the banal conception that the higher rate of profit of the backward countries is the cause of capital exports. We argued earlier that on the world market the technologically more advanced countries make a surplus profit at the cost of the technologically backward nations with a lower organic composition. This is what stimulates and simultaneously drives capital to keep developing technology, to force through continuous increases in the organic composition in the advanced countries. Yet this only means that as progressively higher levels of organic composition are introduced, a field is simultaneously created for more profitable investments. However high profits may be in the colonial countries, they would appear to be higher still in the chemical and heavy industries at home which, given their organic composition, are making surplus profits. So the question remains – why is capital exported at all? Bauer can't explain this.

It is not necessarily true that in countries recently opened up to capitalist production the organic composition is always lower. While West European capitalism may have needed 150 years to evolve from the organisational form of the manufacturing period into the sophisticated world trust, the colonial nations do not need to repeat this entire process. They take over European capital in the most mature forms it has already assumed in the advanced capitalist countries. In this way they skip over a whole series of historical stages, with their peoples dragged straight into gold and diamond mines dominated by trustified capital with its extremely sophisticated technological and financial organisation. Does Bauer mean to suggest that British capitalists invest in railway construction in Africa or South America because the organic composition of the railways there is lower than in England? Argentina's beef industry works on huge refrigerated plants equipped with the most modern technology with large sums of capital invested by the meat-processing firms of Chicago. An industry of this type could only have developed after a revolutionary change in transport and refrigeration techniques, and this again presupposes a high organic composition of capital.

Bauer senses that there is no factual basis in the argument about higher rates of profit in less developed countries, so he drags in various other factors in the conviction that piling up doubtful arguments is a good enough substitute for one correct one. 'At any given time', he says, 'a part of the social money capital always lies fallow' (1924, p. 462). 'If too much money capital lies fallow the consequences can be disastrous for capitalism' (p. 462). Therefore there is a drive for spheres of investment that will absorb the superfluous capital. One form of this drive is the export of capital which, according to Bauer, 'reduces the volume of capital that lies fallow in a given country at a given time' (p. 470).

Here two completely different explanations tend to coalesce. One deals with productive capital, the other with money capital that is not active in production. In his second theory Bauer has merely confused money capital which is deposited in banks with capital that lies fallow and searches for investment opportunities. A portion of the total social capital must always exist in the form of money, in the shape of money capital. If reproduction is to be continuous the size of this portion cannot be reduced at will. The period of time which capital, individual or total, spends in any of its three forms is not determined arbitrarily by bankers or industrialists. It is objectively given. And because the size of money capital is not arbitrarily determined, any more than is the size of commodity capital or productive capital, definite numerical ratios must obtain in the division of capital into three portions. Marx says:

> The magnitude of the available capital determines the dimensions of the process of production, and this again determines the dimensions of the commodity capital and money capital in so far as they perform their functions parallel with the process of production. (1956, p. 106)

Summarising the results of his analysis Marx writes:

> Certain laws were found according to which diverse large components of a given capital must continually be advanced and renewed – depending on the conditions of the turnover – in the form of money capital in order to keep a productive capital of a given size constantly functioning. (p. 357)

He goes on to add that to 'set the productive capital in motion requires more or less money capital, depending on the period of turnover' (p. 361). So although money capital is itself unproductive – it creates no value or surplus value and limits the scale of the productive component of capital – it cannot be arbitrarily diminished or cast aside because it fulfils necessary functions.

Bauer turns all this upside down. In Marx the money capital that lies fallow is only a portion of industrial capital in its real circuit, constituting a unity of its three circuits. In Bauer money capital that lies fallow is a part of money capital 'which has been pushed out of the circuit of capital' (1924, p. 476). In Marx the size of the money capital depends on the length of the turnover period. In Bauer the length of the turnover period depends on the size of the money capital. So instead of a slower turnover tying up too much money capital, an accumulation of too much money capital slows down the turnover according to Bauer.

The upshot is that production does not determine circulation, circulation determines production. Bauer says: 'Any change in the ratio of fallow to invested capital, of productive capital to capital in circulation ... completely transforms the picture of bourgeois society' (p. 463). The mystical power of money capital to do this lies with the banks. In fact expansion is only possible due to the banks: 'Thanks to the scale of resources at their disposal at any given time, they [the banks] can consciously direct the flow of capital to the dominated areas' (p. 472). Capital is exported because the banks decide it. The banks seemingly can do what they like. So what of the objective laws of capitalist circulation? Obviously for Bauer these must belong to the realm of fantasy.

Bauer refers to fallow money capital which is expelled from the circulation of industrial capital and returns to production through the export of capital. But from statistics on international trade, Bauer knows that international capital movements take place mainly in the form of commodities and hardly at all in the form of money or as money capital. It is not money capital but commodity capital which is expelled from the circulation of industrial capital. This merely shows that there is an overproduction of commodity capital which is unsaleable and which cannot therefore find its way back into production. In fact Bauer himself accepts that export of capital creates an outlet for commodities.

Overaccumulation and export of capital in Marx's conception

Marx points to the consistency of Ricardo's argument that if overproduction of commodities is impossible then there 'cannot ... be accumulated in a country any amount of capital which cannot be employed productively' (Ricardo, 1984, p. 193). This proposition is founded on J B Say's thesis that demand and supply are identical. It shows that 'Ricardo is always consistent. For him, therefore, the statement that no *overproduction* (of commodities) is possible, is synonymous with the statement that no plethora or overabundance of capital is possible' (pp. 496–7). Marx then refers to the 'stupidity of his [Ricardo's] successors':

who deny overproduction in one form (as a general glut of commodities on the market) and who not only admit its existence in another form, as overproduction of capital, plethora of capital, overabundance of capital, but actually turn it into an essential point of their doctrine. (p. 497)

The epigones of Marx, for instance Varga, merely reverse this stupidity. They accept the overproduction of commodities and even 'make this a fundamental part of their doctrine', but deny the overproduction of capital.

For Marx there could be no fundamental distinction between the two phenomena. The question is: what is the relation between these two forms of overproduction, the form in which it is denied and the form in which it is asserted or accepted? 'The question is, therefore, what is the overabundance of capital and how does it differ from overproduction?' (p. 498).

Those economists who admit to the possibility of an overabundance of capital maintain that 'capital is equivalent to money or commodities. So overproduction of capital is overproduction of money or of commodities. And yet the two phenomena are supposed to have nothing in common with each other' (p. 498). Against this 'thoughtlessness, which admits the existence and necessity of a particular phenomenon when it is called A and denies it when it is called B' (p. 499) Marx emphasises that when we are dealing with overproduction we are not dealing merely with an overproduction of commodities as commodities. We are dealing with 'the fact that commodities are here no longer considered in their simple form, but in their designation as capital' (p. 498). The commodity 'becomes something more than, and also different from, a commodity' (p. 499).

In a situation of overproduction the producers confront one another not as pure commodity owners but as capitalists. This means that in every crisis the valorisation function of capital is disrupted. A capital that fails to valorise itself is superfluous, overproduced capital. In this sense overproduction of commodities and overproduction of capital are the same thing. 'Overproduction of capital, not of the individual commodities – although overproduction of capital always includes overproduction of commodities – is thus simply overaccumulation of capital' (Marx, 1959, p. 251).

The heart of the problem of capital exports lies in showing why it is necessary and under what conditions it comes about. Marx's achievement was that he did precisely this.

Marx showed the circumstances which determine a tendential fall in the rate of profit in the course of accumulation. The question arises – how far can this fall go? Can the rate of profit fall to zero? Many writers believe that only in such a case can we speak of an absolute overaccumulation of capital. As long as capital yields a profit, however small, we cannot speak of overaccumulation in an absolute sense because the capitalist would rather be content with a small profit than have no profit at all.

I shall show that this idea is completely false, that there is a limit to the accumulation of capital and this limit comes into force much earlier than a zero rate of profit. There can be absolute overaccumulation even when capital yields a high interest. The crux of the matter is not the absolute level of this interest, but the ratio of the mass of surplus value to the mass of accumulated capital.

In identifying the conditions on which this limit depends mere empiricism is quite useless. For instance in the utilisation of fuel the experience of almost 100 years has shown that it was always possible to obtain a greater quantity of heat from a given quantity of coal. Thus experience, based on several decades' practice, might easily suggest that there is no limit to the quantity of heat obtainable through such increases. Only theory can answer the question whether this is really true, or whether there is not a maximum limit here beyond which any further increases are precluded. This answer is possible because theory can calculate the absolute quantity of energy in a unit of coal. Increases in the rate of utilisation cannot exceed 100 per cent of the available quantity of energy. Whether this maximum point is reached in practice is of no concern to theory.

Starting from considerations of this sort Marx asks, what is overaccumulation of capital? He answers the question thus: 'To appreciate what this overaccumulation is ... one need only assume it to be absolute. When would overproduction of capital be absolute?' (1959, p. 251) According to Marx absolute overproduction would start when an expanded capital could yield no more surplus value than it did as a smaller capital:

> As soon as capital would, therefore, have grown in such a ratio to the labouring population that neither the absolute working time supplied by this population, nor the relative surplus working time, could be expanded any further (this last would not be feasible at any rate in the case where the demand for labour were so strong that there were a tendency for wages to rise); at a point, therefore when the increased capital produced just as much, or even less, surplus value than it did before its increase, there would be absolute overproduction of capital. (p. 251)

According to Marx's definition of absolute overaccumulation it is not necessary for profit on the total capital to disappear completely. It disappears only for the additional capital which is accumulated. In practice the additional capital will displace a portion of the existing capital so that for the total capital a lower rate of profit results. However whereas a falling rate of profit is generally bound up with a growing mass of profit, absolute overaccumulation is characterised by the fact that here the mass of profit of the expanded total capital remains the same.

To understand the conditions under which this occurs I shall first analyse the simplest case where population and the productivity of labour are constant.

Absolute overaccumulation of capital with the size of population and technology held constant
Marx says:

> Take a certain working population of, say, two million. Assume, furthermore, that the length and intensity of the average working day, the level of wages, and thereby the proportion between necessary and surplus labour, are given. In that case the aggregate labour of these two million, and their surplus labour expressed in surplus value, always produces the same magnitude of value. (1959, pp. 216–17)

Under these presuppositions capital accumulation runs up against a maximal limit which can be calculated exactly because the maximum amount of surplus value obtainable is exactly given. It would make no sense to continue accumulation beyond this limit because any expanded capital would yield the same mass of surplus value as before. If accumulation were continued it would necessarily lead to a devaluation of capital and a sharp fall in the rate of profit:

> a portion of the capital would lie completely or partially idle (because it would have to crowd out some of the active capital before it could expand its own value), and the other portion would produce values at a lower rate of profit owing to the pressure of unemployed or but partly employed capital ... The fall in the rate of profit would then be accompanied by an absolute decline in its mass ... And the reduced mass of profit would have to be calculated on an increased total capital. (1959, p. 252)

This constitutes a case of absolute overaccumulation of capital 'because capital would be unable to exploit labour ... to the degree which would at least increase the mass of profit along with the growing mass of employed capital' (p. 255). According to Marx this would be the case 'in which more capital is accumulated than can be invested in production ... This results in loans abroad, etc, in short, to speculative investments' (1969, p. 484).

Absolute overaccumulation with a growing population and changing technology (increases in the organic composition of capital)

It would be wrong to conclude that absolute overaccumulation is only possible when population and technology are held constant. Using Bauer's scheme I have shown that it can and must arise on the basis of the assumptions: a) of a progressively rising organic composition of capital and b) of annual increases in population. Under the conditions postulated by this model, absolute overaccumulation does not set in immediately but only after a certain interval. I showed (in Table 2.2, p. 75) that after year 21 the capitalists could have no interest in accumulating at the existing rate (10 per cent for constant capital, 5 per cent for variable) because a capital expanded at this rate would be too large to be valorised to the same degree. The personal consumption of the capitalists would start declining. So instead of accumulating the surplus value (of year 20) – that is, incorporating it into the original capital – they will earmark it for capital export.

Since businessmen are not inclined to cut down their own consumption, there will be a shortage of the portion earmarked for accumulation. By year 36 there has to be a reserve army (of 11 509 workers) and simultaneously a superfluous capital (of 117 174). This is the situation that prevailed in Britain early in 1867 as reported in *Reynolds' Newspaper*: 'At this moment, while English workmen with their wives and children are dying of cold and hunger, there are millions of English gold – the produce of English labour – being invested in Russia, Spain, Italy and other foreign countries' (Marx, 1954, p. 625).

From this moment on accumulation runs into difficulties. The profit earmarked for accumulation cannot be invested in expanding business in the industry in which it was made. This is because industry is saturated with capital. Marx says:

> if this new accumulation meets with difficulties in its employment, through a lack of spheres of investment, ie, due to a surplus in the branches of production and an oversupply of loan capital, this plethora of loanable money capital merely shows the limitations of *capitalist* production ... an obstacle is indeed immanent in its laws of expansion, ie, in the limits in which capital can realise itself as capital. (1959, p. 507)

The limits to accumulation are specifically capitalist limits and not limits in general. Social needs remain massively unsatisfied. Yet from the standpoint of capital there is superfluous capital because it cannot be valorised.

It is absolutely false to argue, as Luxemburg does, that Marx's reproduction scheme 'contradicts the conception of the capitalist total process and its course as laid down by Marx in *Capital Volume Three*' (1968, p. 343). The fundamental idea underlying Marx's scheme is the immanent contradiction between the drive towards an unlimited expansion of the forces of production and the limited valorisation possibilities of overaccumulated capital. Precisely this is the necessary consequence of Marx's schemes of reproduction and accumulation. Because Luxemburg transformed these limited valorisation possibilities into a limited capacity for consumption she could find no trace of that immanent contradiction in the scheme itself. Against this Marx shows that:

> the self expansion of capital based on the contradictory nature of capitalist production permits an actual free development only up to a certain point, so that in fact it constitutes an immanent fetter and barrier to production, which are [sic] continually broken through by the credit system. (1959, p. 441)

The limit of overaccumulation is broken through by the credit system, that is, by export of capital and the additional surplus value obtained by means of it. It is in this specific sense that the late stage of accumulation is characterised by the export of capital.

How does Luxemburg reconcile the fact of capital exports with her theory of the non-realisability of surplus value under capitalism? She devotes a special chapter, 'international loans' (1968, Chapter 30) to this question. Over some 30 pages she tells us how the capitalist countries of Europe export capital to the non-capitalist countries, build factories there, create a capitalist system and draw them by stages into their own sphere of influence. But there is not a word about how the surplus value produced in the former is realised in the latter. Instead we are told how the masses of Egypt and elsewhere have to work for long hours at low wages, how they are drawn into the capitalist nexus. In short Luxemburg shows us not how the surplus value produced under capitalism is realised in the backward countries but how an additional surplus value is produced in these countries, by means of capital exports, and brought back to the countries of advanced capitalism. The existence of capital exports is not only irreconcilable with Luxemburg's theory, it directly contradicts it. Capital exports bear no relation to the realisation of surplus value. They are related to the problem of production, of the production of additional surplus value abroad.

An inductive verification

I have proposed two sorts of argument: i) that the valorisation of capital is the driving force of capitalism and governs all the movements of the capitalist mechanism – its expansions and contractions. Initially production is expanded because, in the early stages of accumulation, profit grows. Afterwards accumulation comes to a standstill because, at a more advanced stage of accumulation, and due to the very process of accumulation, profit necessarily declines. ii) Apart from trying to explain the oscillations of the business cycle I have tried to define the law of motion of capitalism – its secular trend – or, in Marx's words, the general tendency of capitalist accumulation. I have shown how the course of capital accumulation is punctuated by an absolute overaccumulation which is released, from time to time, in the form of periodic crises and which is progressively intensified through the fluctuations of the economic cycle from one crisis to the next. At an advanced stage of accumulation it reaches a state of capital saturation where the overaccumulated capital faces a shortage of investment possibilities and finds it more difficult to surmount this saturation. The capitalist mechanism approaches its final catastrophe with the inexorability of a natural process. The superfluous and idle capital can ward off the complete collapse of profitability only through the export of capital or through employment on the stock exchange.

To take up this latter aspect. Hilferding devotes a whole chapter to speculation and the stock exchange (1981, Chapter 8). All we learn from it is that speculation is unproductive, that it is a pure gamble, that the mood of the stock exchange is determined by the big speculators, and banalities of this sort. Because Hilferding denies the overaccumulation of capital he removes any basis for understanding the essential function of speculation and the exchange. In his exposition the stock exchange is a market for the circulation of titles of ownership, divorced from and rendered independent of the circulation of the actual goods. Its function is to mobilise capital. Through the conversion of industrial capital into fictitious capital on the exchange, the individual capitalist always has the option open to withdraw his capital in the form of money whenever he likes. Finally the mobilisation of capital in the form of shares, or the creation of fictitious capital, opens the possibility of capitalising dividends. According to Hilferding speculation is necessary to capitalism for all these reasons.

In all this there is no reference to the function of speculation in the movement of the business cycle. I have already pointed out that superfluous capital looks for spheres of profitable investment. With no chance in production, capital is either exported or switched to speculation. Thus in the depression of 1925–6 money poured into the stock exchange. Once the situation improved at the end of 1926 and the start of 1927 credits were displaced from the exchange into production.

The relationship between the banks and speculation which is discernible in the specific phases of the business cycle is also reflected in minor fluctuations within any given year. In periods when the banks can employ their resources elsewhere the exchange is subdued; it becomes brisk only when those resources are again released. Speculation is a means of balancing the shortage of valorisation in productive activity by gains that flow from the losses made on the exchange by the mass of smaller capitalists. In this sense it is a power mechanism in the concentration of money capital.

Let us take the present economic situation of the USA as an example of these movements. Despite the optimism of many bourgeois writers who think that the Americans have succeeded in solving the problem of crises and creating economic stability, there are enough signs to suggest that America is fast approaching a state of overaccumulation. A report dated June 1926 notes that:

> Since the War the capital formation process has advanced with extreme rapidity. Capital is now looking for investment outlets, and due to its overflow, it can only find these at declining rates of interest. Naturally this has meant an increase of all … real estate values … Furious speculation in the real estate is one result. (Wirtschaftsdienst, 1926, I, p. 792)

The basic characteristic of the economic year 1927 is that industry and commerce have watched their production fall, their sales decline and their profits contract. Reduced sales and lower production release a portion of the capital which flows into the banks in the form of deposits. The banks attract industrial profits for which there are no openings in industry and commerce. At the end of 1927 the holdings of the member banks of the US Federal Reserve System were $1.7 billion more than a year earlier. This constitutes a rise of 8 per cent against the 5 per cent considered normal. The retrogression in industry and commerce contrasts sharply with the overabundance of cheap credit money.

The discount policy of the Federal Reserve Board has to be seen in this context. It is not that capital flows into Europe because rates of interest are higher. On the contrary US rates of interest have been cut in order to promote an outflow of capital. The financial expert Dr Halfeld reports that there were two reasons why in August 1927 the US banks of issue reduced the discount rate from 4 per cent to 3.5 per cent. Firstly to create an outflow of gold to Europe which is short of capital and, secondly, to revive domestic business. Yet this discount policy failed. Despite the substantial outflow of gold, US interest rates continued to remain low in the open market and vast sums of money were directed into speculation. The depressed state of industry is reflected by an expansion of speculative loans and speculative driving up of share prices. According to estimates of the US department of commerce, in 1927 the USA invested $1.648 billion of new capital abroad. While this was partly matched by a reverse flow of $919m, the greater part of this money flowed straight into the New York stock exchange for speculation. Advances by New York banks by way of brokers' loans on the stock exchange totalled $4.282 billion at the start of May – 46 per cent higher than in the previous year. On the other side, disbursements to industry and commerce remained low up to the middle of February. Towards the end of March there was a massive outflow of capital from the country, including large-scale buying up of foreign securities.

As a countervailing measure, the federal reserve banks decided on a discount policy which was the reverse of the one followed late in 1927. All twelve banks raised the discount rate from 3.5 per cent to 4 per cent. In April 1928 the Chicago and Boston bankers increased the rate a second time to 4.5 per cent and several banks followed suit. The discount rate thus returned to a level not seen by American money markets since early 1924. The results of the new discount policy appear to have been a complete failure if we go by the staggering bout of speculation on the New York stock exchange in the last week of March 1928. In fact despite the measures taken by the clearing house association against further extension of speculative credits, the flood of speculation reached a feverish pitch by August.

The fever of speculation is only a measure of the shortage of productive investment outlets. Dr Flemming is therefore quite right in saying that loans to foreign countries offer one way of eliminating difficulties since income from production cannot be redeployed on the domestic market. Not higher profits abroad, but a shortage of investment outlets at home is the basic underlying cause of capital exports.

Today America is doing its best to avert the coming crash – already foreshadowed in the panic selling on the stock exchange of December 1928 – by forcing up the volume of exports. The recent Copper Exporters Incorporated has been followed by the formation of the Steel Export Association of America, a joint export organisation of the two major American concerns – US Steel Corporation and Bethlehem Steel. When these efforts are matched by a similar drive by the Germans and the British, the crisis will only be intensified.

The result: intensified international struggle for investment outlets, trans-formations in the relationship of finance capital and industrial capital

Lenin was quite correct in supposing that contemporary capitalism, based on the domination of monopoly, is typically characterised by the export of capital. Holland had already evolved into a capital exporter by the close of the seventeenth century. Britain reached this stage early in the nineteenth century, France in the 1860s. Yet there is a big difference between the capital exports of today's monopoly capitalism and those of early capital-ism. Export of capital was not typical of the capitalism of that epoch. It was a transient, periodic phenomenon which was always sooner or later interrupted and replaced by a new boom. Today things are different. The most important capitalist countries have already reached an advanced stage of accumulation at which the valorisation of the accumulated capital encounters increasingly worse obstacles. Overaccumulation ceases to be a merely passing phenomenon and starts more and more to dominate the whole of economic life.

This is the case with France which, according to B Mehrens 'has an almost chronic superfluity of money' (1911, p. 230). This superabundance of capital is interrupted by periods of boom. But these boom periods are becoming shorter and shorter. The revival which started in Germany in 1910 was already over by 1912. The boom was over so quickly that A Feiler asked somewhat melancholically, 'Now was that a boom, or were we already in the purgatory of the depression?' (1914, p. 109).

Since 1918 the economic cycle has become progressively shorter. This is perfectly comprehensible in terms of the theory I have developed in this book. As rationalisation sustained its momentum after the war the accu-mulation of capital lurched forward sharply. A substantial part of plant expansions was carried through with the help of foreign loans. However in economic terms this is irrelevant to the fact that capital expanded enor-mously with the result that the valorisation of the expanded capital became more difficult. Apart from this, the problem of valorisation was further aggravated by the fact that America was now absorbing one part of the surplus value in the form of interest on her loans. At this advanced stage of accumulation booms become less intensive; they have changed their char-acter: 'Today we no longer expect booms to bring increased prosperity to all sectors of the economy ... We are generally quite content if industry as a whole tends to prosper, and especially if the main industries and firms show higher prosperity' (Feiler, 1914, p. 106).

Under these circumstances the overabundance of capital can only be surmounted through capital exports. This has therefore become a typical and indispensable move in all the advanced capitalist countries. Export of capital has thus become a means of warding off the breakdown, of prolonging the life-span of capitalism.

The bourgeois economist proclaims triumphantly that Marx's theory of breakdown and crises is false and contradicted by the actual development. He is generous enough to concede that it bore some correspondence to the formative period of capitalism in the 1840s. But when conditions changed the theory simply had the ground removed from under its feet:

> When Marx worked out his theory of crisis ... one could actually suppose that the recessions following the booms would become progressively worse. It was always possible to extrapolate from the line 1825–1836–1847 and end up with the theory of catastrophe worked out by Marx. In fact, even the crisis of 1857 still fitted into the picture. We know from their correspondence how both Marx and Engels saw in the breakdown of the boom in 1857 ... a vindication of their theory of crisis. (Sombart, 1927, p. 702)

According to Sombart the crisis of 1857 was the last great catastrophe of the classic type that Britain would go through. Germany and Austria had still to go through their own crisis in 1873. After that:

> Europe's economic life was underpinned by a conscious drive to neutralise, mitigate and abolish the tensions; this was a tendency that persisted down to the War and nothing in the War itself or the years that followed it at all weakened or transformed this tendency ... What emerged out of capitalism ... was the very opposite of the prophesised sharpening of crises; it was their elimination, or, 'cyclical stability' as people have been saying more recently. (p. 702)

The one-sidedness of this description is shown by the facts. Bourgeois economists prefer to convince themselves more than others that we are through with crises. Sombart assures us that we have not seen a serious crisis in Europe since 1873. But we know that the French crash of 1882 is reckoned among 'the most serious crises in French economic history' (Mehrens, 1911, p. 197) and that it precipitated a depression that was destined to persist for over one and a half decades. According to Sombart, in Britain 'the full savagery of unbridled capitalism burst forth really for the last time in the 1840s ... Already in the 1850s the drive for expansion was much weaker and therefore also the setback' (1927, p. 703). The facts prove the opposite. The crisis of 1895 was preceded by intense speculation chiefly in South African gold shares:

The real boom started only in 1895 ... Of all the attacks of pure speculative frenzy which the City has lived through, this was the worst, the
wildest and the most pernicious. While it raged, more money was won
and lost than in half a dozen earlier booms and panics. It ruined ten
times as many people as the South Seas swindle and undoubtedly
played its part in bringing forth the Boer War. (*Financial Times*, cited
Weber, 1915, p. 270)

Commentators have tried to explain the novel character of crises by
saying that the banks have succeeded in imposing regulation over economic life:

They can systematically withhold credit and stop capital issues, where
claims are economically unsound. And in this way they can ensure that
the creation of capital takes a rational form ... They can thereby
prevent speculation on the exchange and moderate the over optimism
of industry itself. (Feiler, 1914, p. 168)

The fact that the character of crises has changed is traced back to
increasing planning and conscious regulation of the economy. Changes
that are rooted in complex causes are interpreted as the achievements of
bankers.

The worst orgies of speculation are possible in a period when, with the
transition from individual forms of property to its social form in share
capital, enormous fortunes accumulated over several decades are thrown
on to the market and sacrificed on the stock exchange. These are the flota-
tion periods bound up with vast regroupments and concentration of
wealth. They are therefore periods of wild speculation. But once this
process of concentration of share capital has already reached an advanced
level, with the general progress of accumulation and through the mediation of the stock exchange, the exchange itself is left only with the resid-
ual stock capital in the hands of the public. Under these conditions
speculation is badly debilitated, not of course through the conscious intervention of banks which supposedly centralise command over the economy
into their own hands, but because there is not enough material for the
exchange to digest. At an already advanced level of concentration of share
capital, speculation on the stock exchange is bound to lose its impetus as
its middle-class base of small rentiers, workers, civil servants and so on,
dries up.

Yet this only compels the idle money capital to rush into other outlets,
into export of capital, as the only investments promising greater returns.

This alone is one reason why world market struggles for investment outlets become increasingly sharper.

This brings us to the second reason why the character of crises in Britain has temporarily changed. As long as our attention is fixed on an isolated capitalism it follows that advanced stages of accumulation will necessarily generate crises in their sharpest and most savage forms. During the first 50 years after 1825 when British relations with world economy were still only embryonic, and Britain could thus be regarded to some extent as an isolated capitalism, the crises of capital accumulation were enough to precipitate wild panics and collapses. But the more Britain succeeded in building relations with world economy, expanding foreign trade and discovering foreign outlets for overaccumulated capital, the more the character of those crises changed. But with the progress of accumulation the number of countries grows in which accumulation approaches absolute limits. If Britain and France were the world's first bankers, today the list includes America – as well as a whole series of small donor countries like Belgium, Switzerland, Holland, Sweden. Germany's capital imports are a purely temporary phenomenon. Given the technologically advanced structure of German industry, high productivity of labour and very low wages, the rate of surplus value is extremely high. Therefore the tempo of accumulation is much faster so that Germany will reimburse her foreign debts sooner than people imagine and emerge on the world market as an exporter of capital. Yet in proportion to the growth in the number of countries which export capital, competition and the struggle for profitable outlets is bound to intensify. The repercussions of this will necessarily sharpen the crisis at home. If the early crises of capitalism could already lead to wild outbreaks, we can imagine what crises will be like under the growing weight of accumulation when the capital exporting countries are compelled to wage the sharpest struggles for investment outlets on the world market.

B Harms forecasts that the USA is already approaching the absolute limits of accumulation, so that 'the capital which flows into the USA by way of interest payments over the coming decades, must in some form find its way back into the world markets' (1928, p. 8). This will promote the further industrialisation of the newcomers. But this process of industrialisation, encouraged by American capital, can only revolutionise European exports. In future only means of production can be exported. Yet the development of American industry is driving the US in the same direction:

> In other words we have to reckon with the fact that soon the USA itself will be emerging as one of the world's biggest suppliers of the means of

production. The well known enquiries of the Balfour Report and the proceedings of the last 'Imperial Conference' have produced instructive evidence for such an assumption. (Harms, p. 8)

Should the USA start exporting means of production, 'this must ultimately lead to a situation where the European debtor countries simply cannot sustain debt servicing charges to the US' (Harms, p. 8) and cannot pay for their imports of raw materials and means of subsistence. In other words Harms foresees the approach of one of the most terrible crises involving the bankruptcy of European capitalism – although he consoles himself with the illusion that the USA will voluntarily refrain from capital goods exports so as not to smash completely the solvency of her European debtors.

This makes it possible, finally, to form some more adequate picture of the relation of banking capital, or finance capital as Hilferding calls it, to industrial capital. It is well known that Hilferding sees the basic characteristic of modern capitalism in the dominance of finance capital over industry. He argues that with the growing concentration of banking, the banks increasingly come to control capital invested in industry. As capitalism develops, more and more money is mobilised from the unproductive classes and placed at the disposal of industrialists by the banks. Control over this money, which is indispensable to industry, is vested in the banks. So as capitalism develops and with it the credit system, industry becomes increasingly dependent on banking. An ever-increasing proportion of capital in industry is finance capital: it belongs to the banks and not to the industrialists who use it. With the growing concentration of money and banking capital the 'power of the banks increases and they become the founders and eventually rulers of industry' (Hilferding, 1981, p. 226). As banking itself develops:

> there is a growing tendency to eliminate competition among the banks themselves, and on the other side, to concentrate all capital in the form of money capital, and to make it available to producers only through the banks. If this trend were to continue, it would finally result in a single bank or a group of banks establishing control over the entire money capital. Such a 'central bank' would then exercise control over social production as a whole. (p. 180)

Hilferding needed this construction of a 'central bank' to ensure a painless, peaceful road to socialism. As we have seen already, Hilferding imagines that the socialising function of finance capital can facilitate the overcoming of capitalism.

Hilferding's exposition contradicts the actual tendencies of development of capitalism. It is also incompatible with the fundamental ideas of Marx's theory. For if Hilferding were right in arguing that the banks dominate industry, this would only shatter Marx's theory of the crucial importance of production itself to the structure of capitalism. The crucial role would then be played not by the productive process but by finance capital, or structures in the sphere of circulation.

Given the law of accumulation that we have developed, it follows that the interrelations of banking and industrial capital are historically changeable. We have to distinguish three phases. At a low stage of capital accumulation, when prospects for expansion are unlimited, the capital formation of industry itself is not enough. Therefore industry relies on a flow of credits from the outside, from non-industrial strata. The building of a credit system centralises the dispersed particles of capital and the banks acquire enormous power as mediators and donors of industrial credit. This was the phase France passed through after 1850 and which came to a close in Germany at the start of the present century.

The further progress of accumulation alters the interrelation of banks and industry. In France the initial capital shortage passed over into a chronic superfluity of money. In this phase industry establishes its independence. Obviously the specific configuration depends on the given country and the given sphere of industry. As far as German large-scale industry is concerned, Weber could write:

> On the whole, there is no basis for the widespread fear that industry, and especially large-scale industry, is managed according to the wishes of bank directors; on the contrary, the movement of concentration and the formation of industry associations has made industry far more independent of the banks. (1915, p. 343)

At more advanced stages of accumulation industry becomes increasingly more independent of credit flow because it shifts to self-financing through depreciation and reserves. For instance Feiler cites the example of the Bochumer Verein (by no means one of the industrial giants) which, with an initial share capital of 30 million marks, within nine years declared dividends equal to the entire nominal value of the share capital, and simultaneously earmarked 40 million marks for new investments (1914, p. 112). Nachimson has shown that over the period from 1907–8 to 1913–14, the share capital controlled by the German industrial finance corporations declined from 29 per cent of the total capital of all joint stock companies to 26.8 per cent. In the same period their foreign holdings declined from 90 per cent of the total liabilities of all stock companies to almost half. He concludes, 'These figures strongly suggest that the role of banks has declined in importance' (1922, p. 85). Although Nachimson accepts Hilferding's theory of the domination of industry by the banks, he says:

> However it is important to point out compared with the start of the twentieth century, there has been a distinct tendency for industry to become independent of the banks ... Whereas the banks rely on external capital flows which are basically derived from industry, the equity funds of the industrial companies have been rising continuously ... Industrialists like Thyssen, Siemens, Rathenau, Stinnes ... do not come from banking circles, but from industrial circles and they are increasingly dominating the banks, just as the banks once dominated them. (p. 87)

Finally in a third phase industry finds it progressively more difficult to secure a profitable investment, even of its own resources, in the original enterprise. The latter uses its profits to draw other industries into its sphere of influence. This is the case with Standard Oil Corporation according to R Liefmann's account (1918, p. 172). When the overaccumulated capital of a certain industry finds scope for expanding into other industries defined by the lower degree of accumulation, funds are channelled into 'the New York money market, where they play a crucial role' (p. 172). In countries like Britain, France and especially the USA, it is simply not possible to speak of industry being dependent on the banks. On the contrary industry has recently been dominating the banks. Apart from its own assets in banks, industry sets up its own financial institutions precisely in order to secure a profitable investment for its own surplus funds. In Germany firms like AEG are not only independent of the banks, they stand in a solid position in financial circles due to their own massive bank accounts. In a chapter on recent international trends in industrial financing T Vogelstein (1914) points out that the typical balance sheet of modern large-scale companies shows a completely different picture from the past. There is a tendency for the share of equity funds to increase at the expense of borrowed funds, or for the company to acquire its own assets in the banks. According to Vogelstein, this is one of the reasons why banks have been turning to the stock exchange by way of investments.

The historical tendency of capital is not the creation of a central bank which dominates the whole economy through a general cartel, but industrial concentration and growing accumulation of capital leading to the final breakdown due to overaccumulation.

Notes

1. It is a sign of Bauer's misunderstanding of Marx's method when he uses this provisional, simplifying assumption of a constant rate of surplus value of 100 per cent in his analysis of reproduction, but forgets to modify it later.
2. Opponents of Marxism accept Luxemburg's critique with great jubilation because it entails conceding the defective character of Marx's system on a crucial point.

Bibliography

Bauer, O. (1913) 'Die akkumulation des kapitals', *Neue Zeit*, 31.

—— (1924) *Die Nationalitatenfrage und die Sozialdemokratie* (Vienna).

Beer, M. (1923) *Allgem. Geschichte des Sozialismus* (Berlin).

Berger, P.L. (1987) *The Capitalist Revolution* (Wildwood).

Bernstein, E. (1899) *Die Voraussetzungen des Socializmus* (Stuttgart).

—— (1961) *Evolutionary Socialism* (Schocken: New York).

Bohm-Bawerk, E. von, (1975) *Karl Marx and the Close of his System* (London: Merlin Press).

Boudin, A. (1909) *Das Theoretische System von Karl Marx* (Stuttgart).

Braunthal, A. (1927) *Die Entwicklungstendenzen der Kapitalistischen Wirtschaft* (Berlin).

Bukharin, N. (1926) *Fragen des Sozialistischen Aufbaues* (Berlin).

—— (1971) *Economics of the Transformation Period* (London).

—— (1972) *Imperialism and the Accumulation of Capital* (London: Monthly Review Press).

Cassel, G. (1923) *Theoretische Socialokonomik*, 3.Aufl.

Charasoff, G. (1910) *Das System des Marxismus* (Berlin).

Clark, J.B. (1907) *Essentials of Economic Theory* (New York).

Cunow, H. (1898) 'Zusammenbruchstheorie', *Neue Zeit*, Jahrg 17.

Dehaing. (1925) Die entwicklung des motorschiffbaues', *Weltwirtschaftl Archiv*, 22.

Delaisi, F. (1921) Le Petrole (Paris).

Diehl, K. (1898) *Uber das Verhaltnis von Wert und Preis im Okonomischen System von Karl Marx* (Jena).

Dietzel, H. (1909) 'Ernten', *Handworterb. d. Staatswissensch, 3.Aufl.* Bd.III.

Dressler, W. (1915) *Der europäische Schiffanrts verkehr nach Australien* (Munich).

Elster, J. (1985) *Making Sense of Marx* (Cambridge University Press).

Feiler, A. (1914) *Die Konjunktur-Periode 1907–1913 in Deutschland* (Jena).

Fischer, L. (1926) *Oil Imperialism* (New York).

Freeman, M. (1990) 'Marxism after Stalinism', *Living Marxism*, April.

Grossmann, H. (1924) 'Sismonde de Sismondi et ses theories economiques' facsimile (Warsaw).

—— (1926) 'Eine neue theorie uberimperialismus und die soziale revolution', *Archiv fur die Geschichte des Sozialismus und der Arbeiterbewegung*, XIII 1928, 141–92 (Leipzig).

——. (1943) 'The Evolutionist Revolt against Classical Political Economy', *Journal of Political Economy*, October.

Hansen, F.R. (1985) *The Breakdown of Capitalism: a History of the Idea in Western Marxism*.

Harms, B. (1928) 'Wandlungen in der weltwirtschaftlichen stelling Europas', *Strukfurwandlungen der Deutschen Volkswirtschaft* (Berlin).

Hayek, F.A. von. (1928) 'Einige bemerkungen uber das verhaltnis der geld theorie zur konjunkturtheorie', *Schriften des Vereins f. Sozialpolitik*, 173.2.

Helander, S. (1926) 'Der tonnageuberfluss in der weltwirtschaft', *Weltwirtschaftl Archiv*, 24.

Hess, F. (1925) 'Die neueste der wollindustrie in den uberseeischen wollexport-landern', *Weltwirtschaftl Archiv*, 22.

Hildebrand, G. (1910) *Die Erschutterung der Industrieherrschaft und des Indus-triesozialismus* (Jena).

Hilferding, R. (1912) *Neue Zeit*, 30.

——. (1975) *Bohm-Bawerk's criticism of Marx* (London: Merlin Press).

—— (1981) *Finance Capital* (London: Routledge & Kegan Paul).

Hobson, J.A. (1905) *Imperialism* (London).

Howard, M.C. and King, J.E. (1988) 'Henryk Grossmann and the Breakdown of Capitalism', *Science and Society*, Volume 52, No. 3.

Jacoby, R. (1975) 'The Politics of Crisis Theory: Toward a Critique of Automatic Marxism II', Telos 23.

Kautsky, K. (1899) *Bernstein und das Soz.-dem. Programm* (Stuttgart).

—— (1901) 'Krisentheorie', *Neue Zeit*, 20.

—— (1908) 'Verelendung und zusammenbruch', *Neue Zeit* 26.

—— (1920) *Der Weg zur Macht*.

—— (1927) *Materialistische Geschichtsauffassung* (Berlin).

Kestner, F. (1912) *Der Organisationzwang. Eine Untersuchung uber die Kampfe Zwischen den Kartllen und Aussenseitern* (Berlin).

Kroll, Pr. (1926) *Schriften des Vereins f. Sozialpolitik*, Bd.172.

Lederer, E. (1922) *Grundzuge der Okonomischen Theorie* (Tubingen).

—— (1925) 'Konjunktur und krisen', *Grundr. d. Sozialokonomik*, IV/I (Tubingen).

Lenin, V.I. (1948) *Imperialism: The Highest Stage of Capitalism, Collected Works*, Volume 22.

Lescure, J. (1910) *Des Crises Generales et Periodiques de Surproduction* (Paris).

Liefmann, R. (1918) *Kartelle und Trusts* (Stuttgart).

Lowe, A. (1926) 'Wie ist konjunkturtheorie uberhaupt moglich?' *Weltwirtschaftl. Archiv*, II.

Luxemburg, R. (1968) *The Accumulation of Capital* (London: Monthly Review Press).

—— (1972) *The Accumulation of Capital – An Anti-Critique* (London: Monthly Review Press).

Mach, E. (1900) *Die Prinzipien der Warmelehre*.

Marramao, G. (1975) 'Political Economy and Critical Theory', Telos 24.

Marshall, A. (1890) *Principles of Economics*, eighth edition (1920) (Macmillan: London).

Marx, K. (1954) *Capital Volume 1* (London: Lawrence & Wishart).

—— (1956) *Capital Volume 2* (London: Lawrence & Wishart).

—— (1959) *Capital Volume 3* (London: Lawrence & Wishart).

—— (1969) *Theories of Surplus Value Part 2* (London: Lawrence & Wishart).

—— (1972) *Theories of Surplus Value Part 3* (London: Lawrence & Wishart).

Masaryk, T.G. (1899) *Die Philosophischen und Soziologischen Grundlagendes Marxismus* (Vienna).

Mattick, P. (1981) 'The epigones', *Economic Crisis and Crisis Theory* (Merlin: London).

Mehrens, B. (1911) *Die Entstehung und Entwicklung der Grossen Franzosischen Kreditinstitute*.

Meusel, A. (1928) 'Das problem der ausseren handelspolitik bei Friedrich List und Karl Marx', *Weltwirtschaftl Archiv*, 27.

Michels, R. (1928) *Die Verelendungstheorie* (Leipzig).

Mill, J.S. (1970) *Principles of Political Economy with Some of Their Applications to Social Philosophy* (Harmondsworth: Penguin).

Mises, L. (1912) *Theorie des Geldes und der Umlaufsmittel*, I. Auflage.

Mitchell, W.C. (1927) *Business Cycles* (New York).

Mombert, M. (1916) *Zur Frage von Kapitalbildung und Kapitaldarf in Deutschland* (Munich).

Morgenstern, O. (1928) *Schriften des Vereins fur Sozialpolitik*, Bd.173.2.

Muhs, K. (1927) *Anti-Marx* (Jena).

Nachimson, M. (1922) *Die Weltwirtschaft vor Undnach dem Kriege*.

Nearing, S. and Freeman, J. (1927) *Dollar-Diplomatie: Eine Studie uber Amerikanischen Imperialismus* (Berlin).

Olk, B. (1926) 'Die arbeit', *Zeitschrift fur Gewerkschaftspolitik*, 3.Jahrg.

Oppenheimer, F. (1903) *Das Grundgesetz der Marxchen Gesellschaftslehre* (Berlin).

—— (1913) *Die Soziale Frage und der Sozialismus* (Jena).

—— (1919) *Kapitalismus, Kommunismus, Wissenschaftlicher Sozialismus*.

—— (1923) *System der Soziologie* (Jena).

—— (1927) Aufsatz im *Sozialwissenschaft und Sozialpolitik*, 57.

—— (1928) 'Der heutige stand der theorie des sozialismus in Deutschland', *Die Wirtschaftstheorie der Gegenwart*, Bd.IV.

Parvus, A. (1901) 'Die handelspolitik und die doktrin', *Neue Zeit*, 19.

Pember-Reeves, W. (1902) *State Experiments in Australia and New Zealand* (London).

Ricardo, D. (1984) *The Principles of Political Economy and Taxation* (London: Everyman).

Roemer, J. (1986) *Value, Exploitation and Class* (Harwood: London).

——. (1988) *Free to Lose: An Introduction to Marxist Economic Philosophy* (Radius).

Rosenbaum, E. (1928) 'Funktionen des exports- und importhandels', B Harms herausgegeben, *Strukturwandlungen der Deutschen Volkwirtschaft* (Berlin).

Salz, A. (1925) 'Kapital, kapitalformen', *Grundr. d. Sozialokonomik*.

Sartorius von Waltershausen, A. (1907) *Das Volkwirtschaftliche System der Kapitalanlage im Auslande* (Berlin).

Schachner, R. (1903) 'Die Storungen im deutschen Wirtschaftsleben', *Schriften des Vereins f. Sozialpolitik*, Bd.108.

Schulze-Gaevernitz, G. (1892) *Der Grossbetrieb* (Leipzig).

—— (1906) *Britischer Imperialismus und Englischer Frewihandel zu Beginn des Zwanzigsten Jahrhunderts* (Leipzig).

Schumpeter, J. (1914) 'Epochen der dogmen- und methodengeschichte', *Grundr. d. Sozialokonomik*, IV.

—— (1987) *Capitalism, Socialism and Democracy* (Unwin).

Sieveking, H. (1921) *Wirtschaftsgeschichte* (Leipzig).

Simkhovitch, V.G. (1913) *Marxism versus Socialism* (Jena).

Sombart, W. (1924) *Der Proletarische Socialismus* (Jena).

——. (1927) *Der Moderne Kapitalisimus*.

Sorel, G. (1907) *La Decomposition du Marxisme* (Paris).

Spiethoff, A. (1919) 'Einige Bemerkungen zur lehre von der socialisierung', *Schmollers Jahrbuch*, 43, I.

—— (1925) 'Krisen', *Handworterb der Staatswissensch*, IV Aufl.

Sraffa, P. (1960) *Production of Commodites by Means of Commodities*, London.

Stamp (1918) 'The effect of trade fluctuations on profits', *Journal of the Royal Statistical Society*.

Stedman-Jones, G. (1990) 'Marx after Marxism', *Marxism Today*, February.

Steedman, I. (1981) 'Ricardo, Marx, Sraffa', *The Value Controversy* (Verso: London).

Sternberg, F. (1926) *Der Imperialismus* (Berlin).

Strachey, J. (1956) *Contemporary Capitalism* (Gollancz: London).

Sweezy, P. (1970) *The Theory of Capitalist Development* (Monthly Review Press).

Tugan-Baranovsky, M. (1901) *Studien zur Theorie und Geschichte der Handelskrisen in England*.

—— (1904) 'Der zusammenbruch der kapitalistischen wirtschaftsordnung in lichte der nationalokonomik theorie', *Archiv fur Soz.-wiss und Soz.pol*, Bd.XIX.

—— (1905) *Theoretische Grundlagen des Marxismus* (Leipzig).

—— (1908) *Der Moderne Sozialismus in Seiner Gesschichtlichen Entwicklung* (Dresden).

—— (1913) *Les Crises Industrielles en Angleterre* (Paris).

Varga, E. (1926) 'Der uberimperialismus und das gesetz der ungleichmassigen entwicklung des kapitalismus', *Die Kommunist International*, October, (Berlin).

—— (1926) 'Der Marxistische sinn der rationalisierung', *Die Internationale, Jahrg* (Berlin).

—— (1927) 'Kapitalexport in der weltwirtschaft', *Die Internationale* (Berlin).

—— (1928) *Die Wirtschaft der Niedergangsperiode des Kapitalismus hach der Stabilisierung* (Hamburg).

Vogelstein, T. (1914) 'Die finanzielle organisation der kapitalistischen industrie und die monopolbildungen', *Grundr. d. Sozialokonomik*.

Weber, A. (1915) *Depositenbanken und Spekulationbanken*.

Woytinsky, W. (1925) *Die Welt in Zahlen* (Berlin).

Index